OMBURGER · FRED PICKARD · BUD [...] MCDO
TENSI · TOM WEST · JACK FENWIC[...]ON SE[...]
PS · WILLIE JONES · KURT UNGLAUB · JIMMY JORDAN · MONK
MS · ALPHONSO CARREKER · TOM MCCORMICK · GREG ALLEN ·
ELDON · BRAD JOHNSON · TERRELL BUCKLEY · KEZ MCCORVEY
N · BUSTER DAVIS · HUGH ADAMS · BUDDY STRAUSS · LEE CORSO
NE MCDOWELL · KEITH KINDERMAN · WILLIAM "RED" DAWSON
RON SELLERS · WALT SUMNER · RHETT DAWSON · BARRY SMIT
MONK BONASORTE · REGGIE HERRING · KEITH JONES · RICK S
ALLEN · JAMIE DUKES · DANNY MCMANUS · PETER TOM WILLIS
CCORVEY · WARRICK DUNN · ANDRE WADSWORTH · DAVID CAS
LEE CORSO · BILL PROCTOR · RON SCHOMBURGER · FRED PICI
D" DAWSON · DICK HERMANN · STEVE TENSI · TOM WEST · JAC
RRY SMITH · J.T. THOMAS · JOE CAMPS · WILLIE JONES · KURT UN
· RICK STOCKSTILL · PHIL WILLIAMS · ALPHONSO CARREKER
M WILLIS · DEXTER CARTER · CASEY WELDON · BRAD JOHNSON
DAVID CASTILLO · BRYANT MCFADDEN · BUSTER DAVIS · HUGH A
ED PICKARD · BUD WHITEHEAD · GENE MCDOWELL · KEITH KI
ST · JACK FENWICK · BILLY RHODES · RON SELLERS · WALT SUM

# WHAT IT MEANS
# TO BE A SEMINOLE

## BOBBY BOWDEN
### AND FLORIDA STATE'S GREATEST PLAYERS

### MARK SCHLABACH

## TRIUMPH
B O O K S

Library of Congress Cataloging-in-Publication Data

Schlabach, Mark, 1972-
  What it means to be a Seminole / Mark Schlabach.
    p. cm.
  ISBN-13: 978-1-57243-950-4
  ISBN-10: 1-57243-950-5
  1. Florida State Seminoles (Football team)—History. 2. Florida State University—Football—History. 3. Football players—United States—Anecdotes. I. Title.
  GV958.F56S34 2007
  796.332'630975988—dc22                    2007019526

This book is available in quantity at special discounts for your group or organization. For further information, contact:

**Triumph Books**
542 South Dearborn Street
Suite 750
Chicago, Illinois 60605
(312) 939-3330
Fax (312) 663-3557

Printed in U.S.A.
ISBN: 978-1-57243-950-4
Design by Nick Panos
Editorial production and layout by Prologue Publishing Services, LLC
Photos courtesy of Florida State University unless otherwise indicated.

# CONTENTS

# FOREWORD

*What It Means to Be a Seminole*

WHEN I CAME TO FLORIDA STATE IN 1976, they'd just gone 0–11, 1–10, and 3–8 the previous three seasons. Florida State was doing so poorly that the stadium seated 41,000 and we were averaging 17,000 fans per game. The last couple of seasons, Florida State had been losing money. They were going into the red, red, red. It was getting to the point where they were talking about dropping football. I don't know if they were serious about it, but they were talking about it.

So when I came on board, the only way the football program could keep its head above water was to go play at Nebraska for $300,000, which back in those days was unheard of. So the schedule I adopted was playing at LSU five times in a row, with no home and no return. We played at Ohio State two times in a row with no return. Michigan two in a row with no return. Notre Dame one away with no return. Arizona State four away with no return. That's the schedule we faced in the early years.

In 1981 we played at Nebraska, Pitt, Ohio State, Notre Dame, and LSU. They were all back-to-back and all on the road. We were fortunate in that we won many of those games. We swept two from Ohio State. We split with Nebraska. We beat Notre Dame. We beat LSU four out of five. We took three out of four against Arizona State.

As difficult as that schedule was back then, it's really what eventually put us on the map. Beating Nebraska 18–14 during the 1980 season was a big one because, up until that point, I don't think a lot of people had heard of Florida State. Maybe they had heard of Florida State down in the South, but not all over the country. But after that game, people everywhere were saying, "Who's Florida State?"

Bobby Bowden led Florida State to 14 consecutive seasons with rankings in the Associated Press top five. With a career record of 366–113–4, he is the all-time winningest coach in major college history. He was inducted into the College Football Hall of Fame in 2006.

We had our only losing season here during my first year in 1976. Three years later, we were undefeated during the regular season in 1979. We played in the Orange Bowl and got beat by Oklahoma, which was our first major bowl game. We went back to the Orange Bowl the following year and lost to Oklahoma again. Then there was a drop-off. In 1981 we finished 6–5 and did not go to a bowl game. That was the last time we did not play in a bowl game. We did a little bit better in 1982 and gradually got better the next few seasons.

By 1987 we finished second in the nation and stayed in the top four in either the coaches' poll or press poll for the next 14 years. That's what they called the "dynasty." We won 11 games in 1988, 10 games in both 1989 and 1990, and 11 games in both 1991 and 1992.

You can set your goal to be in the top four every year, and you'll never come close. It just happens. It just stacks up. We won 11 bowl games in a row. We played in 14 straight bowl games, but had a tie [17–17 against Georgia in the 1984 Citrus Bowl]. I don't know how that winning streak happened, but it just did.

As good as we were, we didn't win a national championship until 1993, mainly because we kept losing to Miami on missed kicks. I used to get mad because nobody else would play Miami. Notre Dame would play them, then drop them. We would play Miami and lose by one point on a missed field goal and it would knock us out of the national championship. Well, Florida dropped them. Notre Dame dropped them. Penn State dropped them. I didn't want to play them, either, but I had to play them. That's why I said, "When I die, they'll say, 'At least he played Miami.'"

When we finally won a national championship in 1993, it felt like we got the monkey off our backs. That's really what it felt like. You come out second and then third and then third again and second in the polls, people start saying, "Well, he can't win the big one." When you finally do it, it takes the monkey off your back. We had a special team in 1993 with Charlie Ward at quarterback and with what Warrick Dunn did as a freshman, contributing 10 touchdowns and giving us the edge to win a national championship.

The way we beat Nebraska in the Orange Bowl during that 1993 season, my head still hurts thinking about it. The first thing I remember is somebody hit me in the top of the head with the stinking Gatorade jug. I mean, they nearly put me out on the sideline, and it wasn't even the end of the game. After we thought the game was over and we'd won 18–16, I walked out there to shake hands with [Cornhuskers coach] Tom Osborne. The official came up to me and said, "Hey, Coach, we've got to put one more second back on the clock." Well, it gave them a shot at a field goal.

I'll never forget the way that thing ended. I looked to see where the football was, and it was 51 yards away. I'd been watching Nebraska's kicker kick field goals on film, and he couldn't kick one from over 45 yards. I said, "Okay, we've got it." But then the official came back up to me and said, "Coach, we made a mistake. The ball is on the 28-yard line." Now, he's in field goal range. I was thinking, "Geez, we just aren't meant to win it." But after all those darn wide rights we had against Miami, Nebraska had a wide left [Nebraska's Byron Bennett missed a 46-yard field goal attempt at the end], and we won the game and the national championship.

Winning the 1999 national championship felt more like an accomplishment. The monkey was already off our backs, and we were No. 1 in the nation from the very first day of the season to the last, which was the first time that had ever been done. It felt good to just go out there and win every game and stay No. 1. We had Chris Weinke and Peter Warrick. I believe Warrick would have won the Heisman Trophy that year if he hadn't had that little bit of trouble.

We beat Virginia Tech 46–29 in the Sugar Bowl to win the 1999 national championship. I believe [Hokies quarterback] Michael Vick put on the greatest one-man performance I've ever seen in my life. For one man to just nearly beat you with his talent, I just couldn't believe how talented he was. But we won the game and won a second title.

The one thing I've always tried to instill in my players is that you try to get them to do the right things off the field. Kids have to learn that there's somebody who is their boss and they've got to listen to them. It's just like me; I've got a boss. I tell the parents, "When your boy comes up here, you're out of it. You're way down there and they're up here. I'm going to try to do your job. I know you want your son to go to church. I know you want your son to go to class. I know you want your son to stay out of trouble." I tell them, "I'm going to try to pick up right where you left off." Then I ask them, "Is that okay?"

Somebody might say, "You don't have a right to take your boys to church." I take my boys to church two times a year, once to an African American church and once to a white church. I do that so they know they're welcome at any church in town. I know when I was young, I went to church because Mamma and Daddy made me go. Once I got to college, nobody made me go to church. I just feel like I can help fulfill parents' roles while their kids are off at college.

I'm just amazed that people would complain that a coach talks to his players about religion. In my opinion, with the turmoil we have nowadays, do you really mind me quoting the Ten Commandments to your sons? You really don't want me to do that? We're trying to keep them out of jail. We're trying to keep them out of trouble. I hope somebody does my kids that way. I think it's the thing to do. I'm one of those guys who would rather be spiritually correct than politically correct. If our nation doesn't get with it, we're going to throw our nation away because of that political correctness. We hope we can impact kids' lives, and I've seen so many cases here where we did have an impact on a young man's life.

People ask me all the time, "What was my biggest feat in coaching?" My biggest feat is that I've never been fired. [Penn State coach] Joe Paterno is the same way. How many coaches can say they've never been fired. Paul "Bear" Bryant turned out 29 head coaches, and every one of them got fired, except one. We have a saying in coaching: there are two kinds of coaches—one who has been fired and one who hasn't been fired *yet*. So that's why I believe it's my biggest feat. I've won some games, won some national championships, won some conference titles, but the biggest thing I can say is, I've never been fired. You can be an outstanding coach and still get fired.

We've been blessed to have so many great players at Florida State. Guys like Deion Sanders, Warrick Dunn, Derrick Brooks, Corey Simon, Sammie Smith, Dexter Carter, Reinard Wilson, Peter Boulware, and so many others. We've just been so lucky to have so many great players.

Joining the ACC in 1992 was another important step for the program. It came to the point where you were better off to be in a conference than an independent. There were about 17 independents, teams like Notre Dame, Miami, Florida State, South Carolina, and Tulane. But it became obvious that you couldn't operate by yourself. Notre Dame was about the only school that could stand alone.

We were invited to join the SEC, ACC, Big East, and what at the time was the Metro Conference. We just felt the ACC was the best place for us. We were the only team they were inviting into the league at the time. Of course, they added Miami and Virginia Tech later, and it's become a great football conference. It's always been a great basketball conference, but it wasn't known for football until now.

I never would have thought I'd coach at Florida State for 32 years. In 1970 I was 40 years old and got the head coaching job at West Virginia. A couple of years after that, Darrell Royal resigned at Texas and he was 53 years old. A month later, Frank Broyles resigned at Arkansas and he was around 53 years old. I can remember thinking, "Well, I guess when I get 50, I'll probably retire, too." I thought I was old at 40. But then 60 came along, 65 came along, 70 came along, and then 75. I've just never wanted to retire.

This has just been such a great place to live. I love the South. I love the beaches. I love the warm weather. I love Tallahassee. That's where it's had a big impact on me, my wife, and my children. The fact that the administration has been so good about realizing the importance of athletics is another reason I've stayed here so long. Athletics are important. If you took Florida State, Georgia, or Notre Dame and took away athletics, they wouldn't be the same places. Kids want to go where there is a football team.

Here's how important football is at Florida State. We couldn't get enough students at Florida State when I came here in 1976. I used to go out and recruit players, and the university president would ask me to go by some high school to see if I could recruit a student to Florida State. Maybe it was a straight-A student we wanted here. I had to recruit students here because they couldn't get enough applicants. Four years after I got here, we went undefeated and played in the Orange Bowl. That following year, we had an opening for 2,500 freshmen and had 7,000 applicants. The president said the reason was the success of athletics. You can't put the cart ahead of the horse, but you do need that cart for the school to grow.

I always considered myself a big Bear Bryant protégé, even though I never played or coached for him. When I started coaching at Howard [now Samford in Birmingham, Alabama], Coach Bryant was the coach at the University of Alabama. I was able to watch what he was doing and learn from him, and I knew him personally. I never thought one day I would pass him [Bowden passed Bryant and Paterno as college football's winningest coach with a 48–24 victory over Wake Forest on October 25, 2003. Bowden went into the 2007 season with 366 career victories]. I would have thought, *No way, this is impossible*. But then it just happened.

Joe Paterno has been up there at Penn State for 50 years. It's amazing, isn't it? You're not going to see that anymore. Times have changed so much that they won't let you coach that long anymore. They'll fire you too quickly. When I first started coaching, there might have been somebody fired after

10 years. Then it became five years. Now, they'll get you after two seasons. It has changed so much. The climate of coaching is if you don't win, you're gone.

When you're coaching, you can't look back because you've got another game ahead of you and you're afraid you're going to lose it. So you can't look back and say, "Look what I did. Look what we did." Maybe one day when you're retired, you can look back and see what happened. I just feel like I've been very lucky to be able to coach as long as I've coached and to have had the wins and players that we've had.

—Bobby Bowden

# EDITOR'S ACKNOWLEDGMENTS

MY INTRODUCTION TO FLORIDA STATE football came during my time as a student at Norcross High School in suburban Atlanta. One of my closest friends, Brad McDaniel, was a devout Florida State fan because his father, Jerry, had been a standout sprinter at the school and briefly played football for the Seminoles before an injury caused him to quit.

Jerry McDaniel was the first athlete at Florida State to receive a full scholarship in track and field. In his son's mind, Jerry was Deion Sanders before Deion Sanders was even born. Jerry went undefeated in the 220-yard dash during his three-year career at Florida State, from 1963 to 1965. Remarkably, during his junior and senior seasons, he was never beaten in a single race. By the time Jerry left Tallahassee, he had set school records in the 220, 440, and 4 x 100 relay.

Jerry also was an integral part of two of the greatest days in Florida State sports history. In 1964 he won four events as the Seminoles defeated Florida for the first time in school history. The next day he placed four times as FSU defeated Southeastern Conference powerhouse Tennessee.

I met Jerry McDaniel long after his playing days at Florida State and after his stellar coaching career in Georgia high schools. He was inducted into the Florida State Sports Hall of Fame in 1998. Before then, Jerry was one of my first heroes. He was the first person to put a tennis racquet in my hands, and later the first to replace the racquet with golf clubs. He and his loving wife, Lawre, are two of the most generous and kind people I have ever known. When my parents moved to Arizona before I started college, they opened their home and allowed me to share the basement with Brad. Jerry McDaniel put extra money in my pockets by allowing me to work on his construction sites.

Lawre McDaniel and her daughter, Melissa, are big Auburn football fans. Brad and his father were big Florida State fans. Before Jerry passed away in January 2004, he and Brad spent many memorable Saturdays together at Bobby Bowden Field at Doak Campbell Stadium. Their love for the Seminoles was something they shared, and it produced a truly unique father-son relationship.

This book is dedicated to Jerry's memory. A portion of the proceeds generated from the sale of this book will be donated to the FSU track and field scholarship established in Jerry's name. Contact Seminole Boosters, Inc., for more information about the scholarship and other ways to donate to FSU endowments.

I am grateful to Florida State coach Bobby Bowden and the numerous players included in this book who were generous with their time and candor. They allowed me remarkable access into their memories and recollections of playing football at Florida State. Monk Bonasorte, an All-American safety at Florida State in the 1970s and now executive director of the FSU Varsity Club, was an invaluable help in completing this project. Aside from sharing his wonderful stories about playing at Florida State, Monk provided me assistance in reaching many of the players included in this book. Without his tremendous help, this project could not have been completed.

xiii

The same can be said of Rob Wilson, sports information director at Florida State, and Elliott Finebloom, who works in Rob's office as the primary football contact. Both were instrumental in getting me time with Coach Bowden, as well as organizing the photographs included in this book. Both are absolute professionals and two of the best in the business.

I would like to apologize to the former Florida State players who weren't included in this book but were certainly worthy of inclusion. Because of time constraints and space, not every great FSU story could be told. I hope you agree that this wide sample of former players contains not only some of the best stories in Florida State history but some of the most inspirational.

I received help from three colleagues in the sportswriting profession while completing this book. George Henry, a freelance writer based in Atlanta and a fierce opponent in our longtime fantasy baseball league, secured the interview with Atlanta Falcons running back Warrick Dunn. Ray Glier, another freelance writer based in Atlanta, whose work regularly appears in *USA Today*, *The Wall Street Journal*, and *The New York Times*, also interviewed a handful of subjects included in this book. Bob Thomas, a good friend and longtime FSU beat writer for *The [Jacksonville] Florida Times-Union*, was a good source for Florida State anecdotes and history. Their help was instrumental in completing this project.

I would like to thank my editors at ESPN.com for allowing me the time to complete this book, which included several long nights in hotel rooms on the West Coast while covering the NCAA men's basketball tournament. David Duffey, David Albright, Brian Kelly, Lauren Reynolds, and Andrew Glockner make my life at ESPN much easier and more enjoyable. Covering college football and college basketball for a company like ESPN is truly a dream come true.

I would like to thank Tom Bast, the editorial director at Triumph Books, for his patience, even after I blew deadlines by weeks and months. I would like to thank all the other editors and marketing folks at Triumph Books for their work and support.

More than anything, I would like to thank my caring wife, Heather, and beautiful daughters, Caroline and Jane, who probably sacrifice too much for my career. When toe meets leather each fall, they realize Daddy is going to be spending too many nights away from home.

# *The*

# FORTIES

# HUGH ADAMS
## Tackle/Center
### 1948–1949

I GREW UP IN PUNTA GORDA, FLORIDA, and toward the end of World War II, I had already earned a private pilot's license and enlisted in the Navy B-5 program. I was awarded a diploma with my class at Charlotte High School when they graduated in 1946. At that time, I was at the Naval Air Station in Atlanta and was playing out of high school football and looking for the next step.

I participated in spring practice at Georgia Tech, and then the war and the Navy program ended. I was released late in 1946 and went to the University of Florida on a football scholarship for a couple of years, but I wasn't getting any playing time. I wanted to get busy playing football, so I moved over to Florida State. I played the last couple of years there and finished the 1948 and 1949 seasons at Florida State. I graduated from there in 1950.

I played tackle and center in 1948 and was on Coach Don Veller's first team. He was one of the outstanding positive influences in my life. He was a thoroughly decent man and a disciplinarian. I regarded him very highly over the years. He brought with him from Indiana a couple of assistant coaches, the Armstrong boys, and they had been in the military and joined him on the staff at Florida State. I had the very good experience of having them as coaches.

Florida State had been an all-girls school until two years before I got there. When I got there, most of the male student population was being quartered at an old Air Force base, Dale Mabry Field, and we were bused to the other

Hugh Adams was one of Florida State's first All-Americans and was captain and Most Valuable Player on the 1949 Seminoles team. After serving in the Navy following graduation, Adams returned to his alma mater as an assistant coach and was Dean of Men at FSU.

campus when necessary. We practiced football and lived and dined in the West Campus, which was the former military base.

Where I was staying was in the military barracks. They were not the open-space style but were compartmented into double rooms. They were spartan but quite satisfactory. They were two stories and, if you can picture the military housing of that day, post–World War II, that's what we were in.

They weren't bad at all. I think they might not meet the elegance of today's standards, but they were quite adequate and comfortable. The campus was a very convenient one because it was laid out in military fashion.

We opened the 1948 season against Cumberland and shut them out 30–0. I was just happy to be playing football. As you would guess, we had a lot of ex-servicemen on the team. There was a real mix, and they came from a lot of parts of the country for whatever reason. I look back on it with very good memories. I was named a team captain before we played Erskine, out of South Carolina, and then we elected permanent captains at the end of the season. We lost the game 14–6, and it was one of only two games we lost in the two seasons I was at Florida State.

In 1949 we opened the season against Whiting Field, a team from a military base. During my active duty with the Navy, I had been released to help coach, of all things, the Norfolk Navy Tars for one season. They played a limited schedule, and we had a mixture of some pros and a lot of athletes waiting to complete their duty and get out. So I was kind of happy at Florida State to be playing a military team. I wanted to see what we could do against them. As it turned out, we did okay—we won 74–0 at old Centennial Field, which is where we played before Doak Campbell Stadium came along.

Don Veller was always pictured chewing his fingernails in great anxiety on the sideline, and we were more than 50 points ahead of Whiting Field, and he was still doing it. We all got a laugh from that.

Later in the 1949 season we played at Livingston State in Selma, Alabama, which was coached by Vaughn Mancha, my really good friend. He was later athletics director at Florida State. We got up there and we weren't sure there were enough officials to play the game. We still laugh and talk about that. Before the game, we were talking amongst ourselves as to whether the game was going to happen or not. But we got it started and ended up losing 13–6. It was not a happy occasion for us.

We had a lot of great players on the team. Buddy Strauss was a running back. Bill Dawkins was an outstanding linebacker. I hesitate to put one above the other because those two were exceptional. We had other great players as well. Wyatt "Red" Parrish was on the team and he also was outstanding. We played Tampa at the end of the 1948 season for the Dixie Conference championship where there were a lot of politicians and other dignitaries in attendance. That earned us a spot in the Cigar Bowl in Tampa, and we played Wofford, which was a very good football team. It was a big deal for us, but I can't say how big it was for other people. Those of us who were involved in the building of the football program at Florida State were happy to be there. They treated us royally, and we didn't have to go far from Tallahassee to the game. We had a good opponent. My recollections are all positive. We played a pretty good game and won 19–6.

After graduating from Florida State in 1950, I did what I wanted to do. I became a math teacher and an assistant high school football coach at Leon High School in Tallahassee. I really enjoyed both the teaching and the coaching. But the Korean War started and I had maintained my reserve status, which I did for the rest of my life. I retired as a reserve Naval commander. I stayed in the military as a civilian doing other things. After the Korean War started, I was recalled to active duty and went to OSC and spent the next several years on destroyers all over the world.

I left Navy service and had the opportunity to return to Florida State as a graduate assistant coach in football during the Tom Nugent era in the mid-1950s. I accepted that appointment gladly and wanted to continue graduate work. It was an opportunity to coach college football and, before long, I was coaching the varsity defense. I stayed in that capacity and worked there for the next several years until Nugent left for the University of Maryland in 1958.

We had several good years at Florida State. We had to make some decisions as to whether to move to Maryland and continue coaching or look for another career path. I enjoyed the coaching at the time, but I did not see it as something I wanted to spend my life doing. I completed my master's degree and, when the staff left for Maryland, I got a position at FSU to work on a doctorate. I worked in education for more than 20 years until I retired.

Hugh Adams, a native of Punta Gorda, Florida, was one of Florida State's first All-Americans and earliest stars. He was captain and most valuable player of the 1949 football team, and his teams had records of 16–2 in the 1948 and 1949 seasons. Adams was named Little All-American in 1948 and 1949, the first Seminoles player to receive that honor. After serving in the Navy, Adams returned to Florida State and was an assistant coach on Tom Nugent's staff. He later became assistant dean of men at Florida State and worked as superintendent of public schools and was president of Broward Community College in Fort Lauderdale, Florida. Adams was elected into the Florida State Sports Hall of Fame in 1980 and is retired and lives in Bokeelia, Florida.

# BUDDY STRAUSS
## FULLBACK/DEFENSIVE BACK
### 1948–1949

I GREW UP IN TALLAHASSEE, FLORIDA, and went into the Navy right out of Leon High School. I went to training at the University of North Carolina and was in the preflight school at the University of Georgia. I played football there on the Navy team. I was in preflight training in Pensacola, Florida, when the war ended. After I got out of the military, I went up to Duke University for one year and played football.

Then Florida State changed to a coed college, so I returned home and enrolled at Florida State in 1948. I was on the second football team Florida State ever had and played under coach Don Veller. He was the nicest guy you would ever want to know. He had a bunch of military guys coming back after the war. He was a wonderful coach. Bob Harbison was the offensive line coach, and Charlie Armstrong was also one of the assistants. They were both great coaches.

There were barracks out at Dale Mabry Field, and that's where they housed all the men. But I was from Tallahassee, so I was living at home. We had our practice field and dining hall out at Dale Mabry Field, an old military base. They didn't have football scholarships back then and most of us came back to school on the G.I. Bill. So I lived at home to save money. Kent Strauss, my younger brother, joined the team out of high school and was a lineman.

I was a fullback and weighed about 180 pounds. None of us were very big back then, but I was a little older because I'd been in the military. Ken

MacLean and Wyatt "Red" Parrish were two of the halfbacks. We were running the wing-T offense, and you had the choice of lining up the fullback or halfback behind the center. The primary passer was the tailback, and the fullback did most of the dive running, but I did pass the ball some.

We opened the 1948 season against Cumberland [a 30–0 win] and then played at Erskine in South Carolina the following week [a 14–6 loss]. We played Millsaps in Mississippi during the third week. [Strauss scored the game-winning touchdown in the third quarter of a 7–6 win.] We had bad weather in that game. We traveled to most of the road games on an old school bus.

The Erskine game was the only game we lost that season. We beat Stetson, Mississippi College, Livingston College, and Troy State, then ended the season against Tampa [a 33–12 victory]. We were a small college back in those days and played a lot of small colleges. Most of the schools were still small. Most of the male students had been in the service and most of the players were a little bit older. Florida State had been an all-girls school, so they opened it up for males and brought in a lot of veterans.

We went 9–1 during my senior season in 1949. We opened against Whiting Field and won 74–0. I had been stationed at Whiting Field at the end of the war. It was outside of Pensacola, Florida, and they had military football teams back in those days. Back then, beating any team that bad was a mighty good feeling for us.

We played Sewanee [the University of the South] in Tennessee, and there was really bad weather. A fog came in on the field that was so low, you'd kick the football and the ball would go out of sight. It was a very close game, but we won 6–0. Then we played Stetson at the Gator Bowl in Jacksonville, but it wasn't a very big stadium back then.

We went and played Livingston College in Selma, Alabama, and lost the game 13–6. They weren't sure the game was going to take place. The coaches up there forgot to hire officials, so they went into the stands and got some of the former players to come down and officiate the ballgame. It was pretty tough getting a call. We lost the game 13–6. We came back and beat Millsaps 40–0 and beat Tampa 34–7. We finished the season with a 20–0 win over Troy State.

We played Wofford in the Cigar Bowl in Tampa, and it was a great experience for us. There weren't a lot of bowl games back then. We had a chance to go down there and play a pretty good team. It was a tough ballgame, but we won 19–6. Wofford had won 23 games in a row and was undefeated. But

A home-grown product from Leon High School in Tallahassee, Buddy Strauss was a star running back on two of Florida State's first football teams in 1948 and 1949. He ran for 1,170 yards in his career, which stood as a school record until Lee Corso broke the mark seven years later. He was a Navy veteran and helped found the FSU Booster Club.

it was a small college, too, and we felt mighty good about going to a bowl game.

Never in this world would I think Florida State football would be what it is today. It was an all-girls school. There were no men on campus until the war was over and the veterans started coming back. There was a pretty nice ratio on campus between boys and girls. After being in the service for so long, it was nice to see all the pretty girls around. In fact, I ended up marrying one of the girls I was dating.

After college, I went to work for a company selling tractors and heavy equipment through Florida, Georgia, South Carolina, and North Carolina. We had six children, and five of them attended Florida State.

Buddy Strauss, a home-grown product from Leon High School in Tallahassee, Florida, was Florida State's first 1,000-yard rusher. He was a starting fullback on Florida State's second football team in 1948 and again in 1949. His 1,170 career yards in two seasons was a school record until Lee Corso broke the mark seven years later. Strauss's 747 rushing yards in 1949 was a school single-season record until 1972. Strauss ran for 132 yards in his final college game, a 19–6 upset of heavily favored Wofford in the 1949 Cigar Bowl in Tampa. Strauss, who is retired and still lives in Tallahassee, was active in founding the FSU Booster Club and was elected into the Florida State Sports Hall of Fame in 1980.

# The FIFTIES

# LEE CORSO

## QUARTERBACK/HALFBACK

### 1953–1956

I WAS A QUARTERBACK, GUARD, AND SHORTSTOP from Jackson High School in Miami. Miami, North Carolina, Clemson, and Florida were also recruiting me and offered me scholarships to play football. At that time, I was a pretty good all-around athlete. I made all-state in three sports, which was pretty hard to do. I wasn't very big, though. I was only about 5'9" and 145 pounds.

I was very, very impressed with Florida State coach Tom Nugent as a person. He felt that I could come in with the 1953 recruiting class and help build something at Florida State, as compared to maintaining programs at schools such as Clemson, Florida, and North Carolina. I really felt I could go to Florida State and help build something. Plus, Coach Nugent was the only coach who said I could go to college and play baseball and not have to play spring football. That was really rare in those days.

I played baseball as a freshman in 1954 and was the shortstop [Corso hit .400 in 25 at-bats in 1954]. The Brooklyn Dodgers had drafted me out of high school to play minor league baseball. I had to make a decision about playing college football and college baseball or playing professional baseball. I decided to go to Florida State and get my college degree. I got there and did really well my freshman season.

During football practice in the fall of 1955, Danny Litwhiler, who was my baseball coach, called me and told me to come to the baseball field after football practice. I went over, and he had this nice-looking athlete at shortstop.

Litwhiler hit a ball in the hole, and the guy backhanded it and zipped it to first base. And then he hit another one in the hole, and the kid does the double play across the base. The kid got up to the plate and dragged a perfect bunt down the third-base line, then hit a ball off the right-center wall. Litwhiler looked at me and said, "Lee, how would you like to play center field?" I said, "Center field looks awfully good to me!" That kid was Dick Howser. [Howser was a two-time All-American shortstop at Florida State and made the 1961 All-Star Game as a rookie for the Kansas City Athletics; he later became manager of the New York Yankees and Kansas City Royals.] I played center field the next three years, and Howser was the shortstop.

I left Miami in the summer of 1953, and a few weeks later I was the starting quarterback on Florida State's football team, playing against Miami in the Orange Bowl. I think I lasted one half before they knocked me out of the game. We were running the option, and I kept running down the line until they knocked the crap out of me. We were making all kind of yards, but I couldn't stand up. There was only one option—for me to pitch it. We lost the game 27–0.

We played Louisville in Tallahassee early in the 1953 season. Johnny Unitas was Louisville's quarterback. I felt sorry for him because Louisville had gotten rid of most of its scholarships and he was one of only a few scholarship guys left. Louisville had beaten Florida State the year before, but we beat them 59–0. I was the quarterback at Florida State and had all these studs. Unitas was the quarterback at Louisville and had nothing left. We played both ways, and I played all special teams. [Corso returned a blocked punt 59 yards for a touchdown and kicked an extra point against Louisville.]

11

We were about half and half in 1953. We lost to Miami, which was a big game for us, but beat North Carolina State and Tampa. Abilene Christian beat us up pretty good [a 20–7 loss]. They had a guy, Bobby Morrow, and we'd never heard of him. But he was a world-class sprinter. [Morrow won three gold medals at the 1956 Olympic Games in Melbourne, Australia, winning the 100 and 200 sprints and 4 x 100 relay team.] They had six guys like him and ran right over us. They outran us like crazy. We'd never heard of Abilene Christian.

We lost to Louisiana Tech 32–21 the next week. But then we beat Virginia Military Institute 12–7, and that was a big game. That was the school Coach Nugent came from, and that was the biggest game of the year for him. We went to Hattiesburg, Mississippi, the next week to play Mississippi Southern, and they had the best looking women in the world. They were called the "Dixie Darlings." In fact, we all wanted to stay out on the field at halftime and watch them dance—they were so good looking. We lost the game 21–0. They beat Alabama and Tennessee that year. We were 2–2 against those guys in my career. We lost twice to them in Hattiesburg—because of those girls—and beat them twice in Tallahassee.

Before my sophomore season, in 1954, they moved me to tailback. That's when Burt Reynolds was behind me. He was the second-string tailback. Reynolds was one of the toughest kids we ever had on our team. He was rough, strong, and was a really aggressive runner. His problem was that he was not a great defensive back, and you had to play both ways. Backpedaling and everything, he wasn't good at it. But, boy, I'll tell you what, he'd knock your head off, and he would run you over. He was a very good football player.

We were playing North Carolina State in the fifth game of the 1954 season, and they had a guy throw a touchdown pass late in the first half. It was ruled legal, but the guy ran out of bounds along the sideline and came out behind Reynolds. It was an illegal play that he got blamed for. The coaches got on him at halftime, and he quit the next day. He was one hell of a good running back. If it had been one-way football back then, he could have played in the pros.

We played in the 1955 Sun Bowl against Texas Western. I ran the opening kickoff back about 50 yards and ran two more times down to the 2-yard line, and Harry Massey ran for a touchdown to put us ahead 7–0. They punted, and the ball hit a friend of mine, Carl Green, in the head. The ball rolled over, and I jumped on it. They jumped on me and broke my leg. I didn't play anymore. When I left the field, we were ahead 3–0. When I came back, the score was 47–3. They scored 47 points while I was at the hospital.

I broke my fibula in that game, but the doctors thought it was a sprained ankle. They x-rayed my leg in that hospital, and I was trying to get them to x-ray my ankle. So they wrapped me up and I went dancing that night in Juarez, Mexico. It was a heck of a party. I played half the baseball season in 1954 on a broken ankle before it finally collapsed.

Before my senior season, in 1956, they moved me back to quarterback. I don't know why. When I got back in the fall, Coach Nugent said, "I'm going to put you back at quarterback." I never asked him why. In those days, you just did what the guy told you to do. We never threw the ball. I might have

As a freshman in 1953, Lee Corso led the Seminoles in punt returns and interceptions. In 1954 he led the team in interceptions and kick returns, and then led FSU in rushing in 1955. As a senior in 1956, Corso led the Seminoles in passing. His 14 career interceptions stood as a school record for 26 seasons until Monk Bonasorte broke the mark in 1980.

thrown about 50 times the whole year. We ran the option, I rolled out, and I'd run the bootlegs. All we had was the moving pocket.

We blew out Ohio 47–7 in the first game, then we went to play Georgia in Athens. We drove down the field on the first series, and I handed the ball off to Bobby Renn, who threw a touchdown pass to Bob Nellums. But a phantom flag came out about five yards later, and they called us for holding. They called our touchdown back, and we got beat 3–0 on a field goal with 90 seconds left.

We lost to Virginia Tech 20–7 in Tallahassee, and then beat North Carolina State 14–0. The best game of the year was against Wake Forest and Billy Ray Barnes [who was an All-American and 1956 ACC Player of the Year]. It was homecoming, and it was a battle between Barnes and me. He was such a tough running back. It was a heck of a game. It rained, and our kicker missed a field goal at the end of the game because he slipped. It ended up a 14–14 tie.

We played at Villanova the following week in the Grocery Bowl. Bud Dudley invented a game called the Grocery Bowl, and everybody who went to this grocery store and bought food got free tickets to the game. There were 900,000 people there and we took home $4.13. The stadium was loaded with 60,000 people, and we beat them 20–13. Villanova was a hard-nosed football team, but we beat them.

We played against Miami and we played a good game, but they just had too many good football players. They were a better team, but at least we'd made improvements to be competitive against teams like Miami and Georgia. They were good football teams, and we were playing them head-to-head. At least I finished the game that time. I'd started against them as a 17-year-old freshman and then came back four years later, and we played well against them.

The following week, we played Furman and blew them out 42–7. Then we played Mississippi Southern again, and they were a damn good football team. They were the best team we played that season. They were much better than Georgia and Miami. We had one heck of a game. Johnny Sheppard, who was my catcher in baseball, kicked a late field goal to win the game 20–19. I got knocked out of that game with a concussion but came back and intercepted a pass that helped us win the game.

The 1956 season ended at Auburn the following week. Billy Odom, who was the fastest guy on the team, was running a punt back for a touchdown, ran into our center, Troy Barnes, and fell down. We used to send the center at the kicker and then have him peel back. I never did that as a coach. We lost the game 13–7. I was hurt in that game with a hip pointer and didn't play very well.

Early in my senior season, we were playing at North Carolina State. That game was a night game in Raleigh, North Carolina. That afternoon, Notre Dame was playing North Carolina in Chapel Hill, North Carolina. You couldn't get out at night in those days because there were only so many flights in and out, so all the reporters who were covering Notre Dame—all the great newspaper guys who followed Notre Dame—came to our game against North Carolina State. I don't know what happened, but I was all over the place during that game. I had a touchdown run, was running back punts, and intercepted a pass. Because all those Notre Dame writers were at the game, I was named the National Back of the Week. Do you know who were the two guys behind me that week? Jim Brown and Tommy McDonald. Can you believe that?

I graduated from Florida State in 1957 and was a graduate assistant under Coach Nugent. My assignment was to coach the freshman team. One of my biggest victories was 20–7 over South Georgia Junior College. The head coach was Bobby Bowden. We sent all of our players who couldn't get into FSU to his school. Man, he had some players. We had a great freshman class, though, who moved up to be sophomores the following year and were the reason we won enough games to move up to Maryland. About eight of those guys started in 1958, when we beat Miami at Miami and Tennessee at Tennessee.

We went to Maryland after the 1958 season, and I was a 22-year-old assistant coaching the secondary. I stayed with Coach Nugent at Maryland until 1965, when I left to go to the United States Naval Academy. I coached there for three seasons under Bill Elias, who was probably one of the best defensive coaches I've ever been associated with. Coach Nugent was the best offensive mind I was ever around. He invented the I formation, and we did all the shifty formations and the West Coast offense all the way back in 1955 and 1960.

15

Coach Nugent was like a father to me. He had unquestioned integrity. He taught me the value of never prostituting my integrity to get a job or keep a job in my life. I was with him for eight years, and we never had a scandal. That was one of the things I was most proud of. At the end of 15 years of coaching, I never had an NCAA investigator come talk to one of my players. I was proud of that, and proud that I learned that from Tom Nugent.

Coach Nugent started coaching football, basketball, and baseball at a reform school up in New York, then he went to Virginia Military Institute. He was a disciplinarian, but he wasn't a mean coach. He didn't believe in discipline by force or fear, and I learned that from him, too. There's a difference between discipline and intimidation. A lot of coaches lead by intimidation and, once they start losing, they get killed. Coaches who discipline through self-discipline and all that stuff, guys respect them a lot more. In the long run, players don't respect coaches who are intimidators.

I was named the head coach at Louisville in 1969 and was there for four years. I was there a week, and the school trustees wanted to drop football. They said, "Look, we'll give them one year." I took Louisville to a bowl game in 1970. We won eight straight games and went and played in the Pasadena Bowl against Long Beach State. Before the 1970 season, schools in the NCAA went from a 10-game to an 11-game schedule. So I got on the phone with Vaughn Mancha, the FSU athletics director, and said, "Coach, you've got an opening game and I'd like to bring my Louisville team down there." He said, "Naaah." I said, "Coach, we're nothing." He said, "Okay, as a favor, I'll let you open the season against Florida State in Tallahassee."

We went down there, and I brought a young sophomore linebacker named Tom Jackson, who had never played in a game before, and we scared the heck out of them. They kicked three field goals, and I think it was the only game Bill Peterson coached at Florida State in which he didn't score a touchdown. We lined up to kick the game-winning field goal, and they jumped offside on purpose and hit my holder and my kicker. They got a 5-yard penalty. They left me with my second holder and my second kicker. We missed the 28-yard field goal and lost 9–7. Mancha ran across the field and said, "That's the last alumni favor you get."

After leaving Louisville, I was the coach at Indiana for 10 years and got fired. I went to ABC Television and did the first football games in the United States Football League. I coached at Northern Illinois after that, and then went to coach the Orlando Renegades of the USFL. When that league folded, I went to ESPN and have been there for 20 years.

I've been around college football for 50 years. I don't think there's anybody who's been as fortunate as I've been. I was a head football coach for 15 years in college and then I spent 20 years in television covering football. No one else has done that. Nobody's that old to hang around that long.

When I went to Florida State, I just felt like this was an opportunity for me to help build something that people would always remember. And I've been fortunate to live long enough to see it come true. That's hard to do in this life: to go some place and try to build something and then see it come to fruition. Being a part of the Florida State football program has meant a lot to me.

Lee Corso, a native of Miami, Florida, was a four-year starting quarterback, tailback, and defensive back for Florida State from 1953 to 1956. As a freshman in 1953, Corso led the Seminoles in punt returns and interceptions. In 1954 he led the team in interceptions and kick returns, and then led FSU in rushing in 1955. As a senior in 1956, Corso led the Seminoles in passing. His 14 career interceptions stood as a school record for 26 seasons, until Monk Bonasorte broke the mark in 1980. Corso also was a standout baseball player at FSU. He was a graduate assistant coach at Florida State and later became head football coach at Louisville, Indiana, and Northern Illinois. For the last 20 years, he has worked for ESPN and is host of the popular *College GameDay* show. He was elected into the FSU Sports Hall of Fame in 1978.

17

# WILLIAM "BILL" PROCTOR
## TACKLE
### 1955

COMING OUT OF HIGH SCHOOL, I was recruited to the University of Florida, went there, and was fortunate—I got to play some varsity football as a freshman because the Korean War was on. I played behind Charley LaPradd, who was a senior All-American that year.

I was well-treated; no complaints. But coming out of a small high school, I kind of wanted a smaller situation. I had also been recruited by Stetson, and it seemed like a good idea at the time. It was closer to home.

The fellow I went down there to play under left the next summer. I hung on. I had good years at Stetson, but Billy Odom was a halfback and was there with me. Billy left—he was my roommate—and came to Florida State and told me I should come up there. My older brother [Custis Proctor] wanted me to go there right from the beginning.

So after my junior year, my dad called coach Tom Nugent, and Coach said, "Yeah, come up." So I had a spring practice and a fall redshirt year. I was fortunate in my fall redshirt year because I was drafted by Cleveland that spring. Then I went through another spring practice and played the season of 1955 under Tom Nugent.

I really had, from my standpoint, a fine year. I had matured a lot and was older. I had Vaughn Mancha as my tackle coach, and that was a great experience.

I had good coaches; coaches whom I really related to. Blood chemistry sometimes counts. I really enjoyed working with Coach Mancha.

That was our first major college season. We opened up with N.C. State and beat them in the rain 7–0. Then we went down to Miami and lost 34–0. Then we came back to play against Virginia Tech [a 24–20 loss]. I nearly whiffed a kickoff against Virginia Tech. That was an interesting event. Coach Bill Peterson told me to go out and determine which side of the [Virginia Tech] line was dropping back and kick it there. That's kind of difficult as you're approaching the ball.

I actually didn't whiff it, I just knocked it off the tee a little bit. It didn't go 10 yards. The funny thing was, they gave Virginia Tech the ball. The same thing happened down in Tampa [in the season finale] and they penalized them and had me kick it over.

After losing to Virginia Tech, we had Georgia. We played them a whale of a first half [before losing 47–14]. Then we had Georgia Tech [another 34–0 loss]. The thing I remember most was they told me about this great tackle from Georgia Tech, and he wasn't bad at all, but by the fourth quarter their third-team looked a lot better than their first-team guy because you had seen three of them.

That was one of the best teams we played that season.

The challenge of that year was there were some of us who went a long, long time. There were some of us who played anywhere from 45 to 55 minutes for those ballgames. I know I started off at 227 and weighed in at 198 for the Georgia Tech game. If we didn't play three quarters, we felt neglected. In terms of playing time, back in that era, I guess if you counted it up, I'd played as much as today's players would.

Lee Corso was a prized recruit and a very talented athlete. There were a couple of other guys on that team who I never thought got the credit. Billy Odom and Buck Metts were two fine halfbacks. Billy hurt his knee but he was still sixth in the nation in punt returns that year, if I'm not mistaken. Buck was just a tough, hard-nosed, all-around football player; I thought an outstanding back. Corso was good. I'm not taking anything away from Lee, but Buck was a good back.

Bobby Crenshaw, everybody knows, was a leader and a straight-arrow type. I remember in the Miami game, I heard a lick behind me, and I always marveled that, for a guy his size, what kind of linebacker he was. He was a good one.

Dr. William "Bill" Proctor played only one football season at Florida State and was a standout, two-way tackle in 1955. He later became the president of Flagler College in St. Augustine, Florida, and is currently second-term legislator in the Florida House of Representatives.

20

Tom Nugent had a lot of influence. Tom was an interesting character. He came down and visited me for a number of years when I was at Flagler. We had a little cottage on campus. He was a tough, hard-nosed coach, but imaginative, exciting. Then we had people like athletic trainer Don Fauls, who was just legend; the heart and core of the athletics program.

Then I went into high school coaching, and Vince Gibson, whom I had played with at FSU, was on the coaching staff six years later. Charley LaPradd was up there coaching. They called me and told me I should come back to FSU and take a graduate assistantship and finish my master's degree. By the time I came up that summer to do that, in the summer of 1962, Charley LaPradd resigned. So I ended up taking his position on a temporary basis. That January 1963, Coach Pete [Bill Peterson] put me on full-time.

I coached two years with the defensive staff and, by that time, had completed my master's and was ready to start my doctorate. It wasn't practical to try and stay on the varsity staff and do a doctoral program, so I asked to get the head coaching job for the freshman, and he gave it to me in 1964.

We had a rough year that first year, but the next year we had quarterback Gary Pajcic, we had wide receiver Ron Sellers, we had Johnny Crowe. We had a very good group of football players that year. We beat Florida and we beat Georgia Tech.

Then Charley LaPradd called me and said he was leaving the office of the dean of men and asked if I wanted to be the assistant dean of men. So in the fall of 1965 I was head freshman football coach and the assistant Dean of Men. That was an interesting fall.

Coach Pete let me go the next January, and I became the dean of men. I stayed on with that until I got a fellowship with IBM. So I resigned as dean of men and spent the next year down in the cellar of Tully Gym with a computer.

I guess I saw Florida State in two ways. When I came in the Nugent era, I saw a small college program moving into a major one. Then I was out six years coaching high school. Then I came back during the Peterson era, and I saw the beginning of the success with the major program—my next-to-last year we beat Florida, my scouting assignment, and went to the Gator Bowl. That was a super year. We were still playing some schools from the small college ranks but weren't beating the big schools yet. But the first year I was there was a funny year. We tied Kentucky, Georgia Tech, and Auburn. Actually, we played .500 ball in the SEC because we beat Georgia, lost to Florida, and tied three times. I think it was a transitional year.

I had the privilege of coaching with Bobby Bowden, Vince Gibson, Don James, John Coatta; a lot of those guys went on to head coaching jobs.

Bobby may remember it differently than I do, but I had been coaching defensive ends and I was supposed to spend some time with him. That sounds ridiculous, my telling Bobby Bowden how to coach. I'm not sure what position he coached initially, but I think he was on defense.

I know I can remember we were out lining up some dummies and I was talking about our defensive end play. I don't want to sound egotistical, talking about teaching Coach Bowden anything, but that seemed like my job. My job was to make the transition to the head freshman team coach and help him fit in to the defensive scheme, so the defensive ends were part of what he was doing at the time.

He was probably a lot straighter arrow than I was, but the chemistry was good.

I remember we won the Gator Bowl, and boosters gave us the choice of the money or tickets to Nassau, Bahamas. I was a graduate student, and Bobby was married with two or three kids at the time. We both voted for the money and got voted down. So, along with our wives, Ann [Bowden] and Pam [Proctor], we took my car, spent the night in Orlando with my folks, rode the boat to Nassau, and spent the rest of the time walking around Nassau because that was all the money we had.

I can tell you that when they were recruiting Coach Bowden to be Florida State's head coach, a couple of friends of mine who were on the committee called and asked, "What do you think?" I don't want to claim any credit for the selection, but I said I thought he was the one person in American football who could do that job.

I knew Bobby could recruit and I knew he had been at a small school. When you've been at a small school, you know what it's like to have to do with less than your opponents have. It's tough for somebody to come from a big-time program to a place where you don't have what you need. But Bobby had been at a small school. He knew what it was like, and I thought he would be well-received in Tallahassee. I thought he would be a great recruiter, and I knew he was a great football coach. I had coached with him long enough to know that.

Dr. William "Bill" Proctor played only one football season at Florida State and was a standout, two-way tackle in 1955, following in the footsteps of his brother, Custis Proctor, who was a member of the inaugural 1947 team. Proctor earned three degrees from Florida State, including his Ph.D. He spent four years on Bill Peterson's coaching staff, serving as the freshman coach and mentoring Bobby Bowden. Proctor left the coaching staff in 1966 to become FSU's assistant dean of men. After earning his Ph.D., Proctor became the president of Flagler College in St. Augustine, Florida, a position he held for 18 years. A member of the Florida State Sports Hall of Fame, he is currently a second-term legislator in the Florida House of Representatives and still serves on FSU's athletic board.

# RON SCHOMBURGER

## END

### 1954–1957

I GRADUATED FROM WESTVIEW HIGH SCHOOL just outside of Pittsburgh in 1949. I worked for a couple of years, then played a little semipro football and got drafted into the service in 1952. I played service football at Fort Benning, Georgia, and in 1954 [FSU assistant coach] Vaughn Mancha recruited a number of us from Fort Benning to come to Florida State to play football.

Among those was a good friend and roommate at Florida State, Bill Cullom, also Jimmy Trado and Pete Overton. I might add that we all got there in 1954 and graduated in 1958, which was quite a comment about us wanting to go to school and get our education.

We arrived in 1954, and Tom Nugent was the coach. There were a lot of guys who came in and out of here during the tryouts. There must have been hundreds of them, coming in and out, day after day. I don't know what the rules or regulations were back then, or if there were many, but apparently they were pretty lax because we had guys come in here by the busload. They would come out to practice, and when you went back to the dorm after practice, the guy's stuff would be out in the hallway. Somebody would come in while we were practicing. That was the indication that you were not going to be around anymore.

Some of the drills were pretty tough, and some guys would slip away on their own in the middle of the night; pack their stuff and leave. It wasn't what they thought college football was or should have been. There were tons of guys coming in and out of here. A lot of guys played a lot of years, at Livingstone State or somewhere else, and came here for a stint. I don't think you had to get four years in five, or whatever the rule is now. I made the football team, played for four years, and graduated in 1958. I was the team captain in 1957, and I was honored to be a scholastic All-American.

What I remembered most was the fact I thought we had a fine coaching staff. I had never been that deeply immersed in football through high school and semipro and service football. At Florida State, we had a coach for each position. You got clean jocks, clean T-shirts, and clean stuff every day. You turned in the old and got the new. I never had been in a situation like that.

That first year, in 1954, actually was a good season [FSU finished with an 8–4 record]. We went to the Sun Bowl in El Paso, Texas, and played a school that was called Texas Western at the time. It's called UTEP now. They beat us 47–20. I remember we had a little trouble getting used to the altitude out there. We didn't think about Texas being a little mountainous there. We had oxygen on the sideline and all that stuff.

I don't remember much about the game, except the fact we lost. I do remember we had a good time. We were out there about five or six days. Being in El Paso, Suarez, Mexico, was right across the river, and there was a lot happening in those border towns. It was kind of enlightening to some of us. We had a good time there, and that bowl treated us beautifully.

One time, my roommate, Ted Rodrigue, and I took off our sweats after practice and [the rooms] had those floor heaters. It was actually an open flame—a gas flame—and we put our sweatpants on top of that to dry them out. We got dressed and, as we were getting on the bus, somebody said, "There's a fire in one of those rooms over there." We got on the bus and left, and when we came back, our room was the one all smoked up. We had to move to a different room.

What I remember most, aside from the team, was some of the professors I had. The campus was quite small then, probably 6,500. If you didn't know somebody personally, you either had a class with them or passed them on campus going from place to place. It was a friendly campus; a lot of beautiful women. The professors were all helpful and as nice as they could be. It was just a fun time to be in college.

The whole campus atmosphere was so friendly and nice, it was one of the best times of my life. The fact that we were on the football team and getting some recognition, playing a game we liked and having all those good friends with us, going through some adversity—I think that's what bonded us closer together.

I think it helps us maintain our fun with getting together and seeing each other through all these years.

Tom Nugent was an outstanding coach, and a lot of the assistants were the best coaches I had ever been associated with. Bill Collum, who was in the service with me and who came here with me and was my roommate, got injured right after spring practice of our sophomore year and was kept on scholarship, even though he couldn't play football any longer. Al Makowiecki, who was from Monaca, Pennsylvania, was an All-American tackle at Florida State and is in the Hall of Fame. He was a good friend because we grew up not that far away from each other.

Tom Feamster, who was the biggest guy on the team at 6'7", 250 or 260 pounds, was out of the ordinary. Al Makowiecki and our other tackles weighed 215 or 220 pounds. We weren't nearly as big as all the teams are now. They were just outstanding players. Bobby Crenshaw, who was team captain and went to the service right after college and died in a jet crash while we were still in school, was outstanding.

Lee Corso, who played many, many positions—he played where he was needed—was just an outstanding athlete; a running back, quarterback. He could play any of those positions.

Actually, when Tom Nugent got here with his innovative coaching style and formations, he really got the program moving forward, growing and attracting better players. We always looked at being an integral part of getting the program really going; not that we were the first or that the five or six teams before weren't. But once Tom Nugent got here, we really got some recognition because he got us playing some high-profile teams. We played Auburn, Georgia, and Georgia Tech, who at that time were—and mostly still are—outstanding football teams.

Once we got better and would give them a little more competitive game, they didn't want to play us anymore. For a non-conference game, they didn't want to take a chance on losing to Florida State. Certainly, since then, and through Bill Peterson and Bobby Bowden and all that they have done, the program has progressed to where it's a national power and one of the premier football programs.

We probably felt like Burt Reynolds was going to be our premier running back. He had all the skills. He was fast, he was shifty. He could just play football. I don't think he was as strong defensively as he was offensively, but back then we had to play both ways. Then he just had a series of mishaps with injuries that just curtailed his going on.

I don't remember what year he was injured the first time, but he came back [in 1957] and played again and then was reinjured. I think at that point, those injuries were going to keep him from being as good as he was. I guess he just thought then to go into something else.

I admire him as somebody, I think, who has the same feeling about Florida State, the football team, and the players, as most of us do. There's just a strong bond that's there and that's why he has supported it so much and why he keeps coming back. In fact, he comes back to as many of our Nugent Boys reunions as he can.

He was on campus last fall [in 2006] doing seminars for the theater school, so we had a chance to visit. He's a little stove up. He's not doing any more stunts. He's moving a little more gingerly now, but still just as nice and charming a guy as you could ever meet.

I almost think of him in the same category as James Dean, who died in a car accident. He wasn't hyper or in-your-face. He was just laid back and had that air about him that, "I'm good looking and a good athlete and I know that," but he didn't need to announce it to everybody.

26

When he came here, besides his football uniform, he had a dress uniform for classes—jeans and a T-shirt. Most of the guys didn't have much of a wardrobe back then, but every time you saw him, he had on his sneakers or loafers, his jeans, and a white T-shirt.

The music at that time was all ballads and soft; there was some rock and roll, which we all enjoyed. A group of us used to think we were quite good singers, and we'd get in the stairway of old Senior Hall and attempt to harmonize and sing those songs. We thought we were as good as any of those groups.

It was Ted Rodrigue, Jerry Henderson, sometimes Burt, myself, and several others who would show up and attempt to sound like whatever song was popular at the time. We could perform as well as those groups.

Freddie Pickard and some of those other guys who were a little bit younger were called Nugent's Sons. Any time there was some roughing up [on the field] where tempers really got hot, Nugent would say, "Who hit Schomburger?" Nugent was trying to take care of the older guys getting hurt.

Almost every game before the kickoff, I'd be saying a prayer and saying, "What the heck am I doing out here?" Everybody is coming from 50 [yards]

Ron Schomburger was a standout two-way end for the Seminoles. A three-sport high school star in Pittsburgh and an Army veteran, he arrived at FSU in 1954 and played four seasons. His aggressive style and indomitable will were immediately evident as coach Tom Nugent described him as a "tough, complete package."

apart, colliding or trying to get to your running back or blocking you. It happened every game—"What the heck am I doing out here?" Once [the game] started, though, [the hesitation] was gone.

One recollection I have: we were playing Auburn, and they kicked off to us. We all did our assignments, and I threw a block and was rolling over to get up, and Billy Odom was coming up a wide-open hole. Everything worked perfectly. Everybody was blocked. There was nobody in his path. He was going to go for a touchdown. About that time, one of our players had made a block, got up to do something else, and collided with Odom and knocked him on his rear end. We ended up losing to Auburn in a very close game [13–7 in 1956]. It was one of those things that just sticks out in my mind, what could have been.

I remember some of the teams we played, the games we played, and how they went, but what I remember the most about playing football here was the relationships I made, not only with the players, but with the coaching staff and support staff, as well. I made lifelong friends in college; guys I played with, a number of whom I see on a regular basis and still live here in Tallahassee.

We have a group of that we call the "Nugent Boys," which was a group of guys who played for Tom Nugent. He arrived here in 1953 and left after the 1958 season. We get together every year at one of the football games. This past year we had some 40 players, plus wives and families, come back. We always have some get-together in the last eight or 10 years at Bobby Carnes's lake house over near Quincy and have a party on a Friday night before a football game.

We carry on and tell lies. The stories get bigger and better every year. We're not getting older, we're getting better. We just really have a close, strong, tie. Some of the same guys keep coming back to that football game each year. Occasionally, we'll get somebody back who hasn't been for a long time, and it's always good to see some of those old friends come back and hear the stories of what they've done and where they've been.

Up until two years ago, Tom Nugent came back to each one before he passed away. He came right up to the end, and his wife, Peg, used to come with him as well. She passed away probably a year or so before that. But Tom still came with his son and daughter-in-law, and they would hang around with the guys as well and just reminisce and talk about old times. We had great fun doing that.

Ron Schomburger was a standout two-way end for the Seminoles. A three-sport high school star in Pittsburgh and an Army veteran, he arrived at FSU in 1954 and played four seasons. His aggressive style and indomitable will were immediately evident as coach Tom Nugent described him as a "tough, complete package." An All-State player, Collegiate All-America Academic Team member, he was a member of the FSU men's leadership honor society and Gold Key. Schomburger was inducted in the FSU Hall of Fame. He lives in Tallahassee, Florida.

# FRED PICKARD
## HALFBACK/DEFENSIVE BACK
### 1956–1959

I GREW UP IN COLUMBIA, TENNESSEE, and Florida State had an assistant coach who played for the Washington Redskins. A guy named Max Peoples, who was a junior high coach in Columbia, also played for the Redskins. Peoples had a nephew on my high school team who was a big lineman. He got Florida State to recruit us, and they offered us scholarships.

Smaller schools, such as Tennessee Tech and Tennessee State, were looking at me. But FSU flew us down to Tallahassee, and it was the first time I'd been on an airplane. It was different and scary. When we landed, they drove us around campus for a little while, and I saw more pretty girls in one day than I'd seen in my whole life. So I thought Florida State would be a good place to go to school.

When we arrived at Florida State that summer, they had 133 freshmen at practice on the first day. They killed people on that first day of practice. Back then, there were four-year scholarships, but at FSU, they were four-year scholarships one day at a time. The coaches tried to run you off pretty quickly. We had three practices the first day, and they ran off about 30 freshmen. Every drill you could think of, we did it in practice at FSU.

Coach Tom Nugent was a nice guy, but he wasn't nice as a coach. He was rough. He was my coach my first three years. I was on the freshman team in 1956. We were live dummies. They used to have those dummies you could hit and they would bounce back up. They did the same thing to us. We used to have to practice against the varsity all the time. We played about four to six games as freshmen, against teams from Eglin Air Force Base and some junior colleges. But we didn't ever get to practice as a freshman team; we were always practicing against the varsity.

I got to be really good friends with some of the guys I finished with: John Spivey, Abner Bigbie, and Joe Majors. Majors, whose brother was Johnny Majors [who became the longtime football coach at the University of Tennessee], had transferred to FSU from Alabama. He lost a year of eligibility, so he was practicing with the freshman team. Burt Reynolds's foster brother, Jimmy Hooks [now Jimmy Reynolds] also was on that freshman team.

You played both ways back then, and I was a running back and defensive back. I moved up to the varsity team in 1957 and started after about the third game and finished the rest of the season in the starting lineup. They moved Bobby Renn around quite a bit, and he was a great football player.

We opened the 1957 season against Furman [a 27–7 win] and then played at Boston College and Villanova. That was a treat. Believe it or not, we flew on an airplane to those games. Most of the games we went to, we'd leave on a Friday. But we had to leave on Thursday to get up to Boston and Philadelphia. It was the first time I'd been up North. It was different.

We played in that big stadium in Philadelphia, and they had about 20,000 people in the stands. They were big and had huge kids. We lost to Boston College 20–7 and lost to Villanova 21–7. I started against Villanova, but they didn't run me a lot in the game. They got after us pretty good, I know that. Both of those teams were pretty good.

We went back to Tallahassee and lost to North Carolina State 7–0. That was the game when Burt Reynolds left. The coaches got on him at halftime. N.C. State had two great backs, and they were two of the top runners in the country. One of them caught a little pass and ran it in for a touchdown in the first half, and the coaches blamed it on Reynolds. They got on him, and the next day he'd quit the team and gone back to Hollywood.

We beat Abilene Christian College 34–7 [Pickard ran 16 times for 62 yards in the victory] and then we beat Virginia Tech 20–7. In that game, believe it or not, I had just screwed up the kickoff return in the first half. Back in those days, if the kickoff went into the end zone, you had to bring it out. I fumbled the football into the end zone and had to bring it out, and they hit me in the end zone. I got it back to the 20-yard line, and Nugent was getting ready to take me out and kill me.

Fred Pickard was a standout halfback and defensive back at Florida State from 1957 to 1959. He led the Seminoles in rushing three straight seasons and set school records for career rushing yards (1,546) and carries (339). He was a longtime high school coach in Florida and was coach at Tennessee-Martin.

But on the next play, I ran it up the middle and a guy hit me as I was falling down. He knocked me straight up into the air, and I landed on my feet and was on a dead run. It was one of the luckiest runs you'll ever see. One guy knocked me down, and the other guy knocked me straight up.

We played Miami the next week and lost 40–13. The score was only 7–6 at halftime, but then they psyched us out. We beat Miami my junior year, but the only other time FSU had beaten Miami was during my freshman season. We met them halfway near DeLand, Florida, and beat them up pretty good.

After losing to Miami, we went to Hattiesburg, Mississippi to play Mississippi Southern, and it was tough. We lost 20–0. We played Auburn at our place the following week, and they were ranked No. 1 in the country. Both of their defensive ends were All-Americans and were great. But we gave them a great ballgame and hung in with them for most of the game. We lost 29–7. We went down to Tampa to finish the season and won 21–7.

We finished my sophomore season with a 4–6 record. We were better my junior year, with a 7–4 record in 1958. We played Tennessee Tech and Tennessee during my junior season. Playing two schools from my home state was fun. We opened the season against Tennessee Tech, which had offered me a scholarship, and won 22–7.

We came back to Tallahassee and played Furman [an easy 42–6 win], and then went to Georgia Tech. We lost the game 17–3, but we should have won. Georgia Tech was a big, big name back then. Where I grew up, Tennessee and Georgia Tech were like pro ball. I'd never heard of Florida State. Georgia Tech just psyched us out, and Bobby Dodd was coaching on the sideline. If we had the confidence they had, we would have won the game.

We upset Wake Forest 27–24 the next week, and our quarterback, Vic Prinzi, was just great. He threw those passes end over end, but he was tough. Wake Forest had a bunch of great receivers and always threw the ball very well.

We played Georgia in the Gator Bowl stadium. Georgia was a big name, and we just didn't play as well as we could have played and lost 28–13. That was a pretty good schedule for Florida State. They'd never played so many Southeastern Conference schools and Miami. It was kind of just like going through the process. We had to get the confidence to play those schools.

But we were getting confidence. We beat Virginia Tech 28–0. Virginia Tech was always good on defense and it was always a really physical game. We had a little bit of confidence and had to go up to Tennessee to play. We played them up there, and it was a great experience. Somehow, we won the game 10–0. Tennessee was the first Southeastern Conference school that FSU beat. We played good against them, there was no doubt about it [Pickard had 133 yards in the game]. It was special. Most of my family, my mom and dad and brothers and sisters, were at the game.

We'd beaten Tennessee and played Georgia Tech and Georgia, so we had some confidence. We beat Tampa 43–0 in Tallahassee, and then we had to play Miami. Going into the Miami game, they were just rubbing it in our faces that we'd never beaten them. Well, we won the game 17–6. It wasn't the best team Miami ever had, but they were always pretty good.

I caught a touchdown in that game after the football bounced off someone else. They faked the football to me running out of the backfield. No one tackled me, so that tells you I didn't fake very well. They threw it over in the corner and got to the goal, and dang if the pass didn't bounce right over to me. It went about 10 yards and bounced right to me.

After beating Miami, we played Florida for the first time in Gainesville. They wouldn't ever play us because we were a smaller school and everything. We played them tough. We scored first and had them 7–0. They killed Prinzi and took him out of the game. Back then, you had to play all kinds of positions. He was blocking for the punter, and one of the big ends went back and killed Prinzi. That really hurt us because Vic was a great player. They had a better football team than we did, and they had more troops than we did, but we still gave them a good ballgame. We lost to Florida 21–7, but we had a good season and went to a bowl game.

We went to Louisville, Kentucky, after the season to play Oklahoma State in the Bluegrass Bowl. We had on those little Florida uniforms, and it was freezing cold up there. They had a tarp on the field, and it was still frozen. They had barrels on the sideline with fires in them, but it was rough. It was the first Bluegrass Bowl and the last one. Oklahoma State was big. It was just an awful experience, and we lost the game 15–6.

After my junior season, Coach Nugent left for Maryland. I couldn't blame him because Maryland had a better program than we did. Years later, he told us that Maryland was going to let his kids go to school for free, and Florida State wouldn't. He had about seven or eight kids.

Florida State brought in Perry Moss, who had played at Wisconsin and coached at Miami. He was mean. In practice, he dug a big hole in the ground. You could get in it and someone would have to help you out. He'd put two players in there and would say, "The toughest one gets out." He was pretty tough. Moss went to the Canadian Football League after only one year, but I thought he was a really good football coach. He just didn't get along with people. He had everybody at Florida State mad at him.

During my senior year, we weren't very good. We lost to Wake Forest 22–20 in the opening game, and things got worse from there. When Perry Moss came in, he ran off a lot of people who had played a lot for us the year before. It was like a war zone. We didn't have any depth at all. He sent them all to the house.

We came back and beat The Citadel pretty bad [a 47–6 win], but then we lost to Miami 7–6. We tied the game really late [Pickard scored on an eight-yard touchdown run with less than three minutes left to make the score 7–6] and we went for the two-point conversion. It was the first two-point conversion we tried, and it was a killer. It surprised me that we decided to go for it. I took a pitch out and ran left. I cut up, and the goal line was at about my waist line when I was tackled. I'm telling you, if you look at the film, I was halfway into the end zone. But they said I didn't get in, and we lost the game.

We played Virginia Tech the following week and stopped a two-point conversion to win the game 7–6. They tried to run the fullback around end on the two-point try, but Tony Romeo knocked him out of bounds. Boy, I'm telling you, Tony Romeo could play. We went to Memphis after that, and we just weren't ready to play. Memphis State beat us 16–6. They just whipped us.

We just couldn't get it together during my senior season, and we had a bunch of starters back. Coach Moss was just rough. We came back and beat Richmond 22–6. But then we went to Georgia. The Bulldogs had Fran Tarkenton at quarterback. We were losing 21–0 at halftime, and Coach Moss walked in the locker room and said to us, "Boys, try to keep them under 100." Then he turned around and walked back out. That's just the way he was. I can remember running back five kickoffs and we weren't blocking anyone. They just killed me.

After the Georgia game, we were really thin. Everybody was getting hurt in practice or Coach Moss was running them off. Everybody was whipped. We lost to William & Mary 9–0, and then we had to play at Florida. I didn't play in the Florida game. I'd hurt my knee in practice, and the coaches hadn't decided whether or not they were going to give me a shot of novocaine and play me in the game. They decided they wouldn't do it. I thought they'd killed me. My knee was messed up and swollen, but they never did surgery on it.

I came back and played against Tampa two weeks later. I really had the knee wrapped up and didn't run very well. We won the game 33–0. I always played well against Tampa. [Pickard caught a 62-yard touchdown from Joe Majors and ran for an eight-yard touchdown in the game.]

After my senior season, Coach Moss left for the Montreal Alouettes of the Canadian Football League. He called me and asked me if I wanted to come up there with him. No one else called me, so I went. I made it all the way to the end of training camp but didn't make the team. He liked big backs, and I wasn't very big. Probably the heaviest I ever played at Florida State was 165 pounds.

So I went back to Florida State and graduated. I was a graduate assistant coach under Coach Bill Peterson and coached high school football for 13 years and later coached at a small college, Tennessee–Martin. I came back and finished up at Terry Parker High School in Jacksonville, Florida, where I coached for 21 years before retiring.

Fred Pickard, a native of Columbia, Tennessee, was a three-year varsity halfback and defensive back at Florida State from 1957 to 1959. Pickard led the Seminoles in rushing in each of those seasons and set school records for career rushing yards (1,546) and career carries (339) before graduating. Pickard scored 14 touchdowns during his Florida State career, and scored the first touchdown ever scored in the Florida-FSU series. He also led Florida State to one of its most important early victories, a 10–0 win at Tennessee on October 25, 1958, the school's first win over a Southeastern Conference school. In that game, Pickard ran for 133 yards, more than the entire Volunteers team. Pickard was chosen honorable mention All-American by both the Associated Press and United Press International as a senior in 1959. He was a longtime high school coach in Florida and was coach at Tennessee-Martin from 1982 to 1985. He was elected into the FSU Hall of Fame in 1982, is retired, and lives in Jacksonville Beach, Florida.

35

# BUD WHITEHEAD
## HALFBACK/DEFENSIVE BACK
### 1957–1960

I GREW UP MARIANNA, FLORIDA, and I guess I was recruited to Florida State just like they do today. Guys came over from the college coaching staff and scouted my high school games and talked to my coaches about whether I was worthy of a scholarship. I had other opportunities to go to Florida, Auburn, Alabama, and Georgia. Those are the schools I remember recruiting me the most.

But I think Florida State made a bigger commitment in spending time with my family and me and showed more interest in me. One of my very best friends, Bobby Conrad, was the quarterback of our high school team. He was a high school All-American and probably could have gone to any college in America because he was such a good athlete. Florida State might have been thinking that if I went to Florida State, he probably would come, too, because he was one of my best friends. We did go to Florida State together and played football.

I knew Florida State was an up-and-coming program. It had been an all-girls school until the late 1940s, and they definitely weren't a powerhouse football program. My high school coach told me a lot of schools wanted me, but Florida State *needed* me. The opportunity to be close to my hometown was a big factor in choosing Florida State, too. We could drive to Tallahassee in about an hour and 15 minutes, and it would give my parents and grand-parents an opportunity to come over and watch me play. That was appealing.

My younger brother, Willie, was a year behind me and came over to Florida State to play football the following year. It was great having my brother there. My brother and I are very tight. I love Willie very much and we came from a tight-knit family. It was great to have him at Florida State with me. He enjoyed it as much as I did, and has great ties and friends from the university days. It was great to have family so close by.

I graduated from high school in 1957 and was on the freshman team at Florida State that fall. They probably brought in more than 100 freshmen that year, and they had a lot of older guys who were getting out of the military. They were 21- or 22-year-old guys. They were cutting people pretty quickly with so many freshmen that year. We were having three-a-day practices—morning, noon, and night—because I guess they wanted to see who had the stamina and will to go through all that ruggedness and wanted to stay. They eliminated a lot of people that first week and cut people really fast.

I moved up to the varsity team in 1958 and played halfback. I was playing behind Bobby Renn and Fred Pickard, who were our two big-name athletes in the backfield and were both great players. I still say Freddy Pickard was probably the best pound-for-pound athlete I ever played with, even after my pro days. I just thought he was a wonderful athlete and I don't know if he ever weighed over 160 pounds. He was a small guy who just had catlike agility and balance and was so strong for a little guy. Boy, I don't ever remember him being hurt.

We opened the 1958 season against Tennessee Tech and Furman [both easy victories], and then we played at Georgia Tech. When I was a young kid, I just really respected and loved Georgia Tech. I remember as a middle school student, they had all the college yearbooks in the library. I was just a Bobby Dodd fan. I thought he was the epitome of college football coaches because he was such a great guy and had such a wonderful reputation. He was the man in the South, along with Bear Bryant at Alabama.

It was just awesome to play against Georgia Tech. Florida State had been a small school, and we weren't used to playing powerhouse football programs like Georgia Tech, Florida, and Alabama. These were building blocks, and we were picking up two or three games a year against those powerhouses. Most of our schedule was against schools that were our size with similar stadiums and facilities, like Furman, The Citadel, Tennessee Tech, and William & Mary. We weren't yet what you would call a Southern football power.

So going up to Georgia Tech and playing in their stadium in front of a huge crowd was kind of mind-boggling for a small-town boy. We lost the game [17–3], but it was a wonderful experience. We came back and upset Wake Forest [27–24]. Norman Snead, who went on to play football in the NFL for a long time, was their quarterback. They had some great football players on that team.

We went to Jacksonville and played Georgia in the Gator Bowl stadium and, boy, were they good. Georgia might have been the best team we'd played that season. Fran Tarkenton was the quarterback, and they were as good as anybody we played. [Florida State lost the game 28–13.]

After beating Virginia Tech 28–0, we went up to Tennessee and won 10–0. It was the first time Florida State had beaten a Southeastern Conference school. That was the biggest victory in my career at Florida State. We had to be heavy underdogs for that particular game, and I think one of the Majors boys was their quarterback. That was a really huge victory for Florida State.

That was Tom Nugent's last season as Florida State's coach. He left for the University of Maryland after the 1958 season. One of my assistant coaches on Nugent's staff was Lee Corso. He was a football player at Florida State and came onto the coaching staff. Even now, you can just see his enthusiasm and love for athletics. He always kept things lively, and it was never dull around Coach Corso. He was a good athlete. He was a small guy, but a very fine athlete. His personality was just bubbly and exciting, and it rubbed off on you. You really picked up on that energy he had.

Coach Nugent was such a great motivator. That was one of his real strengths. He was such a classic coach in the way he approached a game. He really preached staying together as a team and believing in one another. He told us, "Yeah, we are a small school and we are an up-and-comer, but that doesn't mean we can't go out and compete and hold our heads high. If we give it our best shot, then good things will happen."

After beating Tennessee, we played at Miami later in the season. They were always good and had a lot of All-Americans and a lot of terrific athletes. We lost to Florida to finish the season and then we played Oklahoma State in the Bluegrass Bowl in Louisville, Kentucky. That game was the coldest I've ever been in my entire life. They didn't know what to wear, sneakers or football cleats because the field was frozen. I think the old helmet face guards were made of plastic and, boy, they would just shatter. Every time you had a good lick on somebody, your face mask would shatter. I can remember getting on the sideline where they had straw, and you'd try to put the straw on your legs and feet to stay warm. That was, by far, the coldest I've ever been in my life. I just couldn't believe it could get that cold. I do remember it was miserable.

Coach Nugent left after the 1958 season, and they brought in Perry Moss as the new coach. We were all very excited about having that good year in 1958. We were all looking for big things the following year. The school had really blossomed under Nugent, and we thought he was going to be there for a long time. But you could certainly understand his position for leaving. The Maryland Terrapins were a powerhouse team and were going to major bowl games year after year. It was a huge stepping stone for Coach Nugent. As players, we were all disappointed and a little hurt that we were going to lose our coach and some of the staff. We were almost like a family going through all those struggles and hard times together, and you love your coaches and love your teammates. When it breaks up, there's a down time.

But we were young and we rolled with the punches. I felt like Coach Moss was a really good coach and did his best and the best he could do for us. He only stayed for a season and then went up to Canada. But we only had him less than a year, so he wasn't there long enough to put his program in place and leave his mark on Florida State.

We struggled as a team during my junior season in 1959. We opened against Wake Forest, and Norman Snead was their quarterback again. [Whitehead returned an interception 81 yards for a touchdown, which still ranks as the 10th-longest return in FSU history.] It was just one of those plays where you're in the right place at the right time. Their passing attack was probably as good as I ever played against. Back in those days, it still wasn't opened up like it is today. But Wake Forest threw the football all over the field.

We played at Georgia that season and lost 42–0. I think in all my football experiences, in high school, college, and the pros, that was the worst thing I'd ever been exposed to. At halftime, Coach Moss told us, "Guys, try to keep it under 100." They flat put a spanking on us. Georgia's quarterback, Fran Tarkenton, was just a stellar athlete. I later worked as an assistant with the New Orleans Saints and coached defensive backs, and I hated to play against Tarkenton.

You would come up with schemes to put pressure on him, and that was probably the wrong thing to do. When you put pressure on him, you're

Bud Whitehead grew up close to Florida State in Marianna, Florida, and was a three-year letterman, from 1958 to 1960. A star two-way player at defensive back and halfback, Whitehead led the country with six interceptions and ranked eighth with 31 pass receptions in 1959, both of which were school records at the time. He was elected into Florida State's Sports Hall of Fame in 1981.

creating holes in other places and putting people in one-on-one situations. He would just wear your defensive linemen out because they couldn't tackle him. He'd run back and forth across the field, and those big guys would try to tackle him and they'd just be exhausted. You had to have two linemen at every position because he'd just wear you down. If you got pressure on him, he'd just juke them. He was like a rabbit because he was so elusive. He could buy time and throw the ball as well as anyone I'd ever seen.

During my junior year, Moss liked to throw the football. Joe Majors, our quarterback, could really throw the football. [In the last game of the 1959 season, Whitehead had nine catches in a 33–0 win over Tampa to set a single-game record at FSU.] You really wondered why a running back would catch that many passes, but I guess we just emphasized throwing to the backs and flooding the zone coming out of the backfield. I guess we threw a lot of short passes instead of trying to go down the field with long passes to the wide guys. We weren't too shabby in the passing game that season because Majors was such a good passer.

Before my senior season, in 1960, Moss left for Canada and Bill Peterson came from LSU. The one thing I really liked about Coach Pete was he really brought in a good staff. Coach Pete wasn't a micromanager, either. He was the key guy in charge of the whole operation, but he wanted to hire people who could do their jobs, and then he would let them coach. That doesn't mean he didn't have a lot of input. Most of his input came on offense because he had been an offensive line coach and he liked offense. He spent a lot of time with his staff in pro football camps, and he loved to throw the football. He loved Sid Gillman, whom I played for with the San Diego Chargers, and I really think Gillman was the guru of the pro passing game. If you throw the ball and say you weren't influenced by Sid Gillman, you're fooling yourself.

We didn't throw the ball as much during my senior season. Joe Majors had graduated, and Ed Trancygier and Eddie Feely were splitting time at quarterback. I don't think either one of those guys was as good of a passer as Majors overall, but they each had other skills. We probably ran more than we passed that season.

We started the season against Richmond [a 28–0 victory] and then played at Florida and lost 3–0 after we missed a field goal in the fourth quarter. Even though we never beat Florida in the years I was there—it was three or four years down the road before Florida State pulled it off—we had some good games against the Gators. They always had great talent and good football players, and I always respected their personnel. It was the game you always wanted to win—always has been and always will be. They were always the team you wanted to play, and it took a long time for us to get the opportunity to play them. I got a chance to play them three times and we never won, but we did have some great football games against them.

We came back and beat Wake Forest [14–6], and then we went to Charleston and played The Citadel. The game ended in a 0–0 tie. We lost to Mississippi Southern and beat William & Mary and then finished the season with four straight losses. You would have liked to have played your last season in college and go out on a high note. You'd like that senior season to be the milestone or the anchor of your college career. Actually, mine was my sophomore year. I was thankful I was on a team good enough to play in a bowl game. We were no powerhouse; those years came later.

After college, I wasn't even thinking about pro football. When I got drafted by the Los Angeles Chargers, I was like, "What's this all about?"

41

I didn't think I'd had a good enough career to even consider professional football. One of the scouts from the Chargers told me later, "We picked up on you when you played up at Virginia Tech." I intercepted three passes in that particular game, so I guess somebody was looking on film and saw me. I guess they thought they should bring me in because they had to bring in some players anyway. I wouldn't have even been drafted today.

I was really kind of shocked to get the opportunity to play pro football, but I was thankful I got the opportunity because it was a marvelous experience. I played eight years for the Chargers and played for the AFL championship four times—we won once. We beat Boston in the AFL championship [51–10 in 1963] during my third season, and one of my good friends at FSU, Tony Romeo, was the Boston Patriots' tight end. He was on that team, and we talked quite a bit during the game and were having a great time playing the game. I just remember Keith Lincoln, our halfback, had one of the greatest games ever. Offensively, it was the best game we ever put on. To get 51 points against the Boston Patriots was really something.

I broke my shoulder during my last season with the Chargers in 1968. I knew that my time was limited anyway, and I got the opportunity to coach at Florida State, so I jumped on that right away. I coached under Bill Peterson, was there two years, and moved on to New Orleans after that. I was the Saints' secondary coach for five years.

I got out of coaching after that. My wife wanted to live closer to her parents in California, and we were seeing a lot of coaches being fired every two, three, or four years. She said she wasn't sure that's what she wanted to do the rest of our lives. I kind of agreed and thought maybe it was a good move to do something else. I loved football and, if I had been a bachelor, I'd still be in it today.

I remember going back to Florida State after my fourth year in the NFL and watching the Seminoles play Oklahoma in the Gator Bowl. I couldn't believe how much they'd improved, and they were just really kicking people. It was only four years after I'd left, and here they were beating the University of Oklahoma. I was really proud. I was just so thrilled. I don't know that I never thought FSU would get to that point, but I never thought they'd get there that quickly.

My memories, like most athletes, are of the guys I played with. Someone once said being a football player is almost like you're getting ready to go to war. You're out there in those hot, miserable, humid days and you're beating each other up and struggling, and you're going around the country playing in stadiums where everyone is against you. You get attached to those guys and go through a lot of pain and stay together. It was a great experience.

A native of Marianna, Florida, Bud Whitehead was a three-year letterman on Florida State's varsity football team from 1958 to 1960. A hard-hitting defensive back and versatile halfback, Whitehead led the country with six interceptions and ranked eighth nationally with 31 pass receptions in 1959. Both totals were Florida State single-season records, and he also broke the school single-game records for receptions (nine) and interceptions (three). Whitehead played in the 1960 North-South All-Star Game and was drafted by the Los Angeles Chargers in the 1961 AFL draft. He played eight seasons for the Chargers and was a member of the 1963 team that won the AFL championship. Whitehead later coached at Florida State and was the secondary coach for the New Orleans Saints for five years. Whitehead was elected into the FSU Hall of Fame in 1981. He is retired from sales and lives in Fresno, California.

# The

# SIXTIES

# GENE McDOWELL
## DEFENSIVE TACKLE
### 1960–1962

W E PLAYED BOTH WAYS BACK THEN. The first thing was, you had to be in good shape. If you were in good shape and had the ability, there's not a whole lot left to it. You just did it. We didn't have All-Americans at every position, so you didn't have to be great to play both ways and play in those days. We were a kind of middle-of-the-road program in 1960 and 1961, but then Bill Peterson brought it from nowhere to somewhere.

They had good football teams when Tom Nugent was there, then it went down for a year. Peterson's first year was down, but then it went up really quickly. His system on offense was really good, and one of his great strengths was hiring really good football coaches to work with him. He knew how to push their buttons. The two biggest things were hiring the right guys and then pushing the buttons to make them do the work. He stirred the pot quite a bit.

Coach Pete's system offensively was a key. He was one of the few early guys who threw the ball a lot, and he had coaches who understood the passing game better than most coaches at that time. He had a really good defensive coordinator, Vince Gibson, who went on to coach at Kansas State, Tulane, Louisville, and Tennessee.

The 1964 season was the real breakout year. That was the year that the "Magnificent Seven" defense led the way, and Fred Biletnikoff was a great receiver. We beat Oklahoma pretty good in the Gator Bowl. I left after the 1962 season, went in the Army for two years, and then came back.

The 3–3 tie with Florida in 1961 is pretty memorable for me. It was especially pleasing to me that we never lost to Georgia while I was in school because I was from Waycross, Georgia, and they didn't want me when I was coming out of high school. Georgia beat us in 1959 when it was my freshman year, but I don't count that because I wasn't playing. They tied us, then we beat them two or three times.

Everybody who was part of the program back then has reason to have pride. We made a lot of strides, but there is a lot of history and success to the program from the 1950s that is being forgotten and stories that are not being told. I have always felt the administration at Florida State has not given them their due. They have a wall down there with all the All-Americans, but what about those guys who were All-Americans at the level we were playing at?

It bothers me some that they don't give those guys like Freddie Pickard, who was as good of a back who played there, the credit they deserved. They were competing at the level they were competing at and succeeding. It bothers me when they say I was the first All-American at Florida State, but that's not true. They beat Tennessee one year; they got national honors and everybody has forgotten about them. Somebody needs to find their pictures and put them up. They had those pictures up on the wall. Where are they now?

47

I was light for a guard, but I was not light for a linebacker. There were a lot of small guys who played back in those days. You didn't have the huge body types you have today. I was in great shape to start with and I had great strength because we worked hard in our summer jobs. That kind of thing paid off in sports. I worked at a tobacco warehouse, and one of the things you had to do was handle those tobacco sheets that averaged 300 pounds. I worked at a planing mill where you threw hot boards off a stack. It was very serious and intense labor. That helped me become a football player as much as anything.

Bob Harbison was my offensive line coach, and he was one of the all-time greats at Florida State. Vince Gibson coached me as a linebacker. He was really intense and really smart. We ran mostly a five-man front.

On offense, Bill Peterson insisted on the passing game. He stayed in touch with Don Coryell. He sent us Joe Gibbs, Dan Henning, and Don Breaux. All of them had some understanding of the passing game. Bill Parcells went through Florida State. Peterson hired him, too. Peterson was very intense, and he researched these guys through the NFL. He probably hired only one guy who was a bad hire, at least that I was aware of.

Gene McDowell was a star lineman and guard for Florida State, then returned to his alma mater as a longtime assistant coach. While working on Coach Bobby Bowden's staff, McDowell earned the reputation as a very organized and tireless recruiter. He later became head coach at Central Florida. (Photo courtesy of University of Central Florida)

48

The 3–3 tie in the 1961 Florida game was big because people said we had no chance to play with them. We didn't really have the personnel to compete with them back then. There was a guy in that game, Roy Bickford, who was the reason we didn't lose that game. He intercepted two passes, blocked a punt, and made six tackles. He played safety. That sort of thing should be up in lights.

It gave us a lot of heart for every time we played somebody like Florida. We knew if we could tie them, we could beat them.

We were just getting to be good again. Playing well against those kinds of teams in the early 1960s really set the table for the 1964 team. Our team really took off that year. The big thing for me was beating Georgia. My senior year we beat them 18–0 up there in Athens. My friends still recount some of the stuff they said I did in the game when I see them in Waycross. They were disappointed with their team; they were kind of down on their team. They were happy for me, which overcame what happened to their team.

I was extra motivated for that game. And in 1961 we beat them, so I was 2–0 against them as a player. We had a lot of guys from south Georgia, so we were all extra motivated. They could sign 30 or 40 guys, but they never got around to us.

As for Florida, [the game] was bigger to us than it was to them back then. It was never any other game for us.

It went downhill in 1970, then Larry Jones left and they brought Darrell Mudra in to coach. I thought he was a good coach and would have been successful if he had stayed. That didn't work out for me, and they brought Bobby Bowden in and it took off immediately.

I always thought if Peterson had stayed there, he would have had great success for another 10 years. He went to Rice for one year and then went to the Houston Oilers.

The best recruiting class we had there was the 1985 class with Deion Sanders. That was a big one for us. I came in as the lead recruiter, and we got better organized in recruiting. Coach Bowden didn't realize what was about to happen. Brad Scott did a nice job, and another guy, Larry Strahm, helped me administratively. He played basketball at Florida State and was a retired businessman, and between the two of us we got really organized.

I don't think people understand the impact Larry had in helping me get that organized. They continued to use our setup for some time after that. We knew where all the players were and we had them ranked.

We decided to recruit speed, and that was a big ingredient. We began to realize in the 1997 team that speed was important. We had guys who could fly on that team. We were really fast and went 11–1 with that team.

Bobby's game-planning was outstanding. He was a great Xs and Os guy. Comparing Peterson and Bobby, they were strong disciplinarians. Bobby was pretty demanding in what he expected out of me as an assistant coach as far as discipline; he didn't let any infraction go unpunished. His hiring was really good in the early days.

Gene McDowell came to Florida State from Waycross, Georgia, and stayed to become one of the Seminoles' greatest linebackers and an outstanding assistant coach later in life. McDowell played guard and linebacker from 1960 through 1962. He was captain of the 1962 Seminoles and that season was named third-team All-American by the Associated Press, the first FSU player to be so highly honored. In 1962 McDowell was named the team's MVP and Florida's College Player of the Year. He also played in the North-South All-Star Game. McDowell was an assistant coach under Bill Peterson at FSU in 1968 and 1969, then moved to Kansas State for four seasons. He returned to Bobby Bowden's staff in 1974 and coached the team's linebackers and was an outstanding recruiter for the next 10 seasons. He was named coach at Central Florida in 1985. McDowell is retired and lives in Tallahassee.

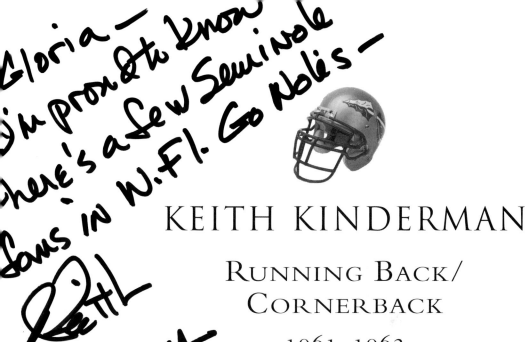

*Gloria —*
*I'm proud to know!*
*there's a few Seminole*
*fans in W. Fl. Go Noles —*
*Keith Kinderman*

# KEITH KINDERMAN

## RUNNING BACK/
## CORNERBACK

### 1961–1962

I GREW UP IN CHICAGO AND GRADUATED from high school in Crystal Lake, Illinois, which is 40 miles northwest of Chicago. I started my college career at the University of Iowa and played on the freshman team in 1959. Ed Trancygier, the quarterback on the Iowa team, was my roommate, and we had a good time drinking beer and such. We'd read the books before the tests, and I'd pass the tests, and he'd fail them. He flunked out of Iowa and got accepted to Florida State, and he talked me into going down there the following year in 1961.

I went to Gulf Coast Junior College in Panama City, Florida, in 1960. The reason I went there was because there were two NCAA rules at the time. One said if you transferred from one Division I-A school to another one, you had to sit out one season. Another rule said if you graduated from a junior college, you were eligible to play at any Division I-A school. There were conflicting rules, so we responded to the one that benefitted us. The only reason I went there was to get a junior college degree. I had enough hours, and only had to get a few more hours at Gulf Coast Junior College. I had to be in residency for at least one semester to get the junior college degree.

I transferred to Florida State before the 1961 season. My first game at FSU was against George Washington, and I played a little bit. We played Florida

Keith Kinderman was a rough, hard-nosed running back from Chicago, who began his college career at Iowa. After playing two seasons for the Hawkeyes, He transferred to Florida State for two years. He was perhaps best known for his sometimes outrageous off-field antics, and was briefly suspended from the team. He later attended FSU's College of Law and was a practicing attorney in Tallahassee for several years.

the second week, and it was a 3–3 tie. The officiating was pretty one-sided, and it always was when we played the Gators over there. I returned kickoffs in that game and caught a kickoff at the 1-yard line. I bent down slightly at the knees and returned it about 60 yards. But the referee said my knee touched at the 12-yard line and gave us the ball there. It was total [hogwash]. They were SEC officials. We missed a long field goal at the end of the game.

We played Ole Miss in Oxford, Mississippi, and they were ranked second in the country. After the game, they were ranked No. 1 because they beat us 33–0. Our total rushing yardage in that game was about 78 yards. I think I had about 76 of them on three- and four-yard bursts. I think that was the first game I started. We went back to Georgia and won 3–0. They had Larry Rakestraw at quarterback and had a really good team. I had 101 yards in that game, and we kicked a field goal in the first quarter and held on.

We beat Richmond 13–7, and I ran for 142 yards in that game. We played at Virginia Tech and lost 10–7. We were getting ready to play at Kentucky, but before that game I got caught with a dorm room sink full of ice and beer. That was kind of the second strike because the night before the Georgia game, I snuck out with Eddie Feely, the goody-two-shoes quarterback, and we both went to the fraternity parties on campus.

We got all beered up, and I stole an iguana from one of the fraternity houses. It was about a two-foot lizard. I got the pass key from the resident manager. I snuck into rooms where people were sleeping and put that lizard on their chests and then flipped on the lights. That was a little prank I pulled, and Coach Peterson found out about it. He let me play that game, but I was gone soon after. Nowhere did it ever come out that Feely was with me. I think it was the resident manager who turned me in.

I only started four games in 1961. I ended up with 385 yards rushing and only played six games. One of my booster friends ran Mike's Texaco, and he had one of the top 10 beer distributorships in the country, selling beer in Tallahassee out of a gas station. He was big in the boosters, and he and a couple of other boosters went to Coach Pete and asked, "How in the hell are you going to play those teams in 1962 without Kinderman?"

Peterson went and had one of the deans in the School of Education call me at home in Illinois about two weeks after I was sent home. I already had a job and was working construction. I thought my life was over. The dean told me, "Keith, you were kicked off the team. You weren't kicked out of school. You still have a scholarship." He said, "If I were you, I'd get down here just as soon as you can and catch back up in all your courses and get your degree." The next morning, I was in my 1953 Mercury on the road to Tallahassee. It was snowing up there, and I was working construction in about 10 degrees. All I could envision was the good-looking Florida State honeys walking around campus with their short skirts. I couldn't get out of there soon enough.

When I got back in town, it was relayed to me that because of the team's discipline plan, they couldn't let me back on the team in 1961. But if I would make some concessions, they might let me back on the team the following year. The concessions were I had to quit smoking and drinking beer. I grew up smoking and drinking beer. I told them, "I don't want to be disingenuous, so I'll quit smoking during the season and I won't drink beer in public." They said, "Deal!"

We had a great defense and had three platoons. Steve Tensi and Fred Bilet-nikoff were sophomores on that 1961 team. We went 4–5–1 in 1961, but all those games were close. Trancygier was on the team, but he wasn't playing because nobody could catch the ball because he threw it so hard. He was the most sought-after athlete coming out of high school, but we didn't have the athletes to catch his passes. He just sat the bench and eventually left to play in Canada.

In 1962 we had the best scoring defense that has ever been at Florida State. We started the season by shutting out our first three opponents. We beat The Citadel 49–0 and tied Kentucky 0–0. In that Kentucky game they called a pick play on us. I scored a touchdown in that game on a quick toss to the weak side from about the 6-yard line. Kenny Russom, our wideout on that side, came in and made a perfect block on the linebacker. They called it a crack block, but he hit him right in the chest. We should have won that game.

Then we beat Furman 42–0. The following week Miami beat us 7–6, with George Mira at quarterback. They beat us on an illegal pick play. Our safety, Charlie Calhoun, was covering the first back out of the backfield. They came out and picked Charlie and knocked him down, and I was the cornerback on defense. The guy burst out of the backfield, and I caught him right at the goal line, and they threw a pass to him. Everybody thought it was my man, but it was Charlie's man. He had been illegally picked.

We went to Georgia and won 18–0. Georgia quit playing us after that game. We beat Virginia Tech 20–7 in Tallahassee, and I scored two touchdowns in that game. We lost to Houston 7–0 at home during homecoming. I had a pilonidal cyst on my tailbone, but they took me out of the hospital to play in that game. The first time I ran in that game, somebody put their helmet in my tailbone and my legs went numb. I played the whole game, though.

Georgia Tech, which was coached by Bobby Dodd, had to come from behind to tie us 14–14 in Atlanta. They had an All-American linebacker, Rufus Guthrie, and I was the lead blocker for Dave Snyder. I just about put Guthrie up in the stands, and Snyder broke about five tackles for a touchdown. Snyder was a tough little kid. Later that season, Tucker Frederickson and the Auburn team came from behind to tie us 14–14.

We went 4–3–3 during the 1962 season. We were playing great defense, and that's why the scores were so low. We didn't have much offense. I was bigger than a lot of our linemen, except for the right tackle, Don Donatelli, who weighed about 225 pounds. Gene McDowell, one of our captains, weighed about 180 pounds and was a pulling guard. Jim Sims was the left tackle and weighed about 190. They were all tough, but those big linemen we played against pushed them around. We had a good scheme and offense, but we'd have 180-pound guys blocking Jim Dunaway at Ole Miss, who weighed about 260 and went on to play in the pros for 12 or 14 years.

I was a pallbearer for Coach Bill Peterson when he died. He gave me a shot and helped me get into the pros. Iowa wasn't giving me a shot. At Iowa, I had the best spring practice of any running back, but I couldn't get into the lineup. They put four guys ahead of me. Coach Pete taught me not to give up on myself. I think that's the biggest thing he ever did for me.

I was drafted by the San Diego Chargers in the third round of the 1963 AFL draft. I was drafted by the Green Bay Packers in the eighth round of the NFL draft that same year. I went with the Chargers because I got some bad advice. The AFL draft was on a Friday, and the NFL draft was the following Monday. That was by design. I got really pressured Saturday and signed with the Chargers Sunday afternoon. I was told by some people that they had already talked to all the NFL teams, and the NFL teams weren't going to draft me. So they told me to go ahead and sign with the Chargers. "Get your bonus and go on your honeymoon," [was the advice] since I was getting married that week. I signed, and Bart Starr called me on Monday and said the Packers had drafted me. He said, "What do you think about Green Bay?" I said, "I've already signed with San Diego."

55

Keith Kinderman, a native of Crystal Lake, Illinois, was a starting running back and cornerback for the Seminoles during parts of the 1961 and 1962 seasons. Kinderman ran for 142 yards and one touchdown in Florida State's 13–7 win against Richmond in 1961, and had 101 yards in a 3–0 victory over Georgia during that same season. He led the Seminoles with 393 rushing yards and caught seven passes for 65 yards in 1961. Kinderman ran for 249 yards in 10 games during the 1962 season. In 1963 he was drafted by both the San Diego Chargers in the third round of the AFL draft, and by the Green Bay Packers in the eighth round of the NFL draft. He played two seasons for the Chargers and one for the Houston Oilers before retiring after the 1965 season. Kinderman was a member of the charter graduating class from Florida State's College of Law and was a practicing attorney for 30 years. He is retired and lives in Tallahassee.

# WILLIAM "RED" DAWSON

## TIGHT END/
## OUTSIDE LINEBACKER

### 1961–1964

I GRADUATED FROM VALDOSTA HIGH SCHOOL in South Georgia in 1960. After I graduated, they won the state championship the following three years. My only other scholarship offer to play football was from Western Carolina. I don't know how I ended up being recruited by Florida State. I guess one of the assistant coaches was watching film and confused me with another one of the players.

I was kind of awkward in high school. I was tall but I wasn't very big and hadn't filled out yet. When I finally got in shape at Florida State, I weighed about 175 pounds. I was slow, too. I certainly wasn't a standout in football, but I worked hard. I went to Florida State in 1960 and was on the freshman team. I played end in high school, and the Florida State coaches immediately tried to run me off. I didn't have anywhere else to go, what can I say?

But I started lifting weights, and that wasn't a big thing back in those days. We didn't even have a weight program. But there was a weight room in the basement of the basketball gymnasium, and I became a regular over there. I started eating right at the training table. They redshirted me in 1961, as well, and I probably weighed about 215 pounds.

When I got to the varsity team in 1962, we had a three-platoon system. The Chiefs were the two-way players who played most of the time. The Renegades played on defense, and the Warriors played offense. We beat The

Citadel 49–0 in the 1962 opener. Then we went up to Kentucky and tied them 0–0. We went up to Kentucky and they had their home officials working the game. We had two touchdowns called back for some penalty. We were down in Kentucky territory several times and never scored. That's one of the good things they've done to college football—put in overtime so there's never any ties.

We lost to Miami 7–6, and George Mira was their quarterback. Late in the game, we went down to their goal line to score. Our running back, George Roberts, hit the goal line and fumbled. But we came back and went up to Georgia and won 18–0. Georgia told me I was too small, so they didn't even recruit me out of high school. That's why they didn't offer me a scholarship. Georgia Tech did the same thing. That's why I always enjoyed playing them, and I usually played pretty well against them. In that particular game at Georgia, I intercepted a pass and recovered a fumble to help us win.

We came home and beat Virginia Tech 20–7, then we played Houston for homecoming. It was a tough defensive game. Because of all the rain, we didn't get anything going on offense. After that, we went up to Atlanta and played Georgia Tech. Dave Snyder had a great 22-yard touchdown in the second half that got us back in the game. After the game ended in a 14–14 tie, [Georgia Tech coach] Bobby Dodd said it was one of the greatest runs he had ever seen at Grant Field.

57

We finished that season losing at Florida 20–7, and we went to Auburn and tied that one 14–14. We finished the season with a 4–3–3 record, and although you're never satisfied with losing, we felt like we belonged in every game. We felt like we'd done a pretty good job on one side of the football in every game.

We opened the 1963 season at Miami and won 24–0. Fred Biletnikoff caught a couple of touchdowns and ran back an interception 99 yards for a touchdown. He was probably one of the best athletes I've ever seen in my life. He didn't have burning speed, but he was pretty quick and he could jump. He probably would have been a better basketball player than a football player because he could jump so well. He had great hands and plenty of stickum.

I remember we played Texas Christian during the worst rain storm I'd ever seen. I remember thinking I was going to drown when everybody got on top of me, and I had my helmet down in the water. That's how much water was on the field. TCU ran back an interception for a touchdown, and we lost

13–0. We played Wake Forest and won 35–0. Our quarterback, Steve Tensi, started breaking out about then.

We went and played Southern Mississippi in Mobile, Alabama, and that game ended in another 0–0 tie. We lost to Virginia Tech 31–23, and just never really got it going the rest of the season. We played at Georgia Tech late that season and lost 15–7. I scored a touchdown in that game, and they had a picture of the play in the *Atlanta Journal-Constitution* the next morning. I looked the lion from *The Wizard of Oz* cradling the football.

Finally, we won a homecoming game when we shut out North Carolina State 14–0. I broke my nose in that game, went out for a couple of plays, and went back in. I blocked a guy off the line of scrimmage and right at the last second, he came right around with an elbow and broke my nose. My first play back on the field, we were on defense and I put the guy that broke my nose out of the game. That meant I was the winner.

I thought the face mask on my helmet was interfering with my ability to catch the ball, so I told the equipment guys to take the face mask off. During my induction speech into the FSU Hall of Fame in 1993, I mentioned that everyone else in the Hall of Fame had broken a record at Florida State, and I couldn't find any records I set. I told them I finally came up with something—I was the last person to ever play a whole college football game without a face mask. That was my accomplishment.

We played next at Auburn and lost 21–15. I hurt my knee in the Auburn game, so I didn't get to play in the last game, a 7–0 loss at Florida. Every game that year was pretty close. We were pretty close to being a big-time winner during my junior season, and that set the stage for 1964.

In 1964 we played our opener at Miami and won 14–0. After the game, Andy Gustafson, the Miami coach, said, "When you have a 240-pound tackle blocking, a 220-pound tight end blocking, and a 215-pound fullback running, and you can't make six inches, you don't deserve to win." Back in those days, 240 pounds was pretty big. They came at Avery Sumner and Dick Hermann and me, and we stopped them fourth-and-one at our 40-yard line and that ended the game for them.

We shut out Texas Christian 10–0 and beat New Mexico State 36–0, so we didn't give up a point in our first three games. The following week, we were playing Kentucky, which was ranked fifth in the country. The Dunkel System had never had an upset of that magnitude before. They came down, and they were heavily favored by three or four touchdowns over us. It must have

Red Dawson was a premier receiver and menacing outside linebacker for the Seminoles from 1962 to 1964. He co-captained the 1964 team with receiver Fred Biletnikoff and helped lead the Seminoles to a 9–1–1 record, including the school's first win over rival Florida and a 36–19 victory over Oklahoma in the Gator Bowl.

been 85 or 90 degrees that day, and there was no wind. Those old boys from Kentucky just got suffocated. I remember looking over at their sideline, and they were spent. We beat them 48–6, and they scored the six points after we put our reserves in. We put the first team back in there to stop them, but they scored anyway.

I got to play Georgia one more time during my senior season, and we beat them 17–14. We beat Georgia every year we played them and always played well against Georgia Tech. That made me feel good. I remember late in the Georgia game, I was fussing with our receivers coach, whose name was Bobby Bowden. They were double-teaming Fred Biletnikoff and double-teaming Donnie Floyd, and they were covering me with a linebacker, who I was continually beating. I fussed at Coach Bowden at halftime, and Steve Tensi came back out and threw me a pass right away. The ball bounced right off my chest. It kind of upset me, but what can you do? I was trying to catch it.

We had a 5–0 record and went to Blacksburg, Virginia, to play Virginia Tech. That game was just a series of errors. Biletnikoff had 182 yards receiving, and Virginia Tech's entire team didn't have near that much production. We would drive the ball between the 20-yard lines with ease, but we couldn't get the ball in the end zone. Everybody was waiting for someone else to step up to the plate. You have games like that. We lost 20–11, and it was a big upset.

We went home and beat Southern Mississippi 34–0, so I guess we kind of took out our frustration on them. We went and played at Houston, and Biletnikoff had a bad bruise in his thigh. We led 13–0 in the fourth quarter, but Houston scored two touchdowns in the fourth quarter. We got called for pass interference in the end zone, which set up one of their touchdowns. We were an independent back then, so we couldn't take officials to road games like everybody else. We never did get any calls. Les Murdock missed a 24-yard field goal at the end of the game that would have won it. [They tied 13–13.]

We came back and beat North Carolina State 28–6, and then got ready to play Florida. That Florida game was a real thrill. When I first went to Florida State, they had a sign in the cafeteria where we ate lunch. It was a big print that said, "This space reserved for the first team that defeats Florida." My freshman season, we beat the Florida freshmen. We demanded our picture be put up there, and it was. They found a bigger place for the first varsity team to defeat Florida, and we got that one, too. Florida's players came out in warm-ups wearing T-shirts that said, "Never, FSU, Never." They just never thought they'd lose to us. We called ourselves the Florida rejects.

After finishing 8–1–1, we played Oklahoma in the Gator Bowl. They had four starters declared ineligible for the game for signing pro contracts, and we were just hot. We beat them 36–19. I never would have imagined it would be that easy.

After college, I played one season with the Boston Patriots and then I went to Montreal in the Canadian Football League, and they didn't like me, either. Perry Moss, who had been the coach at Florida State, called me to play with the Orlando Panthers of the Continental Football League, and that's probably the most fun I had playing football. It was more of a relaxed league. I think we all liked to win football games, but we had fun playing.

I went back to Florida State as a graduate assistant in 1967 and recruited my younger brother, Rhett Dawson, to play at FSU. He was a high school All-American wide receiver. I was a graduate assistant into the 1968 season, and my younger brother got stuck in practice one day. The next morning when I got to work, he was sitting on the steps and said something was wrong with him. I took him to the infirmary, and he had ruptured his spleen, so they took him right to the hospital and had emergency surgery. I just felt like I didn't want that additional worry, so I decided I'd get a job and let him have his career there.

I took the first job offer I got, and that was at Marshall University. Perry Moss was the coach there, and they had some recruiting violations, and Moss and an assistant coach were relieved of their duties in 1968. They named Rick Tolley, a Virginia Tech graduate, the interim coach, and I was the defensive coordinator under him. I coached with Rick Tolley during the 1970 season and, of course, there was the plane crash in November 1970. [On November 14, 1970, while the Marshall football team was returning to campus at Huntington, West Virginia, the chartered Southern DC-9 jet crashed into a hill near the airport. All 75 passengers were killed, including 37 players and eight members of the coaching staff.]

I had driven a university station wagon to Ferrum Junior College in Virginia on Thursday that week. Then I met the team at East Carolina. Because of this big linebacker at Ferrum, I wanted to meet their team when they came back from their game that Saturday night. A graduate assistant, Gail Parker, and I drove the wagon back toward Ferrum. We heard the news on the radio and went straight back to Huntington.

It was a hell of a shock. It was disbelief. The hardest part for me was when the families came in right after the plane crash to claim the bodies. Having to talk to them was very tough. A year ago at this time, there is no way in hell I could have talked about this. There is no way I could have done it. I was the acting head coach until they hired an athletics director, and he hired Jack Lengyel as the coach. Initially, I was very involved in trying to keep the football program. The day after the crash, the president of the university initiated a team meeting with all the freshmen and the players who were not on the trip. I told the president to ensure them that we would have a football team next year and the program would continue. But there was no way we could have played a game the next week. The freshmen wanted to play the game the next week. It would have been a massacre against Ohio University.

The NCAA ruled that freshmen could play the following year so we could field a team. I walked away after a year because I was burned out. There were other issues. It was just hard. Right after you go through something like that, you're going to have weaknesses. I didn't talk about it for years. I didn't want to stir up the spiders and snakes in my head, so I just didn't talk about.

But the movie that was released last year, *We Are Marshall*, has been very good for Marshall, and I wanted to be supportive of Marshall. I think they did a great job.

Red Dawson, a native of Valdosta, Georgia, was a premier receiver and menacing outside linebacker for the Seminoles from 1962 to 1964. He co-captained the 1964 team with receiver Fred Biletnikoff and helped lead the Seminoles to a 9–1–1 record, including the school's first win over rival Florida and a 36–19 victory over Oklahoma in the Gator Bowl. After graduation, Dawson played with the Boston Patriots of the AFL and Orlando Predators of the Continental Football League. He later became a graduate assistant coach at FSU and was defensive coordinator at Marshall University. After a tragic plane crash that killed 75 passengers, including 37 players and eight members of the coaching staff, Dawson was named the team's acting head coach. He left coaching the following year and owns a construction business in Huntington, West Virginia. Dawson was elected into the FSU Hall of Fame in 1993.

# DICK HERMANN

## LINEBACKER

### 1961–1964

*To Gloria*
*My Best wishes*
*Dick Herman*

I GREW UP IN MARIANNA, FLORIDA, and Bud Whitehead was kind of a target for me. A lot of the guys from Marianna High School went to the University of Florida but didn't stick it out. Bobby Conrad, a quarterback, and Whitehead went to Florida State, and Whitehead ended up being the star back in the 1950s.

Whitehead finished in 1960, and he was kind of a mentor for me because it was tough at Florida State back in those days. They had 85 players in our freshman class, and they'd recruited guys from Alabama, Georgia, Florida, Ohio, and Pennsylvania. We had a good group of people. Coach Bill Peterson said it was the best group they'd ever recruited to Florida State.

They had all 85 freshmen in the room, and one of the coaches was walking around when they had all of us crammed in this little room. He was preaching to us, telling us how hard it was going to be. He said, "If you're faint-hearted, you might as well go and leave because we're going to put you through the mill at Florida State." He said, "I'll tell you what, you've got 85 big, strong boys there, but I guarantee you there probably won't be 11 of you that finish here." Everybody was looking around saying, "My gosh." It was kind of a scary situation at the time. We were all thinking, "Who's going to be left when the dust settles?"

Back in those days, the coaches were absolutely mean and they got away with a lot of stuff players wouldn't tolerate today. They'd take us out there and run our butts off until people were puking. If you weren't in pretty good shape, you were going to be one of them. Then the practices started.

There was a lot of innovation out there, and they were trying to find out who was going to be tough enough to endure the rigorous schedule they put you through. We did "bull in the ring" and we had all the chicken wire business. They tried to toughen you up as much as you could toughen up. Of course, scrimmages were always a pleasure just to get out of those drills because the drills were so tough. If you could survive the drills, the scrimmages were easy to take.

We were not able to play on the varsity as freshmen in 1961; we had to play on the freshman team. We played Miami, the University of Florida, and Southern Mississippi. We played about four or five games. That was kind of the measure. If you were good enough, you were promoted to the varsity as a sophomore. If you weren't good enough, they held you back as a redshirt. Most of our team were held back as redshirts.

I was fortunate to get promoted to the varsity team in 1962. There were about eight of us who were promoted: Fred Biletnikoff, Steve Tensi, Phil Spooner, Dale MacKenzie, and Avery Sumner. We opened up the 1962 season against The Citadel and won 49–0. Then we went to play Kentucky in Lexington. On the way up there on the airplane, coach Vince Gibson, who was a legend at FSU because he was such a terror and mean coach, said to me, "Richard, if you don't satisfy us in this game Saturday, we're going to leave you up here and not bring you back." It scared me to death. Of course, as a young kid, you believed those kinds of things. I had one of the best games of my life against Kentucky, and it ended up a 0–0 tie.

We didn't have much offense. We didn't have an offensive machine, but we had a great defense. Nobody could score on us. Nobody would move on us. But our offense was just sluggish. In all the years I played at FSU, we had great defenses. We were tough. They had us so tough that we were able to go out on the field with teams like Miami, Georgia, Florida, and Auburn. The toughness and regimen we went through, we were able to go through four quarters and finish.

We beat Furman 42–0, our third straight shutout. We went down to Miami and played the Hurricanes in the Orange Bowl and lost 7–6. They won the game on a pick-off play. George Mira was Miami's quarterback, and they picked Keith Kinderman off in the end zone. Mira whipped the ball side-armed, and they scored their touchdown and kicked the extra point. We should have won that game. We beat Miami's butt.

During my freshman season, we had a donnybrook against Georgia. I was a freshman and was sitting in the stands watching Georgia and Florida State play in Doak Campbell Stadium. There was a big fight at the end of the ballgame, and they had to turn on the sprinklers to stop the fight. Don Donatelli had one of the Georgia players down on the ground and had his helmet off, and Donatelli was beating him in the head. I ran out off the stands and got in between Donatelli and the Georgia player because I didn't want him to hurt the Georgia player. I told him, "Back off! Back off!" Finally, the sprinklers came on, and everybody got wet and that kind of cooled things off. But that was a heck of an experience.

We went to Georgia in 1962 and won 18–0. We beat Virginia Tech 20–7 at home. We lost to Houston 7–0 and tied Georgia Tech 14–14. That was one heck of a game at Georgia Tech. Bobby Dodd was still coaching there, and we played as hard as we'd ever played in our lives. If we'd had some offense, Florida State would have been on the scene a lot sooner.

Then we went to Florida, and we always ended up on the wrong side of the score whenever we went to Gainesville. We had a split end who kept jumping offside in that game, and there was a Florida defensive end who just kept knocking him in the mouth every time he did it. Our split end probably did it four or five times. We'd get penalized and he'd get hit in the mouth. That was just a really frustrating game, and we lost 20–7. We got intimidated and were rattled and didn't play very well. Most of the time we played pretty good against Florida.

We finished the 1962 season at Auburn, and that was a great game. Auburn had [quarterback] Jimmy Sidle and [fullback] Tucker Frederickson. Frederickson and I had played against each other in the Florida high school all-star game, and old Tucker was the "Freight Train." Jimmy Sidle was a great one, too. He'd come up to the line and start shaking his head. He had a nervous twitch and he'd start calling signals and bobbing his head. You'd sit there and say, "What in the world is wrong with this guy?" Of course, he'd call the signals and plays, and there they would go. I guess we did pretty good to stay on the field with them, tying the game 14–14.

The SEC teams were always pretty good. They'd sit there and say, "Who are these Florida rejects?" But we always tried to prove we weren't Florida

Dick Hermann was the leader of the 1964 Florida State defense that was affectionately known as the "Seven Magnificents." The 1964 team finished 9–1–1 and upset fifth-ranked Kentucky and beat rival Florida. A rough-and-tough linebacker, Hermann played one season for the Oakland Raiders and three years for the Orlando Panthers of the Continental Football League.

rejects and could stay on the field with anyone. We went 4–3–3 in 1962, but nobody scored in those ties. Their offense couldn't score on our defense. You might as well say if we'd had any offense whatsoever, we could have had eight victories.

In 1963 we opened against Miami, and that was one of the best games I've ever played in my life. Coach Peterson was scared to death of Miami because the Hurricanes were supposed to be loaded that season and had everybody's All-Americans. We thought we were going to have a good football team that year, too. We were using a three-platoon system, the Chiefs, Warriors, and Renegades. The Chiefs were the starting team and went both ways. The Warriors were the offensive unit, and the Renegades were the defensive unit.

We went down there to Miami, and Peterson was really rattled. He said it was going to be the greatest Miami team we ever faced. When we went out and warmed up, and came back and were getting ready to go out on the field and start the game, Peterson told everybody to take a knee in the locker room. He said, "Let's say the Lord's Prayer." But he started off the prayer, "Now I lay me down to sleep." It was like he was praying for his little boy. Chuck Robinson was one of the captains that year, and Peterson stopped the prayer and said, "Chuck, take over." By that time, we were just about to bust a gut from laughing. But it loosened us up so much that we went out to the football field almost chuckling through the tunnel. We got out there and lined up, and, from that point forward, they were all tight and we were all loose from Peterson's goof. We just blew them out 24–0. That was a great win.

They didn't score on us. Our defense was so good they couldn't score on us. People forget defense. Defense is great. Offense wins football games; defense wins championships. People forget that. It's the truth.

We played TCU in Tallahassee the next week, and it was raining so hard that the water was just pouring into Campbell Stadium. It was just pouring in there and the field couldn't handle it. I remember I made a tackle and was on the bottom of the tackle pile. There was so much water, I was afraid I was going to drown before I got out of the pile. All TCU did was run that big fullback right up the middle. They had a big center, who was about 255 pounds, and I had to block him on offense. We took him all over the field. If we hadn't had the rain, we would have beaten them. But we lost the game 13–0. We just didn't have any offense.

We blew out Wake Forest 35–0 and gave up about 200 yards. We tied Southern Mississippi 0–0 in Mobile, Alabama. Those guys were about 25 years old. They had beards, and we were just kids. I think I was 18 or 19 years old, and those guys were men. We were better athletes, but they would look at you and they had beards. Southern Miss was always a rag-tag bunch that you had to watch out for because they could get you.

We lost to Virginia Tech 31–23 in Campbell Stadium. Virginia Tech was always a big rival back then, and it was a game where we never knew if we were going to win or lose. Virginia Tech always had a good football team. They had an offensive tackle who was really good, and he just ate Avery Sumner's lunch. Avery wanted to get out of the game because that guy was just eating his lunch. They just kept running over that tackle and running over that tackle.

67

Then we went and beat Furman 49–6 and went back up and played Georgia Tech in Atlanta. We lost that game 15–7 but played well on defense once again. We came home and beat North Carolina State 14–0, and they were playing for a bowl game. We lost at Auburn 21–15 at Jordan-Hare Stadium. We finished the season against Florida and lost 7–0.

There were a bunch of close calls during that 1963 season. We just couldn't seem to get it together and couldn't gel. We had good people who were potentially great football players, like Biletnikoff and others, but we just couldn't get it together like we did in 1964. During my senior season, we realized these kids had grown up to be men and we just weren't going to let it happen again. We didn't want it to happen again. It was just a feeling underneath the surface that, "You know what? We're tired of getting run over by these bigger schools. It's time for us to kick some butt." I believe we did a pretty good job in 1964.

Once again, we opened the season at Miami and we kicked their rears. We shut them out 14–0. Miami had a hard time with Florida State. Miami was one of the first major college football teams that put us on their schedule, so there never was that much bad blood between Florida State and Miami. It was always a good rivalry, but there was never any bad blood. Recently, there's been some heckling and things like that. A lot of people say they hate Miami, but Miami was one of the schools that helped put Florida State on the map.

During that 1964 season, we shut out our first three opponents. After beating Miami, we shut out Texas Christian 10–0 and beat New Mexico State 36–0. I remember hitting a guy in the TCU game and his head just kept flying back. Every time I hit him, his head would do that. Because we were going to win that football game no matter what, that was one of the most brutal games I ever played. I thought I was going to kill that guy. Finally, he just quit.

We were dominant. FSU's defense at that time had what we called the "Seven Magnificents." That defense came together, and we were all for one and one for all. We were a team. We were an army. We were a band of brothers. Nobody really cared who made the tackle. We just wanted to make the tackle and stop those guys. That's what happened with that defense.

George D'Alessandro was the guy who came up with the idea of calling ourselves the "Magnificent Seven" because the movie *The Magnificents* had come out that same year. He said, "Hey, let's do something different. Let's cut off our hair and call ourselves 'The Seven Magnificents' and see what we can do." I don't know what it was, but it just kind of bound us together. We weren't going to grow any hair until we lost. It kind of molded us as a football team, and we had a great group of guys.

In the fourth game of the 1964 season, we were playing Kentucky at Campbell Stadium for homecoming. That was absolutely ecstasy. It was ecstasy. Kentucky was ranked fifth in the country and they'd beaten Mississippi and Auburn. Rodger Bird was one of the best tailbacks in the country. I remember working out the day before the game, and they were prancing around like prima donnas. But nobody was going to beat us. We weren't going to let prima donnas come out and beat us on our own field.

We were just quietly preparing for the game, and when it started, we unleashed a fury on Kentucky. They didn't know what hit them. We were blitzing them. We were knocking them down. We just killed them. We beat them 48–6. We were trying for a shutout because we hadn't been scored on in three games. Coach Pete put the third team in because we were so far ahead, and Kentucky started driving. He put the first-team defense back in the game, but they still scored one touchdown. That's the only way they scored. They shouldn't have scored. It should have been another goose egg.

Georgia had a really good football team, and we went up there to play in the fifth game. That was a hard-fought contest "Between the Hedges." If you win "Between the Hedges," you've accomplished something. That game could have gone either way, but it was decided on one play when Biletnikoff went down the sideline and scored a touchdown.

But the play I remember was when Georgia ran a sweep and took off around the end. They knocked down all our guys on the left side, and I was trailing because I was the right linebacker. I started to trail the play and saw what was happening. They went down the sideline, and the running back was going down the sideline wide open. I realized if I didn't catch him, he was going to score and that would be the ballgame. I hooked my fingers underneath his pads and pulled him down. Of course, we held them after that and won the game. That's a play I'll remember for the rest of my life. It was a play that caused Al Davis to give me a contract with the Oakland Raiders. He said, "If you can run like that for us, you can play for us."

We went up to Virginia Tech the following week and beat them all over the field. We ran up and down the field. Before the game, Coach Peterson told our fullback, Lee Narramore, that he was starting. Peterson said, "Narramore, I coached Billy Cannon at LSU, and I believe you're in a better position than Cannon was at this age. I think you're a better running back than Cannon was." Narramore went out and ground up the yards between the 20 and the 20. But then he would fumble. He fumbled and kept fumbling.

Bob Schweickert, their quarterback, kept running a tackle-eligible play, and we didn't know what a tackle-eligible play was. They'd drop the receiver off the line and make the tackle eligible. Of course, they'd run a sweep to the other side with Schweickert, and we'd run over there to stop him. He'd stop and turn and throw back to the tackle, who was standing there by himself, for a touchdown. We didn't know what was going on and hadn't been coached for that. They beat us on two tackle-eligible plays, and we lost the game 20–11.

Biletnikoff and Tensi were having a rough day. We finally scored in the fourth quarter, and Biletnikoff was so mad he threw the football up into the stands after he scored. We had over 400 yards and ran up and down the field, but we could not score. After the game, I remember walking off the field, and those VPI guys would come up to us and say, "Man, you guys are fantastic! You're good! I don't know how we beat you." I told all of them, "I don't know how you won, either!" We should have been 6–0.

We came back and played Southern Miss and won 34–0. We just crushed them. We were frustrated and knew we shouldn't have lost that game at VPI. We ran all over those guys but lost the game. Of course, we had to go back out to Houston the following week, and that was tough. Those Texas boys are tough. I don't care which team it is, those Texas teams are tough and mean. We ran up and down the field again, but couldn't put it in the end zone. Biletnikoff didn't play in that game because of a bad leg.

I kept telling Bill McDowell, "We're going to screw around and lose this football game." He said, "Nah, we got this game in the bag." Of course, we were in position to kick a field goal at the end and win, but our kicker missed it. It ended in a 13–13 tie.

When you know you should have done something that you didn't do, and you come back home, you take out your frustration on whoever your next opponent is. I don't care who we played the following week, we were going to beat the stew out of them. That's just the way our team was that season. It was one unit working together. When we got beat, we just felt so mad about it. We felt like we'd let ourselves down and took out our frustrations.

After losing at Houston, we came home and played North Carolina State. They caught us on a bad day. We won the game 28–6. Then we played Florida in Tallahassee, and we had never beaten the Gators. Florida came out on the field and on the back of the jerseys, it said, "Go for seven." That was the seventh time we were playing them, and we were winless the first six times. The year before, it read, "Never, FSU, Never," on the back of their jerseys.

But with the schedule we played that season, we were ready to play Florida. We knew that had to be the year, because it was the first time we were able to play them at Florida State. Every other time, we had to play them in Gainesville. We were bound and determined that there was no way Florida was going to beat us again. Steve Spurrier and Tom Shannon were the two quarterbacks, and they alternated back and forth. It was over. We dominated that football game, winning 16–7. They said Spurrier cried after that ballgame. I remember Bill McDowell intercepted one of Spurrier's passes, and we took it back down the field.

We played Oklahoma in the Gator Bowl, and I don't know if we were ranked equal with them or what. But we started taking them apart from the opening kickoff. We won 36–19. We were able to control the game from the get-go. The first time they were on offense, Howard Ehler intercepted their pass and ran it back 69 yards for a touchdown. Tensi and Biletnikoff had premier games. [Tensi threw for 303 yards and five touchdowns; Biletnikoff had 13 catches for 192 yards and four touchdowns.]

I was drafted by the Oakland Raiders after college and went all the way out to Oakland, California. I was scared to death. The first person I met when I got to Raiders camp was Ben Davidson. Ben, at that time, had a big, handle-bar mustache. He was 6'8" and 275 pounds. He was one of the biggest men I'd ever seen in my life, and he was ugly. But Ben turned out to be my locker mate, and he and I got to be good friends. I ended up playing right behind him; he was the defensive end and I was the outside linebacker. I played for the Raiders for two years, and it was a great experience.

I got out there in 1965, and they recruited 14 linebackers. I just thank God I was tough enough and quick enough to make the roster. They cut all but six of us. The next year, I didn't go back to the Raiders even though they begged me to come back. I just wanted a year off. I was tired. I'd played football for a long time. I went back the next year, and then tore up my leg in Houston and got put on waivers. I decided to leave and go home. I ended up getting a call from the Orlando Panthers in the Continental Football League who said they needed a middle linebacker. They nursed my knee, and I ended up playing three years for them before I retired.

71

Dick Hermann, a native of Marianna, Florida, was a starting linebacker for Florida State from 1962 to 1964. He was the leader of the 1964 Seminoles defense that became known as the "Seven Magnificents." The 1964 team finished 9–1–1, upsetting fifth-ranked Kentucky 48–6 and beating Florida 16–7, the Seminoles' first victory over their in-state rival. A linebacker known for his toughness and durability, Hermann also led the Seminoles to a 36–19 victory over Oklahoma in the 1964 Gator Bowl. He was inducted into the FSU Hall of Fame in 1985. Hermann played a season for the Oakland Raiders of the AFL and three for the Orlando Panthers of the Continental Football League. Hermann owns an insurance firm in Marianna, Florida.

# STEVE TENSI

## QUARTERBACK

## 1961–1964

I WENT TO ELDER HIGH SCHOOL IN CINCINNATI and had a lot of scholarship offers to play at other schools. But when I went to Florida State, I just really liked it down there. Kentucky, Miami, Florida, and quite a few other schools were recruiting me, but I just liked everything about Florida State.

Ken Meyer, one of the assistants on Coach Bill Peterson's staff, recruited me to Florida State. I played on the freshman team in 1961. We played a few games against other freshman teams, but we mostly had scrimmages and things like that. We even practiced against the varsity team a few times, but you were really just trying to impress the coaches enough to get to the varsity squad as soon as you could.

I moved to the varsity team in 1962, and they kind of had a three-platoon system. They had a unit that played both offense and defense, one that played strictly offense, and one that played strictly defense. I was on the offensive unit in that system. Eddie Feely was the quarterback going both ways, but I got to play quite a bit, too.

We opened the 1962 season against The Citadel and won 49–0, then we played Kentucky up in Lexington. Being from Cincinnati, which is close to Kentucky, that was a neat experience to go up there and play. The game ended in a 0–0 tie. When we came back to Tallahassee on the plane, we were in a lightning storm. The plane went down to land, but then they told them to take back off. There were some scared guys up in the air. I'd flown on airplanes before, but I don't know that I'd ever been in a lightning storm before.

We beat Furman 42–0 and then lost at Miami 7–6. We went to Georgia and won 18–0 and beat Virginia Tech 20–7 in Tallahassee. Keith Kinderman scored a couple of touchdowns in that game. We lost to Houston 7–0 at home, and that game was played during a rainstorm. We played our last three games on the road and tied two of them. We tied Georgia Tech 14–14, lost at Florida 20–7, and then tied Auburn 14–14. Georgia Tech had some pretty good big-name players, and we had to play a great game just to tie them. We were down 14–0 at Auburn and came back to tie it.

We finished the 1962 season with a 4–3–3 record. For us back then, those ties were almost considered wins because we were so overmatched. We weren't even supposed to be close in those games but found a way to tie them.

We opened the 1963 season by beating Miami in the Orange Bowl 24–0. George Mira was Miami's quarterback and was a preseason All-American. [Tensi threw two touchdowns to Fred Biletnikoff in the game.] Then we played Texas Christian in Tallahassee, and it was raining so hard you couldn't even see the other team across the field. They'd put the football down to spot it, and it would float away in the water, it was raining so much. It was pouring, and I still can't believe we played the game. I wore cut-down thumb tacks on my right hand because I couldn't grip the ball. The ball was just a slime. They put thumb tacks on my hand with flesh-colored tape so I could grip the ball. We ended up losing the game 13–0.

We beat Wake Forest 35–0 in Tallahassee. [Tensi threw three touchdowns in the game, including two to Max Wettstein.] We tied Southern Mississippi 0–0 in Mobile, Alabama. We lost to Virginia Tech 31–23, and we had something like 400 yards offense and lost the game. We'd move it from our 20-yard line to their 20-yard line in two plays but then couldn't score. They ran a tackle-eligible play to beat us. They were playing two or three yards off the line, basically daring us to run, and we kept throwing it. We just couldn't get the ball in the end zone.

73

We blew out Furman 49–6 and lost at Georgia Tech 15–7. Billy Lothridge was their quarterback, and it was another close game. We beat North Carolina State 14–0, and they were supposed to be really good and were going to a bowl game. We lost our last two games in 1963, 21–15 at Auburn and 7–0 at Florida. We were down 21–7 in the fourth quarter at Auburn and tried to come back. Larry Dupree ran all over us in the Florida game.

We went 4–5–1 during my junior season in 1963, but I had a couple of bad games, one of them against Florida. I was on the second team going into the spring before my senior season. But the second team beat the first team in the spring game, and I won the job back for my senior year. They were thinking about starting Ed Pritchett, a junior that year.

We opened the 1964 season against Miami and won the game 14–0. I remember going down there, and they were supposed to be a really good football team. We just had a really good game against them. I remember Biletnikoff put a really good move on a guy to score a touchdown on a corner route. That guy is probably still standing there because it was just an unbelievable move.

Biletnikoff was the kind of guy who would make me mad. We'd stand about 25 yards apart, and I'd just throw him darts. But he would stand there and catch them with one hand. He'd grin and say, "You know, I could catch your fastballs with a pair of pliers, dude." I'd try to hurt him, but I just couldn't get anything by him. The guy just had unbelievable hands. He wasn't the fastest guy in the world, but he'd just beat you so badly on moves that you couldn't catch him. I remember playing basketball against him, and he could really jump.

Donnie Floyd was a great receiver, too. He was a little bit different than Fred. He didn't quite have Fred's moves, but their speed was really similar. Donnie worked on his moves like Fred did. Donnie kept us in the game when we beat Florida in 1964.

After beating Miami to start the 1964 season, we went to Texas Christian and won 10–0. [Phil Spooner ran for a touchdown in the fourth quarter to win the game.] We beat New Mexico State 36–0, and then we were getting ready to play Kentucky, which was ranked No. 5 in the country. They came to Tallahassee, and they weren't ready for the heat and humidity. You could tell by the first quarter that the game was over because they were just spent after warm-ups. Our defense was outstanding that season. It was the "Magnificent Seven" and the "Forgotten Four." George D'Alessandro, Dick Hermann, and Frank Pennie were really the leaders of that defense, but they were all leaders.

When we beat Kentucky, even though they were ranked in the top five in the country, our defense was mad because Kentucky scored six points against us. Our defense really wanted to shut them out. That's just how those guys were. Our defense really annihilated them, but we played really well on offense, too. We went up 14–0 after Lee Narramore and Biletnikoff caught touchdowns. We were leading 27–0 at halftime, and those guys just kind of laid down. I didn't even play in the second half, and we won 48–6.

Quarterback Steve Tensi led Florida State to a 9–1–1 record as a senior in 1964, including the Seminoles' first victory over rival Florida. Tensi threw for 1,683 yards and 14 touchdowns in his final college season, then played six seasons of professional football.

We went back to Georgia, and they were ahead 14–10 with about eight minutes to go in the fourth quarter. It was fourth down and one yard to go, and somebody came into the huddle and said, "Coach wants you to run a quarterback sneak." I looked at him and said, "What?" He said, "Quarterback sneak." I said, "Yeah, right." I was shocked because I never ran the ball.

I probably ran the ball three times during my entire career there. I was stunned he called a quarterback sneak at such a critical time in the game.

So I called a pass to Biletnikoff, and he caught it for a first down. We went down the field after that, and Biletnikoff caught a 20-yard touchdown with about six minutes to go to win the game 17–14. Peterson didn't say anything to me when I got to the sideline. If the play hadn't worked, I'm sure he would have said something. But it worked.

We had a 5–0 record going into Virginia Tech and, once again, we ran the ball all over them, but we couldn't get the ball into the end zone. We were throwing the ball up and down the field, but we couldn't get the ball in the end zone again. They were sky high and beat us 20–11. It's just like the way it is now. Virginia Tech is in the ACC and they get sky high every time they play Florida State. It's tough to beat them in Blacksburg, Virginia, anyhow.

We came back and beat Southern Miss 34–0 in Tallahassee. We kind of took out our frustration from the Virginia Tech game, I guess. We played Houston on the road, and Biletnikoff didn't play in the game. It was tough because he was our number-one receiver and the guy I looked for first on every pass play. He wasn't there and it hurt. We tied the game 13–13.

Biletnikoff came back to play against North Carolina State the following week. I took a really good shot in that game and threw a touchdown pass to Donnie Floyd, although I didn't know it was a touchdown at the time. I got knocked out on the play, and Don Fauls, the trainer, came out there on the field. He was saying, "Come on, Steve, you're okay. Come on Steve, get up." I asked him what happened, and he said the play was a touchdown. I said, "Oh, hell!" I didn't even see the play because I was on my back. We won the game 28–6.

We finished the 1964 season by beating Florida 16–7 at home. The Gators wore some stickers on their helmets that said, "Never, FSU, Never." But we were ready for those guys. We put in a special game plan for them. Biletnikoff had always played flanker, and we had him playing split end. We just played one heck of a game against those guys. It was the first time we'd beaten Florida, and it was big because they were our biggest rivals. There weren't a whole lot of people who liked each other on either side of the ball.

We went and played Oklahoma in the Gator Bowl in Jacksonville. [Tensi threw five touchdowns in the game to set an FSU single-game record.] We didn't think it would be that easy. But we'd never seen Oklahoma play, except when we watched them play on film. As a team, we had a really good game and won the game 36–19. Howard Ehler ran back an interception for a touchdown, and we just had a great day on both sides of the football. It was a great ending to four great years at Florida State.

Looking back, I think Bill Peterson was really the coach that put Florida State on the map. Before he got there, it wasn't much of a program, and they'd been winning two or three games a season. I remember one time he brought Bart Starr in for two or three days, and then he brought in Sonny Jurgensen the following year. Peterson was really good friends with Sid Gillman, who told him to put in a pro-style passing game at Florida State. We were really the first team to drop back and throw it. Our offense was almost the same as the San Diego Chargers' offense.

I got drafted by the San Diego Chargers in the fourth round of the 1965 draft and played two years there. I thought the biggest difference was how fast everybody was in the NFL. From the line back to the quarterback, it was just so much different than it was at Florida State. I'd say I had time to throw about 95 percent of the time I threw at FSU and there wouldn't be anybody around me. In the pros, it was just a lot different than that. You had a set time to get rid of the ball, and if you didn't get rid of it, you were going to take a loss or throw the ball away.

I got traded to the Denver Broncos and played there for four years under Lou Saban. It was difficult because they weren't the same team San Diego was, needless to say. We never hit on all cylinders. We had some good games, but we weren't consistent. Our defenses were very, very good, but we just never found consistency on offense.

77

Steve Tensi, a native of Cincinnati, Ohio, was a starting quarterback for the Seminoles from 1962 to 1964. As a senior in 1964, Tensi led the Seminoles to a 9–1–1 record, including a 16–7 victory over rival Florida, the school's first win in the intrastate rivalry. Tensi threw for 1,683 yards and 14 touchdowns during his senior season. He threw for 303 yards and five touchdowns in FSU's 36–19 win over Oklahoma in the 1964 Gator Bowl. Tensi was drafted in the fourth round of the 1965 AFL draft by the San Diego Chargers—he also was drafted in the 16th round of the NFL draft by the Baltimore Colts—and played two seasons for the Chargers. He was later traded to the Denver Broncos and played four seasons there before retiring in 1970. Tensi works as a carpenter and lives in Bowling Rock, North Carolina.

# TOM WEST
## TACKLE
## 1962–1964

I GOT TO FLORIDA STATE IN 1962 after playing at Headland High School in Alabama. It was a small town of about 1,500 people, and it's still a town of about 1,500. Georgia, Alabama, and Auburn were recruiting me, too. It was a tough decision because of the pressure in my hometown not to leave the state. But it was right after the Wally Butts and Bear Bryant fiasco between Georgia and Alabama, and Auburn wasn't an option because my high school quarterback went to Auburn and ended up playing guard. I didn't want the same thing to happen to me. I grew up wanting to play for Bobby Dodd at Georgia Tech, but they never recruited me.

I was a slow wide receiver and a slow middle linebacker that just got the job done. In the recruiting process, Florida State wasn't too far removed from being an all-girls school, and the ratio at the time was about 5,000 women and 2,000 men. When a 17-year-old young man goes to Tallahassee, walks across campus, and sees all these girls smile at you, it has its effect. Four years later, I walked away with the prettiest one, and 42 years later, we're still here.

Florida State was recruiting me to play linebacker. I got my receiving credentials from one night in high school when I caught 20-something passes, when all the scouts were at the game recruiting our quarterback. We didn't win many games after that senior class left. My senior year, we probably won four ballgames. We only had 119 people in the high school, and we didn't do a good job of developing the younger guys. The Auburn coaches told me I had good hands but was too slow. They said I'd probably end up playing tight end. That whole experience our quarterback had at Auburn kind of cooled me on them, anyway.

I got to Florida State in 1961, and we had a great freshman class. Fred Biletnikoff, Steve Tensi, Avery Sumner, and Phil Spooner were in that class. There were a whole bunch of great players. That freshman season was intimidating. When you walked to your first class and there were as many people in the class as there were in your hometown, it was pretty tough. There were 29 people in my graduating class in high school. There were more than 100 freshmen who went through the tunnel at Florida State, who were either walk-ons or scholarship players.

I weighed a full 197 pounds, and basketball was my best sport. But I think they probably thought, "Okay, we'll take a chance on this guy with big feet." I was a pretty good athlete all-around. I think, without exception, every guy who went with me, [the coaches] either tried to run off or they tried to quit. They tried to weed it out in a lot of ways. Practices were tough. The drills that I remember the most were "opportunity periods," where you had the opportunities to improve your skills or challenge the guy in front of you for a position. "Bull in the ring" was probably one I didn't enjoy.

After my freshman season, Red Dawson and I ended up playing the same position. So the decision was made to redshirt me during my sophomore year. I had to travel with the team. During the Miami game in 1962, we lost three or four tackles to some kind of injuries. One of the coaches said, "West already knows the blocking assignments. We'll move him to tackle, and he can do the job." That's the day I went from being the slowest end in the country to the fastest tackle, and one of the smallest.

I started my first game at tackle the following week at Georgia, and Ray Rissmiller, who was an All-American, was starting across from me. I graded out at 80 percent, and we won the game 18–0. That wasn't bad. That game solidified my credibility until I had to play against Frank Lasky from Florida, and he beat me like a drum. It was the only time I got beat the whole time I was at Florida State. That earned me the right to sit on the sideline against Auburn, and it was tough. We tied that game 14–14, and I watched the whole game from the sideline.

We finished my sophomore year with a 4–3–3 record, and probably lost three games by a total of 15 points. There were a lot of bad rules that year.

To my friend, Gloria,
Go NOLES!
Jimy West

Tom West was a three-year starting tackle for Florida State, from 1962 to 1964. He helped lead the 1964 Seminoles team to landmark victories over Kentucky, Georgia, and Florida. The Seminoles beat Oklahoma 36–19 in the 1965 Gator Bowl, a game in which West was named the team's emergency kicker. His courageous effort earned him the moniker, "the Toe," from his teammates.

Coach Bill Peterson brought in the three-platoon system, kind of like LSU ran the "Chinese Bandits." We did the same thing. Depending on field position, they decided whether to put our first-team offense in there. The good thing about it was that the guys who lined up on offense that season played together for the next three years, with a couple of exceptions.

We opened the 1963 season against Miami in the Orange Bowl and won 24–0. Bobby Biletnikoff, Fred's brother, was on the Miami team. The following week, we played TCU in Tallahassee, and it was an ugly day. There was six inches of rain on the field, and we lost the game 13–0. We came back and beat Wake Forest 35–0, and then tied Southern Miss 0–0 in Mobile, Alabama. I remember Southern Miss had a player named Bill Freeman who played at Auburn and took me around during my visit there and was in his sixth or seventh year of eligibility at Southern Miss. Everybody on Southern Miss's team had tape running down below their knees because they'd blown them out playing somewhere else other than Southern Miss. If there was a semipro team in 1963, it was Southern Miss.

We went back to Tallahassee and lost to Virginia Tech 31–23. We fumbled the opening kickoff, and it kind of went downhill from there. We beat Furman 49–6, but they didn't have much back then. We lost at Georgia Tech 15–7, and it was a treat to play against a Bobby Dodd team. I had great respect for Bobby Dodd and what he stood for. In a lot of ways, he was very similar to Bobby Bowden. There was a big crowd at Grant Field that day.

81

We beat North Carolina State 14–0 in the homecoming game in Tallahassee. Then we went back to Auburn to play, and I got to play in that one. Jimmy Sidle was their quarterback, and he and I had roomed together during the state all-star game. Jimmy had a great day and scored three touchdowns. They won the game 21–15. I had a lot of family at that game.

We finished the season with a 7–0 loss at Florida, and that was a bitter loss. We should have won that game. Not growing up in Florida, I don't have that emotion or the "Gator! Gator! Gator!" stuff. My wife won't let the word "Gator" be spoken in my house. She grew up in Florida. Pepper Rodgers and some of their coaches referred to Florida State as the "Florida rejects," and that spurred a lot of animosity.

During that time, you noticed the only way we could make any money was to go play SEC teams or whoever would take us and guarantee us a fixed amount. It was $50,000 or something like that to go play them on their home turf. Our stadium only held about 20,000 people at the time, so we never really got to play those kinds of teams in Tallahassee and go home-and-home with those guys.

We had a 4–5–1 record during my junior season in 1963. I thought at the time, and I still think now, that Peterson and his staff had decided the best way to get Florida State on the map was with defense. Looking at the guys who were seniors in 1962, the better athletes were on defense. They had more speed there, and we were just introducing a pro-style offense, which takes an entirely different mindset, especially for the offensive line. But with a few points in either the 1962 or 1963 season, we could have had a respectable season.

We opened the 1964 season with the defense shutting out the first three opponents, beating Miami 14–0, TCU 10–0, and New Mexico State 36–0. Kentucky, which was ranked No. 5 in the country, came to Tallahassee to play in the fourth game. We beat Kentucky 48–6, and it was a great feeling. We went back up to Georgia and won 17–14.

As nice as it was to beat Kentucky and Georgia, all the goodness faded away the next game. We were 5–0 going into Virginia Tech and we lost 20–11. We were moving up and down the field, and Lee Narramore kept fumbling. We might have punted one time that whole ballgame. We had more than 400 yards offense and we were behind 20–0. That was a very frustrating day.

We came back and beat Southern Miss 34–0. They were just out-manned that year. We went to Houston and tied the game 13–13. Fred Biletnikoff didn't play in that game, and Frank Pennie didn't play in that game, either. He was my roommate and was a part of the defense. He had diabetes, and it almost took them three weeks to get him diagnosed.

After beating Southern Miss, we won at North Carolina State 28–6, and then we finally beat the Gators 16–7 in Tallahassee. That's the game I still remember the most. Any time you do something the first time, it's special—whether it's taking a step, flying an airplane, whatever. Playing them at home for the first time, and finally beating them, that was the end to a good season. Florida had every reason to think they weren't ever going to lose to us, but there wasn't a big points differential between us the whole time we were there.

We went and played Oklahoma in the Gator Bowl, and we thought we'd win. Oklahoma had a couple of guys who had been suspended for signing with pro teams. Coach Peterson called a meeting two nights before the game to make sure we didn't have any eligibility problems. Les Murdock, who had been our kicker and who they found in a junkyard or somewhere, had refused to go on scholarship, but he was kicking for us. He was a good kicker. He actually had signed to play football at Florida State but was in a car wreck and never pulled out of his classes. So his eligibility problems put the whole season in jeopardy, and they kind of knew it. He had never practiced or done anything else.

The decision was that Murdock wouldn't dress out. The night before the game, they came to me and said, "You're the only guy we have who kicked in high school. You're going to have to kick off in the Gator Bowl." We went for conversions all day because we never tried to kick an extra point. By the time we warmed up, I couldn't kick the football 35 yards. It looked like we were trying to kick onside kicks each time. Finally, I said, "That's all I've got," and we started squibbing the kick. We won the Gator Bowl 36–19 without a kicker. They still have the golden shoe over at Florida State, and they've always called me "the Toe."

The thing I appreciated more about Coach Peterson than anything else was that he was a guy who understood developing talent in his coaching staff. He was an excellent recruiter of good coaches. It's hard to find a guy like that, especially among his peers, who put together a better staff than Don James, Bobby Bowden, Bill Khoada. The list goes on and on. He let them run the show, which is why we were successful. If he tried to run the show, we would have been in trouble.

It was a different era. We had just enough skill at the skill positions to be a pro-style offense, which was different and gave people troubles. We had an offensive line coach, Don Powell, who took over at the start of our senior season, and he was an exceptional leader of young men. He put all of us in a room and said, "You guys will determine what the blocking rules are, so you don't ever bust an assignment." We busted very few, and it paid great dividends. It was amazing to me. I don't think anybody ever tried to blitz us from the second quarter on because they were never successful doing it before then. They'd try in the first quarter, and we'd be successful, and they'd go into a prevent defense, and Biletnikoff and Tensi would pick them to death.

83

Tom West, a native of Headland, Alabama, was a three-year starting tackle for Florida State from 1962 to 1964. He helped lead the 1964 Seminoles team to landmark victories over Kentucky, Georgia, and Florida. The Seminoles beat Oklahoma 36–19 in the 1965 Gator Bowl, a game in which West was named the team's emergency kicker. His courageous effort earned him the moniker, "the Toe," from his teammates. After graduating with a master's degree from Florida State, West enlisted in the Air Force as a fighter pilot and served 31 years, including two tours of duty in Vietnam. West is retired and lives in Shalimar, Florida.

# JACK FENWICK

## TACKLE

### 1965–1968

BILL PETERSON, WHO WAS THE HEAD COACH, was originally from Toronto, Ohio, or somewhere near there, so they made a swing through Ohio where I was from. Bobby Bowden was an assistant coach and was the one who recruited me. He is a good recruiter now and he was a good recruiter back then. When I was being recruited, I said, "Who's Bowden?" Little did I know.

We had a pretty good class of players come in, and that was in the young years of FSU. That was back in the days when you had unlimited scholarships and schools could sign as many as they could afford. Notre Dame and Nebraska, schools like that, would just run out and sign guys others wanted to sign, and the big schools would have three-deep.

Anyway, they signed a whole bunch of us, eight of us who came down that fall of 1964. I was a fullback in high school and played a lot of defensive end, but when I got to FSU I found myself on the roster as a tight end and defensive end.

That 1964 year was the year Fred Biletnikoff was there and they had that group who all shaved their heads and were called the "Magnificent Seven." We had quite a defense. We ended up playing Oklahoma in the Gator Bowl and beat them. Biletnikoff was a consensus All-American and was an All-Pro.

Back then you had three years to play five. Your freshman year you were just cannon fodder for the varsity, and my sophomore year I started out as a redshirt and was moving up to the varsity. I was going to play tight end, but

I was out catching passes for Kim Hammond and sprained my ankle. I didn't have them taped, so I saved my redshirt year.

Peterson had a lot of receivers and ran a pro passing game. That was his way of competing; not a lot of schools could defense it. We did a lot of split wide and we sent more receivers out than they knew how to cover. The big schools just ran the ball. I was going to be a tight end in that system.

The next year there was an assistant coach there, you may have heard of him: Joe Gibbs. He came to me in the spring and asked me to come to his office. He said, "I really would like you to consider switching to offensive tackle." I about threw up.

He told me to look at how many ends we had and that we really needed help—that if I switched over and if I tried hard, I would have a chance to start. I really liked playing defensive end and tight end, but he sweet-talked me into playing offensive tackle. I thought about it; he was very persuasive, a snake-oil salesman.

Back then you were able to run the tackle-eligible play, so we ran it quite a few times. The wide receiver on the other side of the field—never me—would quietly signal the line judge when we had a tackle-eligible because they could miss it. The receiver would step back off the line on my side, as another receiver on the other side stepped up on the line, and I was eligible.

So that made it easier to switch to offensive tackle. I caught a few. I would always tell people I was the second-leading receiver in the nation…for a tackle. I ended up playing for Gibbs, and he was great. Most coaches are like Bobby Knight, whom I feel sorry for, but Gibbs took a different attitude. Coach Gibbs always made things fun.

When we would get rough in practice and people were going psycho with the offense against the defense, and the defensive coaches were yelling and screaming, and the place was going nuts, Gibbs told us to be calm and think. His offensive lines had to think and not pay attention to them going psycho. He would come back and say, "Let them go crazy, go out and be cool. Do your job." He never berated you; he would get on you if you made a mistake, but then you knew he was right.

The most memorable game was the 1966 game with Florida and the Lane Fenner pass. They say it was the right call and he stepped out of bounds before he caught the pass. There were pictures the next day that showed he caught the pass, but the officials said it was no catch, and we lost the game 22–19. It was on the FSU field.

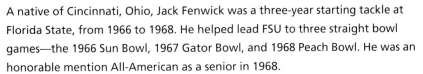

A native of Cincinnati, Ohio, Jack Fenwick was a three-year starting tackle at Florida State, from 1966 to 1968. He helped lead FSU to three straight bowl games—the 1966 Sun Bowl, 1967 Gator Bowl, and 1968 Peach Bowl. He was an honorable mention All-American as a senior in 1968.

That was Spurrier's senior year at Florida, and I believe that's when he won the Heisman. I do remember him because he had an unbelievable ability as a leader and to be able to pull a game out. There was a sixth sense about him. If he was on the field, he was always dangerous. I didn't play defense against him, but I remember the game wasn't over until the final horn.

We had three very good quarterbacks, Gary Pajcic, who recently passed away, Kim Hammond, and Bill Cappleman. Hammond got All-America honors. Ron Sellers came after me and was a great receiver.

Another memorable moment was the 37–37 tie against Alabama and Bear Bryant in 1967. We didn't win it, but everybody was expecting us to lose it. They were actually doing a film of Bear Bryant in Birmingham. It was a game that went back and forth. At one point, the Bear was getting really upset with his team on the sideline because we were hanging with them. It came out in the film that he was stomping around on the sideline, screaming that he wanted the best players out there, and an assistant coach said, "Coach, we have the best players." For us, at the time it was considered a win.

We started that season poorly with a loss to Houston, and people thought we were in trouble. Then we tied Alabama. That was the year we played Penn State in the Gator Bowl and tied them. We won seven straight games. Something just clicked. I think what I remember most and what was impressive is that we averaged less than one quarterback sack a game. We were 7–2–2 and we averaged less than one quarterback sack, which was very good for a passing team.

I remember another memorable game, and we lost this one, too, when we went up and played Syracuse. They had Floyd Little and Larry Csonka. And the thing I remember is Larry Csonka running through our defense and there would be three or four guys hanging on him. All of a sudden they would run Floyd Little around end. It was memorable because it was cold and rainy.

Peterson was a very interesting coach and an unbelievable coach. He was one of the first college coaches who came in and threw the ball. A lot of college coaches believed you could not throw the ball. We had Bob Harbison, who was the defensive coach, and he was really good. Peterson had a great ability to attract very good assistant coaches. He had Gibbs and Don Breaux, who ended up going to Arkansas. Then you had Don James and Dan Henning. They had a whole cadre of assistants who went on to the pros. As we had those good years, those assistants moved on, and Peterson ended up going to Houston.

The draft for Vietnam was going on back then, and I joined the Naval flight program and never thought about having a shot at getting drafted by the NFL. When I started getting contacted by the pros, the first question was "What is your draft status?" I was already committed to five years in the Navy. The Cowboys and Packers were sending me letters, and I only weighed 230 pounds, but they said, "Don't worry about it, we'll get your weight up."

When I came out of high school, there wasn't a weight or a dumbbell. We didn't have them at FSU, either. Everything you accomplished was done on the field. The first weight room FSU had was when Burt Reynolds donated it.

Then FSU fell off and they went 0–10. The next thing you know, Bowden came in and the program took off. I think they have lost that recruiting edge from his Golden Years, though. Florida is picking off great players. It will be interesting to see if they get it back.

We went to three bowl games in three years, which was great because I came out of high school where we won just four games while I was there. It was quite an experience. I felt very good about it.

Jack Fenwick, a native of Cincinnati, Ohio, was a three-year starting tackle for Florida State from 1966 to 1968. He helped lead the Seminoles to three consecutive bowl games—the 1966 Sun Bowl, the 1967 Gator Bowl, and the 1968 Peach Bowl. Fenwick was named honorable mention All-American as a senior in 1968.

# BILLY RHODES

## LINEMAN

## 1965–1968

I WENT TO HIGH SCHOOL IN EUSTIS, FLORIDA. I was recruited by Georgia, Auburn, Florida, and Florida State. I just liked the coaching staff at Florida State. At the time, I really thought I was going to go to Georgia. I was dating a girl who was a year older than me, and she was in school at Georgia. But at the last minute, I went to the Florida–Florida State game, and I really liked Bill Proctor, the freshman coach, and just really liked the atmosphere at Florida State.

I played on the freshman team in 1965. I went to Florida State as a running back. I had played fullback during my junior season of high school, then moved to tailback as a senior. But when I got to Florida State, they had about 10 fullbacks and 10 tailbacks on the freshman team. I played tight end and defensive end on the freshman team in 1965. Before my sophomore season in 1966, Don Powell, the offensive line coach, asked me to move to guard in the spring. I got switched to tackle during the first part of the 1966 season and started two or three games.

Of course, I was probably the biggest guy on the freshman team at 6'3" and 228 pounds. I got up to about 235 or 240 pounds. During the 1966 season, I really wasn't happy at all. I kind of considered quitting the team, but then a new line coach came in—he happened to be Joe Gibbs. He said, "Son, you're going to be a tackle and you're going to be a starter." So I was happy about that and started at tackle in 1967.

We had a great coaching staff. Bobby Bowden was on the staff in 1965. Don Breaux was the offensive coordinator until our senior season, and then Dan Henning came in and replaced him. Don James was on the staff, and he went on to become the coach at the University of Washington. Coach Bill Peterson always brought in the best guys he could find. There were some great coaches at Florida State.

My freshman season, in 1966, we finished 6–5. We lost the first game to Houston 21–13. Then T.K. Wetherell ran a half-back pass on a kickoff return, and we beat Miami 23–20. We lost to Florida 22–19 in Campbell Stadium. We should have won that game. Lane Fenner caught a touchdown late in the game, and the play happened right in front of me. You could see it plain as day, but they ruled him out of bounds. The referee ran down the field and signaled a touchdown, but when he got down there, he said Fenner was out of bounds. The pictures in the newspaper clearly showed he was in bounds. We had a photo of the catch in the locker room right after the game, but the officials never said anything about it. It was a heck of a game. Steve Spurrier, the Florida quarterback who won the Heisman Trophy that year, threw three touchdowns in that game.

91

We beat Texas Tech 42–33 in Lubbock, and Jim Mankins, our fullback, had a heck of a game. He was a really tough player. We played at Syracuse late in the season, and it was an absolutely miserable day. It was overcast and cloudy and cold. That was the first time I saw tear-away jerseys. I don't know how many times Floyd Little changed jerseys, and they had the big guy, Larry Csonka, in the backfield with him. I'll never forget, they were down by our goal line, Csonka got the ball three or four times, and Mike Blatt stopped him every time. A Greyhound bus came up there from Key West or somewhere, and it had a sign on the side of it that read, "Knock 'Em Flat, Mike Blatt." We lost the game 37–21, but they had two great backs in the backfield.

We had a good team in 1966. With a few breaks here or there, it might have turned out a lot better. We were picked to play in the Sun Bowl after that season and played Wyoming. Wyoming had one of the best running backs I ever played against in my life, a guy named Vic Washington.

We opened the 1967 season against Houston in the Astrodome. Nobody liked playing in that stadium. You were just kind of in awe by it because they'd talked about it being the eighth wonder of the world. We had to wear special shoes, and it probably affected the running backs and receivers more

Billy Rhodes was a starting lineman for Florida State from 1965 to 1968. He started on three teams that played in bowl games—the 1966 Sun Bowl, 1967 Gator Bowl, and 1968 Peach Bowl—and was named a member of Florida State's all-time football team.

than the linemen. We lost the game 33–13. Houston back in those days was a powerhouse.

We went to Alabama the next week, and it was the first time we flew on a DC-9 jet to a game. We flew up there the day of the game and stayed in a Holiday Inn. We played right there at Legion Field in Birmingham, and they had about 72,000 people there. ABC Sports was doing a special on Bear Bryant, and they were filming him on the sideline and in the locker room and everywhere else. Walt Sumner had a heck of a punt return, and we were winning 14–0 early in the game. I can remember Bear Bryant yelling, "Somebody tell me what the hell is going on!" They had an interception, and I can remember catching a defensive back from behind. I was still pretty fast for a lineman.

North Carolina State came to Tallahassee the next week and beat us 20–10. They had Ron Carpenter and Dennis Byrd, who were two great defensive linemen. We had played three games and hadn't won a game yet. But we won our last seven games, and the turnaround game was at Texas A&M. It was raining. The cadets were standing and screaming the whole game. Billy Moremen ran a trap play and broke it for a 28-yard touchdown, and we won the game 19–18. It was a miserable game.

We went and played South Carolina, and they had a pretty good team. We won 17–0. We played Texas Tech in a storm and won 28–12. We beat Mississippi State, Memphis State, Virginia Tech, and Florida to finish the season. We played Penn State in the Gator Bowl in Jacksonville, and they had a heck of a defense. Mike Reid [an All-American defensive tackle] played over me. They had a 17–0 lead at halftime and then had a fourth-down play deep in their own territory. Joe Paterno tried to go for it, and we stopped them. We got a touchdown off the short field, and Ron Sellers had an unbelievable game. We ended up tying the game 17–17.

During my senior season in 1968, we started by winning a close game at Maryland, 24–14. Then we played Florida in Tallahassee and lost 9–3. It was a tough loss to take. I remember Coach Peterson saying he really took the blame for that loss because we were down on the goal line twice to go ahead 10–9, and he ran Billy Gunter in there twice. I love Billy Gunter to death, but he was about 142 pounds. The last two times we ran, Pete said, "I just can't believe they think I'll be so stupid to run him again." Gunter got close to scoring, but he was stopped, and they prevailed.

When we all got to Florida State in 1965, we beat Florida's freshman team. We had a great recruiting class, and they had a great recruiting class. We beat

93

them as freshmen and felt like we'd beat them as sophomores. We went to Gainesville during our junior season and beat them, and Ron Sellers and Kim Hammond had a heck of a game, and it was the first time we'd beaten them in Gainesville. It might have been the biggest win we ever had, to beat them there.

After losing to Florida, we won seven of our last eight games. Coach Peterson was a little bit crazy. We beat Wake Forest 42–24 in another rain storm and we got filthy. Pete said Houston was coming to Jacksonville and he wasn't going to let them wash our jerseys. Man, those things were dirty and they smelled. That's just the way Coach Pete was sometimes. We ended up beating Houston 40–20. They had Elmo Wright, who would dance in the end zone and do the "Elmo Shuffle." They had a big running back, Paul Gipson, who was a great player. Ron Sellers and I played in the Senior Bowl after the season, and Gipson told us he'd never been hit so hard in his life as he was during that game.

I'll never forget some of the pep talks Coach Pete tried to give us. People never gave him enough credit, probably, as he deserved. He was a great coach. Sometimes, he got a little carried away during his motivational speeches. During our sophomore season, we were getting ready to play at Miami. Pete said we were going to fly down there in a plane and land right there in the lobby. He said people weren't going to believe it. He'd start out the Lord's Prayer and he'd screw it up. You never knew if he was doing it on purpose or trying to see if you were paying attention.

I loved Coach Pete. My father passed away right before I got to Florida State and he never got to see me play a down of college football. I needed a little guidance here and there, and Coach Pete was there for me.

I played in the Senior Bowl after the 1968 season and got drafted by the St. Louis Cardinals in the fourth round. But the Cardinals released their coaching staff that season, and Red Miller, the offensive line coach, said he wanted me to play right guard behind an All-Pro player who was getting ready to retire. That was fine and dandy with me. I was the first lineman they drafted.

At the same time, the Canadian coaches were at the Senior Bowl, and I didn't realize they were allowed to have only so many Americans on their team. I went to St. Louis and met the owners, and they offered me a contract. It had a signing bonus of about $15,000, and they were going to pay me about $22,000 per season. I started talking to the Canadian coaches, and they offered me $5,000 more in signing bonus and the salary was a little higher. And the Canadian money was worth more than American money at the time. So I decided to go to Canada and play, and it was probably the biggest mistake of my life. I liked it at first, but then I got homesick. I never got home to see my friends, and we were traveling all over the country. I was going to go back to St. Louis, and thought about it for a while, but then decided it wasn't the life I wanted. I went home and worked on the family farm.

Billy Rhodes, a native of Eustis, Florida, was a starting lineman for Florida State from 1965 to 1968. Peterson started on three teams that played in bowl games—the 1966 Sun Bowl, 1967 Gator Bowl, and 1968 Peach Bowl. Rhodes was chosen as a member of Florida State's all-time football team and was listed as the toughest and best lineman who played for assistant Bob Harbison. Rhodes was the second Florida State player chosen to play in the Senior Bowl in 1968, and was a fourth-round draft choice of the St. Louis Cardinals in 1969. Rhodes was elected to the FSU Hall of Fame in 1992. Two of his sons, Billy and Bobby, followed his footsteps and played football at FSU. Rhodes lives in Umatilla, Florida, and operates the state's largest producer of honey.

# RON SELLERS
## WIDE RECEIVER
### 1965–1968

I ATTENDED PAXON HIGH SCHOOL in Jacksonville, Florida, and the quarterback on that team, Gary Pajcic, was a dear friend and the best friend in my life. He was voted the number-one high school football player in the state of Florida during our senior season, and he and I both made all-state in basketball. He just was very bright and was a charismatic guy.

We started in the first grade together, and we were state champions in basketball—I think we only lost nine games in three years of high school. I had three basketball scholarship offers and only three in football. Well, really four, until the University of Florida withdrew its scholarship offer a week before national signing day in 1965 because they said I was not major-college material. Gary was recruited more heavily than I was. I was 6′4″, 160 pounds after taking a shower. I was really tall and skinny.

I also had football scholarship offers from the University of Miami and University of Georgia. Florida's coaches came to the high school about a week before signing day and said, "Gary, we really want you, but Ron, you're just not major-college material." Years later, when I was on the board of directors at the state of Florida's sports hall of fame, Ray Graves, the former Florida coach, was on the board as well. He'd always hate it whenever I used to tell that story in front of him at board meetings. He has told me, "Ron, you were the number-one mistake I ever made in recruiting."

Vince Dooley, the Georgia coach, was recruiting us. Gary and I went up and visited Georgia, and, of course, they ran the ball most of the time. We were a passing team in high school. But Coach Dooley told us, "If you and Gary will come to Georgia, I promise you I will switch to a more balanced passing attack, and we'll throw a lot more than we're passing right now." In 1988 when I was inducted into the College Football Hall of Fame, during the reception at the Waldorf-Astoria Hotel in New York, Coach Dooley came up to me and congratulated me. I reminded him that he told me in 1965 that if I had gone to Georgia, he would have switched to a passing attack and that would be his predominant mode on offense. He laughed and said, "Ron, I'm sure glad you didn't trust me because if you had ever gone to Georgia, I never would have gone to a passing attack!" I told him, "I knew that."

I went to Florida State to play both basketball and football. They said I could play both sports. But after I had a really great year on the freshman football team in 1965—freshmen could not play on the varsity teams back then—Bill Peterson, the football coach, did not want me to play basketball anymore and wanted me at spring practice. Before I quit playing basketball, I was able to play with Hugh Durham [later the basketball coach at Florida State and Georgia] and with Dave Cowens [an NBA Hall of Famer and legendary Boston Celtics center]. I had to quit playing basketball, but I couldn't jump very well, so basketball wasn't going to be my long-term future, anyway. I made the right choice.

We played about five games on the freshman football team in 1965. Gary was our quarterback, and I had 10 touchdown catches and 700 receiving yards. I just wish I could have had my freshman records kept in my career records. I really enjoyed playing on the freshman team. I personally don't think freshmen should be able to play on the varsity. When so few can be lucky enough like I was to go on to pro football, they really need to get an education. Your freshman year is so important in making it academically. My freshman year, we signed 74 freshmen to football scholarships. It was unlimited back then. Four years later, only 13 of us graduated. There were seven or eight who graduated a year later as fifth-year seniors. But the point is, you had 74 freshmen and only a few graduating. We need to get back to the students going to college for their education because that's what's going to carry them through life.

During my sophomore season in 1966, Kim Hammond started the season at quarterback. We played Houston at home in the opener, and I had a really

97

good game. In the third quarter Hammond threw me a 68-yard touchdown, and they called it back because someone was offside. Being my first game and being really excited, I went back to the huddle and said, "Who in the hell was offside?" Kim Hammond looked at me and said, "Ron, you were!" Watching the film the following Monday, I had [close to] a five-yard start ahead of anyone else. After that, whenever I caught a pass and there was a penalty, I never opened my mouth again for the rest of my career. It was a very humbling thing, and I realized it happens to all of us.

I lost 17 pounds during that game and started the game only weighing about 165. I spent the night in the hospital because of dehydration. It was pretty bad. Kickoff was about 6:00 that night, and it was 95 degrees in the middle of a heat wave. I was 6′4″ and only 165 pounds. Some of the sportswriters that night said, "Boy, he looks like Jingle Joints out there." The nickname stuck.

We went to Miami the following week, and Florida State had always struggled against the Hurricanes in the past. They had Ted Hendricks, "the Stork," who was a great defensive end. Miami had been the only team we'd lost to during my freshman season. We were lucky to win that game 23–20, and I scored my first touchdown in that game. Gary Pajcic threw me the touchdown after he took over for Kim. Gary did a great job during our sophomore season. He was a great leader in the huddle. He was very, very confident. I played with Roger Staubach and Bob Griese in the NFL, and Gary had as much command of the huddle as anyone.

We went to Florida the third week in the 1966 season and lost the game 22–19. It was sad because that would have really propelled us that season. We lost on an infamous call by a Southeastern Conference referee when he was on, like, the 16-yard line. After Gary threw a touchdown to Lane Fenner with 17 seconds left, the official called Lane out of bounds, when he was clearly four or five feet in bounds. Traditionally, Lane Fenner was always falling down when he caught a pass. I usually caught the pass and ran with it. Lane wasn't very sure-handed and always cradled it. He was cradling the ball and fell down, and his feet were four or five feet in bounds. A lot of other games have ended like that—it happens all the time, so you just live with it. We should have never lost to Florida in the three years we played them.

We played Texas Tech in Lubbock, Texas, and won 42–33, and then shut out Mississippi State 10–0 in Tallahassee. We lost at Virginia Tech 23–21 up in Blacksburg, Virginia, and Frank Loria had an 80-yard punt return for the Hokies. Frank and I became nice friends after we met each other at an All-

American program on *The Ed Sullivan Show*. My gosh, what a great athlete he was. He was 5′8″ and a hard hitter and a great punt returner. We should have beaten Virginia Tech. We were on the 1-yard line, and Jim Mankins ran the ball three times up the middle and didn't score.

We played at Syracuse during my sophomore season, and they had Floyd Little and Larry Csonka. It was the first time I'd ever seen snow, and it was cold as heck. It was also the first time I ever really got hurt in college. I separated my shoulder but still played the rest of the game. Floyd Little scored three touchdowns, every one of them from the 24-yard line. In 1988 during my induction speech at the College Football Hall of Fame, I told Floyd, "I bet I'm the only one in the room other than you who knows the number of touchdowns you scored against Florida State in 1966 and how long they were." He looked at me and said, "How in the world did you remember that?" I told him, "I'm a darn jock, what can I say?" We were no match for Syracuse, and we lost the game 37–21. They were bigger, stronger, and tougher than we were.

We went back to Tallahassee and prepared to play Wake Forest. I had a separated shoulder, and the coaches weren't sure they were going to let me play. But I played, and, like Gary always used to say, "I threw Ron a 10-yard pass and he turned it into an 80-yard touchdown." I had an 86-yard touchdown in that game, and we won 28–0. We had to beat Maryland to get invited to the Sun Bowl in El Paso, Texas. We should have beaten them and we did [a 45–21 victory].

99

We should have beaten Wyoming in the Sun Bowl. I really enjoyed El Paso. I thought the Sun Bowl people were absolutely awesome. We went to three bowl games, the first Florida State team to do that. I was a Florida boy and thought it was really neat to go out West. Gary hurt his arm late in the season, and Kim Hammond came into the game. Kim threw three touchdowns off the bench and played well, but we lost the game 28–20.

My junior season, in 1967, we opened the season against Houston in the Astrodome. If you've never played in a dome, and never played on Astroturf before, it's really different. Because the Houston Astrodome was used for so many things, [the turf] was just a really flat carpet. It was a strange surface to play on, and the lights were weird. But Houston had a better team than we did, and we got beat by the better team 33–13.

The Alabama game in 1967 was one of the most exciting games I've ever been associated with in my life. We played Alabama at Legion Field in

Ron Sellers still holds Florida State records for catches in a game (16 against South Carolina in 1968), catches in a season (86 in 1968), career receptions (212), receiving yards in a season (1,496 in 1968), and career receiving yards (3,598), in addition to several other marks.

Birmingham, Alabama, and I remember catching the first touchdown to go up 7–0. We punted to them, and we stopped them three plays and out. They punted to Walt Sumner, and he took the punt back about 75 yards for a touchdown.

We were in Birmingham, and there were like 74,000 people in the stadium, and only 5,000 of them were Seminoles. When we scored the second touchdown to go up 14–0—surprise, surprise—the scoreboard broke. We were, like, 23-point underdogs because Alabama was preseason No. 1 and we were their first ballgame. They'd given up only 44 points in 11 games the year before, and they had 10 starters back. Because of some infractions during the offseason, Bear Bryant had suspended Ken Stabler, his starting quarterback, from playing in the first game. He was dressed out, but they said he was not eligible to play in the game. Well, guess who came into the game on the third series? Ken Stabler, absolutely.

Bill Moremen scored a touchdown late in the fourth quarter [an eight-yard pass from Kim Hammond, which cut Alabama's lead to 37–36]. When I came off the field after the touchdown, Dan Henning, the receivers coach, was standing on the sideline. Coach Peterson said, "Dan, what do you think we should do?" Henning said, "Let's go for the two-point conversion and the win." Peterson looked at me and said, "Sellers, what should we do?" I said, "Let's go for it, Coach!" Hammond was sitting there, saying, "Let's go for it!" He got all three of us to say the same thing, and he turned around to our kicker, Grant Guthrie, and said, "Guthrie, get in there and kick it!" The game ended in a 37–37 tie.

Years later, the Alabama sportswriters voted the 37–37 tie in 1967 among the 10 greatest Alabama football games ever played. That game helped me become an All-American during my junior season. I caught 13 passes for 165 yards and had a good game. I loved to play against Alabama. It was awesome. Legion Field was a great place to play, and I loved to play big games against great teams.

101

We went home the third week and lost to North Carolina State 20–10. Chuck Amato [a longtime FSU assistant coach] was a defensive lineman for the Wolfpack. He reminds me they beat us that season every time I see him. They really beat us because we fumbled the ball too much and our quarterback threw too many interceptions. We played a really bad game, and I'm absolutely positive it was a hangover from the tie in the Alabama game.

But we ran the table after that. We went to Texas A&M the following week, and it rained about six inches during the game. It was a monsoon. I caught a 61-yard touchdown from Hammond during the third quarter. It was a broken play. Bill Moremen, our tailback, had one of the best runs I've ever seen to win the game to beat them with about two minutes to go. He ran 27 yards for a touchdown and broke five tackles to do it.

We came back and played South Carolina in Tallahassee and won the game 17–0. I remember that game because Gary Pajcic got married after the game and I was the best man. We beat Texas Tech 28–12 the next week. We should have been a member of the Southwest Conference. We played Houston, Texas A&M, and Texas Tech. I was at the right place at the right time, because we played some really good teams. We played Syracuse, Alabama, Mississippi State, and Miami.

The Virginia Tech game near the end of the 1967 season [a 38–15 victory] was one of the most physical games we played. Virginia Tech put an outside linebacker in front of me before the ball was snapped, and he was trying to jam me and all that, but they weren't very quick. If I can't run around an out-side linebacker, I've got problems. [Sellers caught eight passes for 229 yards in the game.]

We beat Florida 21–16 in the last regular season game of the 1967 season, and it was the first time Florida State won in Gainesville. Kim Hammond, our quarterback, suffered a concussion in the first quarter and was out the rest of the game. Gary Pajcic came in and did an honorable job, but it was tough for him with the crowd. At halftime, Kim didn't know where he was. My nickname for him was "Hambone." At halftime, I said, "Hambone, how you doing?" He looked at me and said, "Where are we?" He literally didn't know where we were. I thought he was done for the day. But late in the fourth quarter, we recovered a fumble at our 6-yard line. Kim came into the game off the bench and threw a 51-yard pass to me on the first play. Two plays after that, he threw me a 38-yard touchdown. We went 94 yards in two or three plays for a touchdown, and that sealed the victory.

The victory over Florida earned us a trip to the Gator Bowl in Jacksonville to play Penn State. We trailed 17–0 at halftime, but in the third quarter Joe Paterno made what he said was the biggest mistake in his career. They were ahead 17–0 and they had fourth and one on their own 26-yard line. For what-ever reason, he went for it and didn't make it. Three plays later, Kim threw me a 20-yard touchdown, and we were right back in the game. We tied them 17–17 in the fourth quarter [after Hammond scored a one-yard touchdown, and Guthrie kicked a 26-yard field goal with 20 seconds left]. The game ended in a tie, but I felt we really should have won the ballgame because the momentum was all on our side in the second half. On the last possession, I was wide open in the end zone, but Kim overthrew me, so we had to kick the field goal.

During my senior season, Bill Cappleman took over at quarterback. Bill had come in with me as a freshman and had redshirted our sophomore sea-son. Bill had tremendous ability and he threw the ball a mile. Bill had a great arm, and fortunately it worked out very well for me. We hooked up and did very well. We beat Maryland [a 24–14 victory] to start the 1968 season and then played Florida at home. Having beaten them the year before in Gainesville for the first time, it was a big game. We were trailing 9–3 late in the game, and Cappleman threw me three or four straight completions and went 70 yards down to the 1-yard line. We had three or four tries from the 1-yard line, and they stopped us every time. We had to have a touchdown, and we ran all four into the goal line. We didn't try one darn pass, unfortunately. But they stopped us on a goal-line stand, we turned the ball over, and they won the game.

We came back from the Florida game and beat Texas A&M 20–14 and Memphis State 20–10. We played South Carolina in the fifth game, and the Gamecocks were coached by Bill Peterson's former boss, Paul Dietzel. They coached together at LSU. Peterson knew what Dietzel liked to do on defense, so they had me play four positions in the game—split end, flanker, tight end, and running back—to get me in different slots. It was a shootout.

What I didn't know was Dan Reeves, who was one of my future teammates with the Dallas Cowboys, had come to the game to watch his younger brother play defensive back for South Carolina. [Sellers caught 16 passes for 259 yards and three touchdowns in a 35–28 victory.] When I got traded to the Dallas Cowboys years later, the first thing Reeves said to me was, "Ron, I saw you play South Carolina that night and you ruined my little brother's career. He never was the same after covering you that night." Of course, he didn't cover me that night.

We were 4–1 and we were getting ready to play Virginia Tech, and that game was a disaster before it started. Coach Peterson decided we were going to change things up. We were playing at home and, for the first time ever, Florida State wore garnet jerseys at home. Virginia Tech's favorite color was garnet. The joke was someone forgot to tell our quarterback, Bill Cappleman, that we were wearing garnet and not white! [Cappleman threw five interceptions in the 40–22 loss.] Virginia Tech had at least two late hits against them. They wanted to take me out of the game, if they could. They did that a couple of other times before, and so did a lot of other teams. It was just a bad night all around.

We played at Mississippi State the following week, and it was cold and wet. I remember all the cow bells ringing, too. We won the game 27–14. We came back and played at North Carolina State. We led 14–7 early in the third quarter but ended up winning the game 48–7. We played Wake Forest at home, and I had a pretty good night. [Sellers caught 14 passes for 260 yards and five touchdowns, setting Florida State single-game records for yardage and touchdowns.] I remember after I scored my fifth touchdown, they were going to take me out of the game, so I gave my chin strap to a young man, who was one of our trainers and was dying of cancer. That was one of the things I remember most. It's nice to have a good game, but those are the things you never forget.

We ended the 1968 season playing Houston. It was my last regular season game for the Seminoles and it was in Jacksonville, my hometown. Jacksonville was nice enough to give me the keys to the city before the game. Houston was the 10th-ranked team in the country, and the week before they'd beaten Tulsa 100–6, which is still a modern game record. It was the highest-scoring game in the 20th century. They had an All-American running back and an All-American defensive back. There were a lot of pro scouts at the game. The first half, I caught 12 passes, and we were ahead 25–0 at halftime. I only caught two passes in the second half, but one of them was a 62-yard touchdown. It was a broken play, and Cappleman saw me open down the field. It was a great game and a great way to go out.

We played LSU in the first Peach Bowl in Atlanta, and it was one of the coldest games I've ever played in, other than the game at Syracuse. It was cold and wet, and we should have beaten LSU. But they had a fourth-and-25 late in the game, and they got it. They threw a Hail Mary and their guy jumped up and beat three of our defensive backs. We lost the game 31–27.

I remember years later, when I was inducted into the Peach Bowl Hall of Fame, I asked them why I was being inducted. I told the director, "We lost the game!" But he said they wanted someone from the first game in the Hall of Fame because it was so long ago!

Looking back at my four years at Florida State, we never really had a complete team. We had some good skill players, which is why we were able to compete. But in the trenches, we got out-manned against teams like Syracuse and Houston. They just had big boys. But we had great coaches. My sophomore and junior seasons, Joe Gibbs [a Pro Football Hall of Fame coach, who led the Washington Redskins to three Super Bowl championships] was my offensive coordinator. He was fabulous, and we all loved him. He left and helped Southern California win the national championship. Dan Henning [who later coached the NFL's Atlanta Falcons and San Diego Chargers] was my receivers coach. We had some great, great coaches.

In the 1969 draft, O.J. Simpson was the first pick and I was selected sixth by the Boston Patriots. It was the last year of the AFL, and I played three years for the Patriots before I got traded to the Dallas Cowboys in 1972. We were only one game away from playing in the Super Bowl in 1972, but lost to the Washington Redskins. They traded me to the Miami Dolphins, who had gone undefeated in 1972. We went back to the Super Bowl in 1973, beating the Minnesota Vikings 24–7, so I was fortunate enough to play on an NFL championship team. I tore my knee up that season and finished out the year and retired. I was a tall, skinny guy who was very lucky to be at the right place at the right time. For what I accomplished, I was very lucky.

Ron Sellers, a native of Jacksonville, Florida, was the most accomplished wide receiver in Florida State history. In fact, he held nearly all of the NCAA Division I-A receiving records from the end of his senior season in 1968 until they were broken in 1987. In three seasons at Florida State, Sellers caught 212 passes for 3,598 yards. He caught passes in 30 consecutive games and averaged nearly 12 yards per reception. Sellers still holds Florida State records for catches in a game (16 against South Carolina in 1968; he actually has the four highest single-game totals and seven of the top 10), catches in a season (86 in 1968), career receptions (212), receiving yards in a season (1,496 in 1968), and career receiving yards (3,598), in addition to several other marks. Sellers was elected into the Florida State Hall of Fame in 1977. Sellers was the sixth choice in the 1969 draft and played four seasons with the Boston Patriots and one each with the Dallas Cowboys and Miami Dolphins. He was a receiver on the 1973 Miami Dolphins team that won Super Bowl VIII. Sellers retired from professional football at the end of the 1973 season and owns an insurance company in Palm Beach Gardens, Florida.

# WALT SUMNER

## CORNERBACK
## 1965–1968

I GREW UP IN OCILLA, GEORGIA, and one of the former athletes in Irwin County, Marion Roberts, went to Florida State on a football scholarship. He was about five years ahead of me, so we always went as a group to Florida State games. When they offered the scholarship, I was ready because that was my goal. South Carolina recruited me, and late in the ballgame, Georgia Tech tried to recruit me.

It didn't hurt that Bobby Bowden was recruiting me for Florida State. There were a couple of guys in town who had played with Bobby at South Georgia Junior College, and they were interested in me going down to Florida State. They had some influence in pushing me in that direction, too.

I graduated from high school in 1965 and played on the freshman team at Florida State that fall. Ron Sellers, Bill Cappleman, and Billy Rhodes came in at the same time. I was fighting to survive. I came out of high school as a quarterback, and I was one of 12 recruited quarterbacks that year. By the time they cut it down to the final four, I was the last one to be cut. They moved me to defensive back, and I was in a whole different world. I had to get used to being a defensive back. I'd never played defense in high school. I played mostly quarterback and returned kicks and kicked. When they moved me to defense, it was just a totally different ballgame.

We went down and played Miami's freshman team in Orlando. I remember I had some people come down to see the game, and I didn't even get off

106

the bench. It was a really high-scoring game, and they went back to Tallahassee the next week and just started all over on defense. They said if it hadn't been for that game, they might not have ever realized that I could play that well. It's odd how things work out sometimes. I had a shot at moving to wide receiver after my freshman season, and playing both ways, but I was moved to defense exclusively after Ron Sellers showed them what he could do.

I moved up to the varsity team in 1966, and they had a couple of seniors who were cornerbacks. I started playing in games more and more, and then I was starting by the end of the season. We lost to Florida 22–19, but we should have legitimately won that ballgame. They ruled Lane Fenner's touchdown incomplete, but it was a catch. I think everybody would agree that it was a catch. Even the Gators, but they just wouldn't admit it at the time.

We beat Texas Tech 42–33 and Mississippi State 10–0 after that. Then we went up to Virginia Tech and lost 23–21. That was the game where Coach Bill Peterson delivered the halftime speech that he didn't carry us up there on a "four-plane engine" to lose. It was a four-engine plane, not a four-plane engine. He was good at using those reversals of words. We beat South Carolina 32–10 in Columbia [Sumner had two of Florida State's six interceptions in the game], and what I remember about that game was meeting the fullback head-on at about the 5-yard line at the end of the first quarter. I got my bell totally rung because they were holding the game up when I came to at the other end of the field.

107

It was interesting going up to Syracuse because we went up there with a defensive line, where the starters and reserves didn't weigh over 220 pounds. Playing a five-man line, we took some of our people out who weighed less and put in all the big bodies we had across the line. We still couldn't do anything with Larry Csonka, their big fullback. I played against him in college and the pros, and he was a load, regardless of who was hitting him. They had the best of both worlds, with the train coming up the middle in Csonka and the jet on the outside in Floyd Little. We couldn't do anything against them and lost 37–21.

We came back and shut out Wake Forest 28–0. We beat Maryland 45–21 and got a berth to play Wyoming in the Sun Bowl in El Paso, Texas. It was a new adventure for a lot of us going that far away to play in a bowl game. It was an exciting time. El Paso had a lot of things that were unique, being right there on the border. What I remember most is we had a bus trip carrying us over into Mexico to eat. One of the police escorting us hit one of the highway dividers and it flipped him totally out. When we got to the border, we went from uniform police to guys who were not in uniforms. That was different.

We opened the 1967 season against Houston in the Astrodome. That is [the place] where I hurt my knee in the pros. We thought we had a really good chance at beating Houston that season. We didn't come close and lost 33–13. We didn't have any offense and couldn't stop them on defense.

We went over and played Alabama at Legion Field in Birmingham. Ron Sellers caught a touchdown, then I had a punt return for a touchdown that made it 14–0. Back in those days, Alabama was looked at in awe. For us to even go play them was exciting. I remember there were so many people there, they broke down one of the fences in the end zone and the scoreboard broke because of it. ABC was doing a special on Bear Bryant that night. Later, they showed it as an hour-long special on TV. They've always teased me about my 75-yard punt return because, as I was completing the run, Bear said, "What in the hell is going on out there?"

We thought the Alabama game was a win, even though it ended up being a 37–37 tie. I'm sure we were down the next week, playing somebody who wasn't Alabama. We lost to North Carolina State 20–10. It was really deflating because we should have beaten N.C. State.

108

When we lost to Houston in the 1967 opener, it got back to chaos in practice. They were trying to eke out the weaklings again. And after we played Alabama and lost to N.C. State, some of the players had a meeting and tried to keep it from where we were going to be knocking each other's heads off again that week. We tried to convince Coach Peterson that we didn't need to do that to play up to our potential. We went out to Texas A&M and squeaked it out 19–18, and it was a saving grace that allowed us to substantiate the argument that we didn't have to kill each other in practice.

We ended up winning our last six games in 1967 [beating South Carolina, Texas Tech, Mississippi State, Memphis State, and Virginia Tech], before we played Florida. Mississippi State and Virginia Tech were always tough opponents. You might have beat them, but you always went away knowing you got some bumps and bruises yourself and you just won on the scoreboard. Some games and some teams had a more physical approach, and I always felt that way about Virginia Tech and Mississippi State.

We went to Florida and had never won in Gainesville. During pregame introductions, they just walked out on the field. That fired us up even more.

Walt Sumner's memorable punt return for a touchdown against Alabama in 1967 caused legendary Crimson Tide coach Paul "Bear" Bryant to exclaim: "What in the hell is going on out there?" Sumner led the Seminoles in punt returns and interceptions in 1968.

Kim Hammond, our quarterback, got knocked out of the game and came back and threw a touchdown to Sellers. I had a great opportunity to pick off a pass and run it back for a touchdown, but I dropped it. Those are the team games that you remember, especially beating Florida in Gainesville for the first time. When you're in the mix, playing at the time, and you haven't been at Florida State for years and years to see and know what people have been through, you're just trying to win a ballgame. But when you reflect on it later, you say, "Boy, that's the first time we ever beat them down there? Why was it so impossible before?" It was just nice to make that come true.

At the end of the 1967 season we played Penn State in the Gator Bowl in Jacksonville. They had a great running back. I hit one guy in the first half and lost control of one of my eyelids. I couldn't see out of but one eye. I tried to get them to tape my eyelid open, but they refused to do it. They wouldn't send me back in with a taped eyelid, so I had to sit the rest of the game. The game ended in a 17–17 tie.

We went 8–3 during my senior season in 1968. We played Florida, and they had a big fullback, Larry Smith, and we did a good job of holding him. We lost to the Gators at home 9–3. We beat Texas A&M in another close ballgame [20–14], beat Memphis State 20–10, and South Carolina 35–28. We lost to Virginia Tech 40–22, but then won our last four games.

Late in my senior season, we were playing up at North Carolina State. I had a hip pointer and hadn't practiced the entire week. I didn't start the game, but they were driving late in the first half. The coaches put me in on a third-down play. N.C. State passed, and the ball was deflected. It wound up being fourth down, and they tried a field goal. I blocked it and ran it back 58 yards for a touchdown. We ended up killing them 48–7.

The 1968 season ended against Houston in Jacksonville. They had beaten Tulsa 100–6 the week before. Everybody was writing Houston up big in the week before our game against them. Coach Peterson tried to use a psychological tool to work on us that week. After we beat Wake Forest 42–24 the week before, he said we weren't washing our uniforms. We played Houston in the Gator Bowl, and before we went out for warm-ups, Peterson said, "I don't want to hear anyone say anything." We went out and everyone was complying with his order—no one was chattering or hollering. We went in for our pregame pep talk and we were all about to go crazy because we couldn't say anything. We were all high as a kite and beat them up pretty good, 40–20.

After the 1968 season, we got invited to play LSU in the first Peach Bowl. It rained and rained, good grief. We played at Georgia Tech's stadium, and there was water all over the field. I had some friends come up to the game, and they might have been the only people left in the stadium.

I played baseball at Florida State in 1968 and 1969, and I was fortunate to get drafted by the Cleveland Browns and the Atlanta Braves in baseball. I decided to play football and played six years for the Browns. I had a couple of knee injuries and had to get out.

Walt Sumner, a native of Ocilla, Georgia, was a star cornerback for Florida State from 1966 to 1968. As a junior in 1967, Sumner had a 75-yard punt return for a touchdown in a 37–37 tie against Alabama, which caused legendary Crimson Tide coach Paul "Bear" Bryant to exclaim, "What in the hell is going on out there?" Sumner led the Seminoles in interceptions and punt returns in 1968. He also played on Florida State's baseball team and hit .300 as a senior, leading the Tribe in runs, doubles, and total bases. Sumner was a five-year starter as a cornerback and safety for the Cleveland Browns from 1969 to 1974. He was inducted into the Florida State Hall of Fame in 1982. Sumner is an accountant and lives in Ocilla, Georgia.

# *The*
# SEVENTIES

# RHETT DAWSON

## WIDE RECEIVER

### 1967–1971

I GREW UP IN VALDOSTA, GEORGIA, and was actually recruited to Florida State by my older brother, Bill "Red" Dawson, who had played at FSU and was a graduate assistant coach there. He was six years older than me, and I graduated from Valdosta High School in 1967. With my brother there, I thought I had a pretty good chance of being recruited to FSU.

I also had scholarship offers from the University of Georgia, Georgia Tech, Florida, Auburn, Alabama, Tennessee, and South Carolina. I was really fortunate. Princeton was recruiting me, and the U.S. Naval Academy recruited me as well. As a small-town kid, I was a little overwhelmed by all the attention. Playing for Coach Wright Bazemore at Valdosta High School, he was a real teacher of teamwork and sportsmanship. There were no prima donnas. It was all about hard work. I think during my playing days, I was so focused on being the best I could be and living up to Coach Bazemore's expectations of me. When I finally looked up, I had all these colleges recruiting me. It was a little overwhelming, to say the least. We won state championships in football during my junior and senior seasons. Around there, it was kind of expected to win championships.

During two-a-day practices in 1968, we were down scrimmaging near the goal line, and I ran a slant pattern. I reached up to catch the football, and a freshman safety, Robert Ashmore, hit me right in the gut. I knew it hurt, but I kept practicing and didn't dare want anybody to think I was hurt. I wanted to make sure I proved myself. But the next morning, I had emergency surgery to have my spleen removed because it had been ruptured. I've heard my brother say that was one of the reasons he left Florida State, and I can better understand it now. All I knew at the time was he'd been given an opportunity to become a full-time coach at Marshall. I had no clue that was why he left there. After that surgery, I was redshirted during the 1968 season.

In the 1969 season I tore cartilage in my knee and had surgery. It didn't keep me out but three weeks. The next spring I dove for a pass and, when I came down on my right shoulder, I was hit on the ground at the same time. I separated my right shoulder and had a pin put in it. It's funny, and I kind of laugh about it now. I look back at the way my mind worked back then. There had to be some sort of insanity because the only thing I thought about was, *How long is this going to take for me to recover so I can get back out there?* I grew up living and breathing to play football. I loved it. I loved to practice. I loved the games. I loved the two-minute drills the most. I'd go out early and stay late at practice. I don't know what was wrong with me, but I just absolutely loved football.

115

After all those injuries, I cracked the starting lineup during the 1970 season. We went 7–4 in 1970. We all have opinions, but I thought if Gary Huff had played quarterback that year, it would have been a whole different year. Tommy Warren was the starting quarterback, but I believe Gary Huff would have been a better bet for us. I can't say enough about Gary Huff. He's certainly one of the best I've ever played with.

We lost three of our first five games in 1970, but then won five in a row. We won at Miami 27–3, and the Hurricanes were one of our rivals. It was especially a thrill to win down there in the Orange Bowl. We beat Clemson 38–13, and I caught a touchdown off a halfback pass from Tom Bailey. Tom was a great athlete. We beat Virginia Tech 34–8, which had Don Strock as its quarterback, and beat Kansas State 33–7, which had Lynn Dickey as its quarterback.

We closed the 1970 season against Houston on Thanksgiving Day in Tampa. We were winning 21–12 at halftime, and they came out in the second half and ran all over us. They turned Elmo Wright loose in the second half. Every time you looked up, Elmo Wright was running down the sideline. He was the guy who invented the end zone dance, and he was busy in the end zone in the second half.

At one point in that Houston game, Warren threw an interception, and their cornerback picked it off on a dead run. He was flying right down our sideline in front of our bench. Bill Parcells was our linebackers coach, and Dan Whitehurst was our great middle linebacker. It was like a love affair between those two. Well, this guy was streaking down the sideline, and Whitehurst was over there standing in front of our bench. Parcells started yelling, "Somebody get that son of a bitch! Somebody get that son of a bitch! Somebody get him!"

Whitehurst couldn't help himself, so as the guy was running by our bench, Whitehurst stepped off the sideline and leg whipped the guy. The officials got together and didn't know what to do. They threw Dan out of the game and gave the guy a touchdown. We were playing the only game on national TV that day, so the whole nation got to see Dan do it. We lost the game 53–21.

After the 1970 season Coach Bill Peterson left FSU and took a job at Rice University. It was a big surprise for us. Coach Pete was a really funny guy. He's known for his funny sayings. We called them "Peterisms." He had dyslexia or something before anyone knew what it was. He said things backward all the time. One week, we were getting ready for practice on a Monday. He called the whole team in for a meeting. He was up at the podium, screaming and cussing and spitting and chewing us out. When he got to the end, he pointed his finger at us and said, "Don't you remember that, either!" You knew it wasn't a time to be laughing, and you had to bite your lip to keep from laughing. He had all sorts of those.

We were at spring practice one year and he had a team meeting. He said, "Men, I've been over in Gainesville and I snuck over to a Gators practice. I was peeking over the fence." We were all like, "What?" He said, "I was watching those Gators practice. All I can tell you is they're locking their chips to get you guys next year!"

I don't think Coach Peterson ever got enough credit for what he did at Florida State. He took his passing offense from [longtime NFL coach] Sid Gillman, and that's the offense we ran at Florida State. I remember going from high school to college and thinking, *Man, I had no idea football could be so complicated*. You really had to study to comprehend and get the complexity of our passing offense. Even after I went on to play for the Houston Oilers and Minnesota Vikings and in Canada, our best and most proficient offense was at Florida State. Bill Peterson was way ahead of his time.

The other thing that I admire about Coach Peterson is that he had an absolute genius in hiring assistant coaches. He hired Bobby Bowden out of an Alabama junior college. Joe Gibbs was an assistant there. Don Breaux, who

Rhett Dawson was one of the great receivers at Florida State and still ranks in the top 10 in school history in season receptions (62 in 1971) and catches per game (5.64 in 1971). He caught 62 passes for 817 yards and seven touchdowns as a senior in 1971 and scored three touchdowns in a memorable 45–38 loss to Arizona State in the Fiesta Bowl.

has been Gibbs's right-hand man with the Redskins, was one of Peterson's assistants. Dan Henning was there. Don James was there. Bill Parcells coached there. I look back and think how fortunate I was to play under those guys.

I learned so much from Bill Parcells, and he was the linebackers coach. We used to jaw bone a lot at practice. I loved all those linebackers. I'd go by Parcells in practice and say, "You know, you've got a lot of sissies at linebacker." We were walking from practice to the field house one day, and Parcells said, "Dawson, come here." He told me, "You're a pretty good receiver. You know what your problem is? You can't make the big catch." I didn't sleep that night because here was this guy I admired so much, and he didn't think I could make the big catch. For the rest of my career, I felt like I had to prove him wrong. I'd jump through brick walls, dive through glass to make the big catch.

I had an opportunity to see him 20 years later when he was coaching the New York Giants and had breakfast with the team in Dallas. He told me they'd played the Arizona Cardinals a few weeks earlier in the same stadium where FSU played in the 1971 Fiesta Bowl. He said, "You know, you made the big catches in that game." That's the kind of guy he is. He was just such a player's coach. You'd be out at practice giving 110 percent, and Parcells would say one thing to you, and you'd dig deeper. He demanded excellence and somehow he could get more out of you than you even knew you had. As a player, you loved him.

118

Larry Jones, the defensive coordinator from Tennessee, was named Florida State's coach before the 1971 season. He brought in Steve Sloan and Pat Hodgson to coach the offense. I learned a lot from Pat, who was the receivers coach. He taught me some really valuable, hands-on lessons and just the little nuances of running pass routes. He had been in the trenches and he was just a great guy. It was a real jolt to have such a turnover in the coaching staff, but I have lots of fond memories of Pat Hodgson.

We opened the 1971 season against Southern Miss and won 24–9. We went down to Miami the next week and won 20–17.

They had artificial turf in the Orange Bowl and there was a thermometer on the field. It was something like 130 degrees. They kept dumping ice in front of our bench, and if we had a drive going, and you'd have to stay in for three or four first downs, the bottom of your feet would just be on fire. When you came off the field, you'd go back over to the bench and put your feet on that ice. We had an offensive lineman who lost 20 pounds that game.

We won our first five games in 1971. We beat Kansas 30–7 and then went to Blacksburg, Virginia, to play Virginia Tech. There was always a lot of hype surrounding that game. I don't know where or how the rivalry started, but it was a rivalry. We won the game 17–3. We beat Mississippi State 27–9.

We were 5–0 when we went to play Florida. Right after the two-minute warning, we were trailing 17–15 and had the ball on our 40-yard line or so. Florida was running a nickel defense, and I told Huff, "Let me get between the cornerback and safety in that gap down the sideline." Gary threw a perfect pass, and I had to stretch out with everything I had.

After the game the Florida State newspaper had a series of four pictures of me with the ball in my hands. In the first picture I was stretched out with the ball in my fingertips; the next picture I had the ball in my chest; the next one I was spinning right before I hit the ground with the ball in my hands; and the last one had me hitting the ground as the safety was spearing me. I spun out of bounds and the ball came out at about their 20-yard line. They called the pass incomplete and we lost. There was a picture of me in the newspaper sitting on the bench with my face in my hands. I was literally crying because I could not believe we'd been robbed like that. That was my fifth year, and we'd never beaten Florida. It was a heartbreaker.

119

We bounced back and played South Carolina. I remember having a pretty good game against Dickie Harris, who was their All-American cornerback. When I was in high school and went to FSU to watch my brother play, I was just mesmerized by Fred Biletnikoff. I'd just watch his every move. When I got there to school, I made them go get all that old film out of the archives. Instead of going to the library to study at night, I'd go to the field house and watch Freddie. I just tried to pick up everything he did. So then I watched Dickie Harris on film so much that I could tell you when he was going to scratch his head. I'd lay in my bed at night with my eyes shut, probably for hours, visualizing which way he'd turn if you ran at him, so I could get him to go the other way. [Dawson caught nine passes for 140 yards and two touchdowns in the Seminoles' 49–18 win over the Gamecocks.]

In the Georgia Tech game the next week I dropped a pass that was branded on me forever. We lost the game 12–6. It was late in the game, and I ran a post pattern. I was right in between two guys, and they were both going for the ball. It was one of those plays where if the receiver catches the pass, the two defenders run into each other and the receiver keeps going. It was one of those, but I didn't catch the pass. It was a nightmare.

We blew out Tulsa 45–10 and beat Pittsburgh 31–13 and received a bid to play Arizona State in the first Fiesta Bowl. The Fiesta Bowl game was the only game I ever played in that we lost and didn't feel disappointed. That game was as close as any game I've ever played in. Danny White was Arizona State's quarterback, and he'd get the ball and drive down and score a touchdown. We'd get the ball and score. It just kept going back and forth and back and forth. By the time the game was over, they won because the clock just happened to run out when they had the ball. It was a game we would have liked to have won, but what a football game. [Dawson caught eight passes for 108 yards and two touchdowns in the 45–38 loss.]

I was drafted by the Houston Oilers in 1972 and played one season for the Oilers. I got traded to the Minnesota Vikings and was the last guy cut in training camp. Bud Grant, the Vikings coach, arranged for me to go play for the Saskatchewan Rough Riders of the Canadian Football League. I got up there on a Wednesday, and on Sunday I was the starter and scored two touchdowns. I thought, *Boy, this isn't bad*. I finished that season and played two more. I loved playing football at Valdosta High School and at Florida State, but it would be hard for me to say that wasn't the most fun I ever had playing football.

Rhett Dawson, a native of Valdosta, Georgia, was a starting wide receiver for Florida State in 1970 and 1971. He led Florida State with 54 catches for 946 yards and five touchdowns as a junior in 1970. As a senior, Dawson was named a third-team All-American after catching 62 passes for 817 yards and seven touchdowns. Dawson's most memorable game came against Arizona State in the inaugural Fiesta Bowl in 1971. He caught three touchdowns and a two-point conversion in the Sun Devils' 45–38 victory. More than 25 years after he last played for the Seminoles, Dawson still ranks among the top 10 in school history in season receptions (62 in 1971) and catches per game (5.64 in 1971). He was elected to the Florida State Sports Hall of Fame in 2006. Dawson, who played two seasons in the NFL and three in the Canadian Football League, is a land developer in Austin, Texas.

# BARRY SMITH
## WIDE RECEIVER
### 1969–1972

I GREW UP IN MIAMI and went to Coral Park High School. I was being recruited by Georgia, Auburn, Tennessee, Alabama, Florida, and Florida State. I was a heartbeat away from going to the University of Tennessee because Bill Battle was initially the offensive coordinator and then became head coach. I ran high hurdles in high school and was the state champion. My junior year, I finished fifth or sixth in the Junior Olympics, and Tennessee had a great tradition of high hurdlers and wide receivers. I came close to going to Tennessee because I liked the program and the facilities were incredible.

But ultimately I decided I was from Florida and wanted to live in Florida. For me, Florida State was obviously the right decision. I loved it when I got there, and I loved watching Fred Biletnikoff and Ron Sellers when I was in junior high and high school. I wanted to play at a place that threw the football and had a pro-style offense.

Joe Gibbs recruited me for Florida State, and then it was Dan Henning. Bill Parcells was the linebackers coach. We had some great coaches. I went to

Florida State because of Bill Peterson, and I loved the offense. It was the right decision for me, and I'm glad I went there.

I arrived at Florida State in 1969 and played on the freshman team. Back then, you could not play on the varsity squad as a freshman. We called it "frosh ball," and you just had your sophomore, junior, and senior seasons on the varsity. Gary Huff was one of the quarterbacks on our freshman team. Gary only played one game during our freshman season. We played a JV game in Tampa, and Gary went to high school in Tampa, so he played that game against Miami. You could really tell there was a lot of potential with Gary. He still had to grow a little bit, but nobody threw the ball better than Gary Huff.

We were running Sid Gillman's offense from the San Diego Chargers. Joe Gibbs left Florida State and went out to San Diego, and Dan Henning had been at San Diego and came back to Florida State. There was a lot of influence from San Diego. That's why it was so much fun. We threw the ball a lot, and it's funny looking back at the offenses we ran.

But the problem we had, and it was the same problem a lot of schools like Florida State had, was that there was no limitation on the number of scholarships you could give out. Schools like Alabama, Tennessee, and Georgia would just come in and gobble up all the great athletes because they didn't want them to go anywhere else.

So when Bill Peterson got to Florida State, he knew he couldn't line up and run anybody over because he couldn't get the big offensive linemen. But you know what? He created a finesse game. Our offensive linemen were 225 pounds. A lot of those guys are still my close friends, and I look at them and think, *How in the heck did you play guard?* We had one guy, Bill Rimby, who was 250 pounds. We thought, *Holy crap, this guy is a big son of a gun!* Our offensive linemen were just quick and tough. We threw the ball, so it was different. You didn't have to run over anybody. We just threw the ball and tried to make something happen. The only time we got blown out is when we got wore down. Our first team was as good as anybody in the country, but we just didn't have the depth that a lot of teams had.

During my sophomore season in 1970, we started 2–1 and beat Louisville 9–7 in the opener, with J.T. Thomas blocking a field goal at the end. I've got buddies who played on that Louisville team, and they still can't believe we beat them. It was a night game on Labor Day weekend, and Coach Peterson was so mad at us for the way we played in that game that we had a scrimmage the next morning. We were back there at 8:30 in the morning he was so upset.

We lost to Georgia Tech 23–13 in Atlanta and then beat Wake Forest 19–14. We played Florida at home the following week, and we were getting clobbered. But Gary Huff came off the bench late in the game and almost brought us back.

That was the day "Huff the Magic Dragon" was born. That's when the legend of Huff started. He was the third-team quarterback, but all of us were going crazy because everybody on that team knew Gary should be the starting quarterback. But the coaches liked Tommy Warren because he was the senior, and Gary was only a sophomore and didn't have the experience. Tommy was a scrambler and had a very average arm, and Gary was just throwing BBs. They finally said, "Okay, Gary, go see if you can do anything." He went out and lit up the scoreboard. I caught my first touchdown and I was laughing my rear off because it was a one-yard catch. A couple of minutes later, he threw me a 66-yard bomb for a touchdown. I was like, *I'm going to like this guy, Gary Huff.*

I ran a flanker reverse in that game, and I remember Tommy Warren pitching me the ball. I was trying to look the ball into my hands, but Jack Youngblood had a bull's eye on my chest. He was coming right at me, and I was like, *Holy crap! This is going to hurt!* About the same time the ball hit my hands, he just nailed me. That was my introduction to Jack Youngblood. That was rough. We lost the game 38–27, but we were kind of excited because of what Gary had done.

Florida always had a lot of talent on their team. But you know that saying, "You can leave your best game on the practice field"? That's the way it was with Florida. Bill Peterson was a very emotional coach; that's why I liked him so much. But the Florida game was just way over the top. I think we always left our game on the practice field. Everybody wanted to beat Florida so badly that we all kind of tightened up when we played them. Thank God we don't have those days anymore. At least we're competitive with Florida now.

We lost to Memphis State on the road, 16–12, and Huff lost three fumbles in that game. We came back and beat South Carolina on the road, 21–13, and then we played against Miami in the Orange Bowl. I always wanted to play in the Orange Bowl. I grew up a Miami Hurricane. My dad raised me to be a Miami Hurricane. Everybody in the world thought I was going to be a Miami Hurricane. But when it came time to decide, I didn't want to go there.

123

That game always meant a lot to me because I was back playing in front of my family and friends in my hometown.

To me, playing in the Orange Bowl was like playing at Wrigley Field or Fenway Park. It was really special. We won the game 27–3, and I had a very good game and scored a touchdown. Tommy Warren, who was from Coral Gables, had a very good game. Tom Bailey was from Coral Gables and had a great game and became the school's all-time leading rusher in that game. Back then, when you got your picture splashed across the front of *The Miami Herald*, that was big stuff. We didn't have ESPN and didn't have every game televised. Everybody gets exposure now, but back then, you had to play big in big games to get exposure when the media was there.

We played Clemson at home and won 38–13. I caught touchdowns from Tommy Warren and Gary Huff in that game. Hootie Ingram, who later became Florida State's athletics director, coached that Clemson team. We beat Virginia Tech 34–8, and Don Strock was their quarterback. We had over 600 yards of offense in that game. We beat Kansas State at home, 33–7, and our defense really roughed up their quarterback, Lynn Dickey.

We closed the season playing Houston in Tampa. It was played on the night of Thanksgiving Day. I remember that game very well. I always ask my buddies this trivia question: Who was the last athlete to score a touchdown for a Florida State team coached by Bill Peterson? The answer is Barry Smith. I caught a 65-yard touchdown right before halftime. We ran a little play-action, and I faked like I was going to come in and block the strong safety. He bit on it, and then I ran up the field. It was a short cut and a nice long run. Charlie Ford, who was an All-American cornerback at Houston and later played for the Chicago Bears, was step for step behind me, but he couldn't catch me. Unfortunately, the second half was like night and day. They just beat the living dog out of us.

It got so bad in the second half that when they were running back one of Tommy Warren's interceptions for a touchdown, Bill Parcells was standing on the sideline, screaming, "Somebody do something!" Dan Whitehurst was standing on the sideline and stepped off and nailed the guy right there. The poor guy never knew what hit him. Back then, it was only a 15-yard penalty from that spot. It was hilarious. I asked Dan why he did it. He said, "You tell Bill Parcells you're not going to do it. When he screamed at me, I jumped!"

Barry Smith was one of Florida State's first big-play receivers, scoring 27 touchdowns from 1970 to 1972, which ranked him second at the time. He also scored 164 points during his three-year career, another Florida State record at the time. Smith, who played for the Green Bay Packers and Tampa Bay Buccaneers in the NFL, is a successful businessman in Tampa and remains an avid supporter of FSU athletics.

Coach Peterson left for Rice after the 1970 season, and I was not happy. When they announced Larry Jones was going to replace him, I actually contacted Bill Battle and said I wanted to transfer. I'd decided I was going to go to Tennessee and wasn't going to stick around with Jones. But then Jones signed Steve Sloan as the offensive coordinator and Pat Hodgson as the receivers coach. They sat down with me and talked sense into me. I liked them. They were like big brothers to me, and we had a lot of fun in 1971.

We beat Southern Miss 24–9 to open the 1971 season. Then we went back down to Miami and played the Hurricanes in the Orange Bowl. It was so hot that I was getting sun-burned on the bottom of my feet from running on the artificial turf. The heat coming off that turf was melting the rubber soles on my shoes. It was wicked. Dick Allen, who used to play for the Philadelphia Phillies, one time was asked about playing on artificial turf. He said, "If cows can't eat it, I don't want to play on it." I felt the same way. You need grass. It was a game where we should have beat them worse. We won 20–17, but they had a lot of talented players who got drafted by NFL teams. They had Chuck Foreman, a great running back. They had a lot of studs.

We beat Kansas 30–7, and I had probably one of my most fun memories between Gary and I. I probably dropped two or three balls that he threw to me early in the game. The passes hit me right between the numbers, and I just dropped them. It was just one of those games. But we kept running this play where the tight end would run out in the flat, and I'd run a turn in. Every time we ran it, the cornerback was biting on the tight end. I told Gary to run the play again, and pump fake the throw, and I'd be gone for a touchdown. We ran it, and I scored an 88-yard touchdown, which at the time was the longest touchdown catch in FSU history. It was fun after I'd dropped those early passes and was the goat.

We played at Virginia Tech and we hadn't beaten the Hokies in Blacksburg since 1959. It was a great game and we won 17–3. Gary Huff set an NCAA record by completing 21 of 25 passes. That was a fun game. Besides winning, it was always good to beat Strock and those guys. Florida State and Virginia Tech always had a great rivalry though the years, and they were always tough. I remember they had some of the best-looking cheerleaders I'd ever seen. You ask anybody who played on that 1971 team. The best-looking cheerleaders we saw were at Virginia Tech, no doubt about it. They had these stands that were right behind our benches and they'd be, like, shoulder-height. They'd do their cheers, and you'd have to keep looking at them because they had the best-looking legs you'd ever seen. They did it on purpose to distract us.

We played Mississippi State the next week, and it was a strange game. I caught a touchdown in that game, and it was a little rainy. We won the game 27–9, but the whole game just seemed weird. It was wet and sloppy.

To this day, I'll never forget the Florida game. We were 5–0 and they were 0–5. Everybody has their own opinions, but we got to a 5–0 record by throwing the ball. We weren't known as being a running team. We went out and warmed up, and everybody was fired up. We went back to the locker room, and Larry Jones told us, "By the way, guys, we're going to show the University of Florida that we can run the football. We're going to run it down their throats." We were all going, "Huh?" Come on, we had Rhett Dawson, Gary Parris, Gary Huff, Kent Gaydos, and me. Come on!

In the first half, Art Munroe, bless his heart because he was a tremendous athlete, was going into score twice and fumbled the football away. The third time, he was running out in the flat, and Jimmy Barr was running at him to make the tackle. The ball went through Munroe's hands and bounced off his shoulder pads, and Barr intercepted the ball and walked into the end zone. We lost two touchdowns and gave up a touchdown. It was like Bill Buckner with the Red Sox. We ended up losing the game 17–15, but I don't blame Art Munroe. I dropped passes, too.

We came back home and beat South Carolina, 49–18. Gary Huff was so hot in that game. They had Dickie Harris, an All-American cornerback, and Rhett Dawson just turned him into a pretzel. Rhett Dawson wasn't the fastest guy, but he could run a route and he could catch the football. He was a lot like Fred Biletnikoff. I was always the guy who went deep. I ran the 40-yard dash in 4.5 seconds consistently. Back then, that was pretty fast. I never got caught from behind. But I didn't learn how to run routes until my senior season. I just always told Gary to throw it deep.

We lost to Houston 14–7 and lost to Georgia Tech 12–6. We came back and beat Tulsa and Pittsburgh to finish the season 8–3.

We played Arizona State in the very first Fiesta Bowl in 1972. They came up with the Fiesta Bowl because Arizona State was a great team. They had Danny White, Woody Green, Benny Malone. I could go on and on about all the guys who played pro ball off that team. But they were kind of a renegade team and scored a lot of points. Back then, you might have had only eight or nine bowl games, not like the 32 you have today. They wanted Alabama to play Arizona State in the Fiesta Bowl. Alabama was extended the invitation and declined, so they took Florida State. Our coaches took the stance of, we'd had a great year, so we were going to go out there and have fun. We were going to work, but we were going to have fun. With Arizona State's coach, Frank Kush, it was back to two-a-days, and he was going to work the hell out of them. He wanted to murder us.

We were heavy underdogs in that game. They beat us 45–38 in the final minute. It was a track meet. We lined up at the beginning, and they were going to play us man to man. We thought they were crazy. It was the first time in any bowl game that the same team had three 100-yard receivers. We had three guys catch over 100 yards a game, and Gary was the offensive player of the game. I ran into Danny White, their quarterback, a couple of years ago. He said, "I'll never forget that Fiesta Bowl. We'd go in and score, and then I'd go and sit down on the bench. As soon as I sat down, you guys would score, and I'd have to go right back out there!"

We lost the game, but we proved a lot to a lot of people. Playing out there, it was a home crowd and they had officials from the Western Athletic Conference. But we had a lot of fun, and that's what it was all about back then. We were going to throw the ball and have fun.

We started the 1972 season with a great team, but we had a lot of injuries and they just took their toll. We got to the last game of the season against South Carolina, and they said all you have to do is either win or tie, and you'll get to the Peach Bowl. That was exciting. We went up 14–0, but we lost our defensive ends—the last two we had—and we had down linemen having to stand up. J.T. Thomas, our stud cornerback, had to play on a broken foot because other guys were hurt. It was just the walking wounded.

It was ironic in that South Carolina game because the very first game we played at FSU in 1970, we won because we blocked a field goal at the end. J.T. Thomas had blocked the field goal, but they called us offside. But he blocked it again, and we won the game. In that South Carolina game, the score was tied at 21–21. In the 1972 game they attempted a field goal and the kid missed it, but they called us for being offside. They moved it up five yards, the kicker made it, and we lost 24–21. We didn't play in a bowl game that season.

I was drafted by the Green Bay Packers in the first round of the 1973 draft. The fans in Green Bay are the greatest fans in the NFL. I made some very dear friends. The Lombardi era and great times were over. We had some pretty ugly games. But in my very first game, we were playing on *Monday Night Football*, and I was watching Joe Namath. It was pretty cool.

I had a blast at Florida State. I had a lot of fun. Did we lose some games we should have won? Sure. But we had fun. At this point, 35 years later, it's not about how many games you won and lost, it's about the friendships you made and that you still have. Those are very unique friendships. A lot of those guys have gone on to become successful businessmen, and those were unique times that we shared. You can't manufacture those times. You can become a millionaire, but I guarantee you're not going to have as much excitement or have the stories that we have.

Barry Smith, a native of Miami, Florida, was a standout wide receiver for Florida State for three seasons, from 1970 to 1972. In three seasons he scored 27 touchdowns, an FSU record at the time, and scored 164 points, another then–school record. As a senior in 1972, Smith caught 69 passes for 1,243 yards and 13 touchdowns. He caught 11 passes in a 44–22 victory over Kansas, and had 10 against both Virginia Tech and Florida. He was named a first team All-American after the 1972 season and was drafted in the first round of the 1973 NFL draft by the Green Bay Packers. Smith played three seasons for the Packers and one for the Tampa Bay Buccaneers. Smith is a successful businessman in Tampa, Florida, and remains an avid supporter of Florida State athletics.

# J.T. THOMAS
## CORNERBACK
### 1970–1972

WHEN I WAS A JUNIOR IN HIGH SCHOOL, the big football schools in the South weren't integrated yet. The black schools were recruiting from the black high schools, and I had just integrated a large white high school in Macon, Georgia, so I wasn't being recruited by the black colleges, either. I had no idea where I would go to college, and I definitely knew that my parents couldn't afford to send me to college on their own.

My father, James Thomas, was an aircraft refueler at Warner Robins Air Force Base, and my mother, Annie Ruth, was a homemaker. It was a typical family where the father worked and the mother raised the kids. It was an extended family, with my grandmother and my aunts all living in the same house. I was the oldest of four children, so I was kind of the pacesetter there in a lot of areas.

Not until my junior year did the opportunity present itself. They actually started integrating the schools and would be recruiting African Americans in the Southeast to play football. Harley Bowers, the columnist at *The Macon Telegraph* in my hometown, knew Georgia coach Vince Dooley very well and called and talked to him. But Vince Dooley indicated that the University of Georgia wasn't quite ready to accept African American players.

But Florida State was ready. Bobby Jackson, one of the assistant coaches there, came up to Macon and saw me play in an all-star game. He let me know they were interested in my coming to Florida State. I don't think they

James "J.T." Thomas was the first African American football player at Florida State. After earning All-America honors as a senior in 1972, Thomas was a first-round selection of the Pittsburgh Steelers in the 1973 NFL draft. He was a member of the Steelers' famed "Steel Curtain" defense and won four Super Bowl rings while playing in Pittsburgh.

knew what the challenges would be, and he couldn't talk about something that hadn't happened. I knew the challenges as an African American.

I had integrated the schools in Macon when I was 14 years old. I was one of 17 African American students who integrated the junior high. I'd gone through the whole process of being accepted and going through the whole racial attitude that existed in the 1960s. Obviously, there were a lot of things that were happening with desegregation, so I grew up in the midst of desegregation. I was a part of that process, so I knew what to expect.

I went to a Catholic school at a very young age, and most of the nuns were white. From kindergarten to eighth grade, most of my teachers were white. My influence and perception of people was probably different than most African Americans. I knew at an early age that all white people weren't bad. The nuns had a lot of influence on my life, as far as how I saw and perceived other people. They told my mother that I should go to one of the all-white schools they were integrating. They told her I shouldn't go to one of the predominantly black schools. Whatever the nuns said, my mother bought into it. Whatever they said, that was it.

I knew the dangers and I knew the things that were lurking out there. But when you're young, you don't fully understand the dangers. That's why they send young men to war; you think differently when you're young. I had been there and wanted the opportunity. I was always taught and felt that I belonged and could do anything anyone else could do. It was something that was instilled in me as a child. It was a challenge I wanted.

I got to Florida State in 1969, and they brought in four African Americans at the time. I wasn't by myself on the freshman team. You were 18 years old, and the walls of desegregation were still tumbling. But in football, when you make contact and you're physical with anyone, there's a transmission of identity. When you tackle someone, it's kind of subliminal and you feel their character and who they are. You feel their strengths and their weakness. You feel their anxiety. You feel what's driving them. So every time you hit someone, you're feeling their character. That's why athletes have a tendency to bond very quickly. You get to know the core person very easily in that process. When you get to know a person like that, you get to know who a guy is really well. You find out 95 percent of that person is just like you, and the other 5 percent is insignificant.

I think because of that, we were accepted by our teammates first. If you weren't accepted by your teammates, you weren't going to be accepted. But our teammates invited us to certain things and took us to certain places where we weren't really allowed to be. People didn't want us there, but our teammates took a risk in associating with us. It wasn't a good idea at the time to be hanging around with black people, so they took a risk, too. Guys like Barry Smith, Dan Whitehurst, Gary Huff, and David Snell were pioneers. You'd never hear about those guys. You'd hear about the protesters and the people taking over the university, and I was a part of that, too. But my teammates were a part of breaking down those barriers, and with me becoming comfortable at that university.

Our coach, Bill Peterson, was very humorous. Sometimes, you wondered if he took life seriously, but he was a great coach. Peterson was intimidated by the blacks when we first got there, though. We all had Afros. Pete was from the old school and had his own ideas about Afros. He'd seen the black militants wearing them. He had a meeting after practice one day, and he only called the black players to stay after practice. I didn't know why he was only calling us over. But he started talking about our hair. He wanted us to cut our hair, and he didn't have a good reason for it. We knew why he wanted us to cut it—he thought the hair provoked a militant-type persona, and he didn't want that on his football team. We heard him out, but we didn't cut our hair.

Peterson was a great guy. He would always come and ask how things were going and if we needed anything. He worked in the background a lot. There were a lot of things that happened, which I knew he was behind. It was very obvious. There were things that set up, even in the off-season, that I knew Peterson put together. He made sure that you went to class. Class and study hall were mandatory.

Peterson made sure we worked out and were in good shape. We had the "room." The "room" was a place with a chicken-wire ceiling, and you went in there to do all these drills with the coaches. They outlawed the "room" later because players changed and started to complain. It was like going to the death chamber. Your whole day was ruined because you were going to the "room." You never walked out of the "room"; you crawled out of it. You were totally exhausted. The coaches pushed you around like rag dolls, and it was constant movement. The last thing you had to do was wrestle and you couldn't move. It was the hardest thing I ever had to go through. It almost became barbaric. In fact, I joined the track team so I wouldn't have to do it anymore.

I played on the freshman football team in 1969. I was a wide receiver. They used to call me and Barry Smith the "Golddust Twins." Gary Huff was the quarterback, and we scored when we wanted to score. Barry was a sprinter and state hurdles champion out of Miami, Florida. He was a bad white boy. He was an awesome athlete. We became great friends, and our goal was to become the starting receivers for the Seminoles. We used to go up in practice against the varsity secondary and we would just smoke them. So in our minds, we were going to be starting as sophomores no matter what.

But they moved me to cornerback before my sophomore season, and Barry started at receiver. You have to understand that Florida State was still a white university, and they'd had only white players on offense. They weren't accustomed to having an African American on the team, let alone on offense. Those receivers, like Fred Biletnikoff and Ron Sellers, were sacred. This was still a work-in-progress, believe it or not.

Obviously, I had the talent to play defense, and I'm sure the coaches thought I was better for defense. But I thought I was going to be on offense and I wasn't even thinking about playing defense. I think it worked out for the best, and I believe things happen for a reason in life. Sometimes things might not go the way you think they should go, but they go the way they should go.

I ended up starting at left cornerback in 1970, and it was an awesome thing. But I also was taking on the burden of being the first black football player at Florida State, and those were the headlines in the newspapers. As you can imagine, I felt a little bit of pressure. Back then, I wasn't just playing for my parents or for me. I never even loved football. Football was the vehicle for me to get from point A to point B. I enjoyed playing football, but I don't think I ever loved it. As a matter of fact, I know I didn't love football.

But I was playing for the Deion Sanderses and Terrell Buckleys who would come behind me. You realized you had to make it athletically on the football field and had to make it in the classroom. You had this pressure building that you couldn't fail. Because if you failed, you fell into those stereotypes that African Americans can't compete and they're not good enough. A lot of people were looking for me to actually succeed. Nowadays, guys are playing for their parents and for themselves. They're playing for an opportunity to go play pro ball. Those weren't the reasons I was playing at the time.

I had people from the NAACP, from Macon to Tallahassee, supporting me. It was almost like an Underground Railroad. When I got to Tallahassee, I had a contact person already there. It was the Reverend Charles K. Steele of the Bethel Baptist Church. One of the ministers in my hometown told me to call Reverend C.K. Steele and he would be my mentor. Reverend Steele was one of the founders of the Southern Christian Leadership Council. When I got to Tallahassee, he was the first person I called, and he was waiting for my phone call. I went to his church, and he was a mentor. I also was adopted by a family in the Tallahassee area. I had a support system in place because of the challenges I was going to face.

I got hate mail on several occasions. I got hate mail before games. Some of it was signed by the Ku Klux Klan. I got it more so than other players because they weren't the focal point. I was because I was going to be the first black to play in a game at Florida State. I got quite a few hate letters the first year, but after that, it stopped. I never felt like I was in danger. I never feared life or death because I started at a very early age being in that type of environment.

We were getting ready to start the 1970 season, and I still remember the Friday practice before the first game. Bill Parcells was Florida State's linebackers coach, and you always thought he was going to run the show one day. He was loud and intimidating. He was the kind of man that if he thought you were soft, he'd ask you if you had lace around your jockstrap. He was the kind of man who would break you or make you.

135

Parcells didn't bother me for the most part, but on this particular Friday he really got under my skin. We were leaving the practice field, and Parcells was three practice fields away from me. I was getting ready to talk to some reporters, and Parcells called me out. He said, "Thomas! You know what? You haven't showed me sugar, honey ice tea! When you get back inside there, you call your momma! You tell her to send me some of those trophies and newspaper clippings because you haven't showed me [expletive] out here today!" That was war talk. You don't talk about somebody's momma. I was mad. I was embarrassed because he'd called me out in front of all those reporters. All I wanted to do was slap my helmet upside his head.

After that, I wasn't thinking about all those reporters being there or even being the first black player at Florida State. All I could think about was Bill Parcells calling me out. I went inside, and he came in after me and we stared at each other. It went on the entire weekend. We went out to the pregame meal at the Spring, and he was looking at me like I was road kill. I looked at him like he was road kill. It was the same thing during the meetings the morning before the game. I was still upset. I wasn't thinking about the football game or anything. I was only thinking about getting my hands on Parcells.

We went to the stadium to play Louisville, and it hit me during pregame introductions. I was standing under the goal post ready to come out, and it was like a moment of silence. These fans were like, "There he is. That's him." That's when it hit me. But I ran across the field and everybody was cheering. I realized how big of a thing this was.

We were beating Louisville 9–7 late in the game. In the last few seconds of the game, Louisville was inside our 25-yard line and was about to kick a field goal that would win the game. Our coaches called "Field Goal Block Left," and I had a knack for coming off the corner and really almost taking the football off the tee. I came off the corner and blocked the kick, and everybody started cheering. We had the game won. But then there were yellow flags all over the place. I was down. I thought I'd let down my team and let down myself. I thought I was really a spectacle on the field now.

I went back to the huddle, and Ron Wallace, who was from my home-town, came over to me and said, "J.T., don't worry about it. You'll do it again. We're going to block this kick again." I thought, *Block it again? Are you kidding me?* But we called "Field Goal Block Left" again, and somehow I blocked the kick again. This time, Ron Wallace picked the ball up and ran a few yards. We won the game. It was a great experience. I couldn't have asked for a better ending to the game. Going back into the locker room after the game, Parcells looked at me and had the same look on his face. But then he smiled and hugged me and said, "You a bad man!" To this day, I still don't know if that was just Parcells being himself or if that was a tactic he employed to get my mind off the idea of my being the first black football player at FSU. I never asked him and never talked about it, but I'll never forget how it made me feel at that moment.

We played Kansas State later that season [a 33–7 victory], and I had three interceptions against Lynn Dickey. It was awesome because my father was there for Father's Day. My father was honored as "Father of the Day," and that was probably the apex of his life, being in that environment on the field. We were an independent back then, so we got an opportunity to play a lot of great athletes whom I played against later in the NFL. [Dallas Cowboys receiver] Drew Pearson was at Tulsa. Elmo Wright was at Houston. I got an opportunity to cover all those guys. But that Kansas State game, of all games, kind of put me on the map. There were a lot of pro scouts looking at Florida State, and other African Americans were watching black players at FSU.

We finished 8–4 during my junior season in 1971 and played in the first Fiesta Bowl. We played Arizona State, which had nothing but speed at every position. They had a great receiver, Steve Holden, who became a good friend of mine when he played for the Cleveland Browns. [Former Dallas Cowboys star] Danny White was their quarterback. They had such great talent. It was just unreal. It was a great game, and it went back and forth. It was a high-scoring game. We had a lot of guys rise to the occasion. We lost the game 45–38, but it came down to the clock.

We had a lot of speed. Eddie McMillan, another black player, started at the other cornerback position. He was a sprinter on the track team. I ran track, and Barry Smith ran track. We were part of the 4 x 100 relay team at FSU. We had a lot of talent, and about 10 of us ended up playing pro ball.

I played in the East-West Shrine Bowl after my senior season in 1972. When I was out there, the Oakland Raiders and Pittsburgh Steelers were playing in the AFC playoffs. The Steelers had just had their first winning season during Franco Harris's rookie season. We had a huge party set up at the Shrine Bowl, and they had a nice spread with guys carving meat and everything for us. We started betting on the game, and I didn't know how to bet. Well, I took Pittsburgh, and nobody was taking the Steelers. They gave us about $500 to go out there, and it was time to go home and I had less than $100 in my pocket. I bet about 30 guys around $30 each. The game was almost over, and Pittsburgh was losing. They wouldn't let me out of the room, and I was like, *How am I going to pay all these guys?* I didn't have the money. The chefs were standing at the door with their big carving knifes, guarding the door, and I couldn't get out.

Then all of a sudden, Franco Harris had the Immaculate Reception. Pittsburgh won the game, and I jumped out of the chair. I grabbed those chef's sabres and dropped a pan on the floor and said, "Pay up, boys!" They were all dropping their $30 into a pan, and I ended up with about $900. I'd never had that much money in my life.

Ironically, Pittsburgh drafted me in the first round of the 1973 NFL draft. Franco Harris chose me as a roommate, and I ended up sharing a room with him. I told him that story about the Shrine Bowl years later, and he said, "Where's my cut?"

We ended up winning four Super Bowls when I played for the Steelers. The first time, we were all 23 or 24 years old. We played the Minnesota Vikings in Super Bowl IX in 1974, and they had Fran Tarkenton and the

137

Purple People Eaters. We were standing in the tunnel of Tulane Stadium in New Orleans, and they all looked 8' tall and they all wore beards. They looked like real Vikings. We were like little kids. We had 12 men in that tunnel, and one of them was fear. We didn't want to look at them. Glen Edwards, our free safety, was kind of a wild guy. He was in the back, and I guess the silence and quietness finally got to him. He yelled out, "What the hell is going on here? We're fixing to kick their butts!" That's all we needed, and we got all charged up.

The following season, we played the Dallas Cowboys in Super Bowl X. They were introducing us on one side of the field. You could see the Cowboys in the tunnel. You could see Roger Staubach, Tony Dorsett, Drew Pearson, and all those guys. Dwight White, our defensive end, said, "Look at their eyes." You could just see this glaze in their eyes. Dwight said, "We got them." We knew we had them before the kickoff. [The Steelers won 21–17, then beat the Cowboys again in Super XIII and the Los Angeles Rams in Super Bowl XIV.]

When I look back at it now, my whole approach to life has been like a stealth bomber. My teammates used to call me "Easy B." They'd call me that because I made everything look easy. Dwight White called me "Stealth Bomber." He would say, "You see him taking off and landing, but you never see him in the air. But you know he's raising hell someplace."

My approach has always been that I'm not on the radar screen, so to speak, I just did what I had to do. It hasn't been talked about a lot. A lot hasn't been written about it. People don't like to talk about those times. They like to think things have always been the way they are now, that players had access. Players today just think about playing the games. They don't have to think about being accepted after the game—where do I go and what do I do after I leave the game. Their concern is just about playing the game and having fun. Players don't have to think about their skin color today. Deion Sanders didn't have to worry about being accepted there or racial attitudes.

It's just a different time, and I played for different reasons. We were playing for our manhood and dignity, even in the pros. A lot of the guys I played with in the NFL grew up during segregation. Guys were from Southern University, Florida A&M, and Texas Southern. We were playing for dignity and acceptance more than anything else. The bottom line is that was the driving force for all of us.

James "J.T." Thomas, a native of Macon, Georgia, was a three-year starting defensive back for Florida State from 1970 to 1972. He was the first African American to play football for the Seminoles and became an immediate impact player. Thomas blocked two field goals in his first game for the Seminoles, a 9–7 victory over Louisville on September 12, 1970. Later that season, Thomas intercepted three passes in a 33–7 victory over Kansas State. As a senior in 1972, Thomas was named a first-team All-American by *Pro Football Weekly* and *Time* magazine. Thomas was inducted into the Florida State Sports Hall of Fame in 1979. He was a first-round draft choice of the Pittsburgh Steelers in 1973 and was a member of the team's "Steel Curtain Defense." Thomas won four Super Bowl rings with the Steelers and played nine seasons in the NFL. After retiring in 1982, Thomas and a former teammate opened a successful chain of restaurants in Pennsylvania and West Virginia.

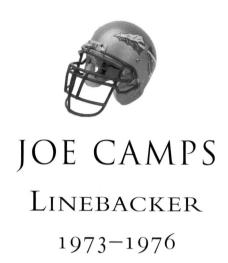

# JOE CAMPS
## LINEBACKER
### 1973–1976

I GREW UP IN GAINESVILLE, FLORIDA, and I went to Gainesville High School. I was a 4-A all-state football player at the time and I was being recruited by Florida, Auburn, Miami, and all the Ivy League schools because I had a 3.5 [grade-point average]. I got inquiries from Yale and Brown, and I felt real good about that, but I wanted to play football.

Larry Jones was the coach at Florida State, and he sent a fellow down to Gainesville by the name of Bill Canty. I happened to be on a high school team that went undefeated, and we had 11 players get major-college scholarships off that high school football team. I was coached by Jim Niblack, who was one of the legendary high school coaches in the state of Florida at the time. I went to school with two guys—Jon Thames and Carlos Dennison— and all three of us decided to come to Florida State.

It made the big paper because it was one of the first times that Florida State had come into Gainesville and had taken three pretty decent football players to come up to Florida State. Of course, I was really excited about that.

I'll never forget coming to a [Florida State] game and watching J.T. Thomas, Eddie McMillan, Gary Huff, Barry Smith; Charlie Hunt was a great linebacker from Jacksonville. I'll never forget coming up here and watching the games, being excited about being in a college atmosphere. I had sort of followed Florida State from Bill Peterson's days.

140

I grew up a Gator. I actually sold Cokes at Florida Field and really, initially, wanted to go to the University of Florida. But every time I think about it I always say, "Thank God, I'm a Seminole," because I don't know that I'd ever want to be anything else. Just the whole spirit of Florida State, I'm just all about it.

I really liked the Florida State Seminoles' Indian Tribe, because I think of the warriors and people who lived off the land, who were just tough.

I came through the era when we were not the big, big program. We had some good, good teams, but we were not the marquee school. Through the years, watching the development of the era of the Seminole Uprising, it all kind of fit with me. Determined to be the best, I guess, is what makes me proud to be a Seminole.

I had come off of an undefeated high school team; two straight years we were undefeated, to going 0–11 [at FSU in 1973]. I was disappointed, but I grew up working hard and we were working hard. When Darrell Mudra came in [1974], he had been a winning coach at Western Illinois. He embodied a will to win and instilled some discipline in the team. My position when I first got in was with Jack Stanton, and then Mudra brought in Deek Pollard. Deek was a real tough, hard-nosed coach who believed in fundamentals and discipline. Even though we were young, I'll never forget that Deek instilled in us a will to win and fight. I felt like even though we were losing, we were fighting very, very hard.

Probably the time I was most afraid in FSU history was when they were about to abolish the program [circa 1974–1975]. We didn't even have uniforms and practice uniforms. I'll never forget, they sent a truck down to the University of Tampa after they abolished their program and they bought their equipment. We actually practiced in the University of Tampa's equipment. I remember the old weight room we had under the stadium. In the winter, when it was cold, all we had was wire. There was no enclosed weight-training facility.

You know, you go through all of that, and here comes Coach [Bobby] Bowden.

Probably the greatest game in that era for me was when we played the University of Miami. We were 0–8 and we beat Miami [21–14 in 1974]. We won and went 1–10. I intercepted a pass in the fourth quarter when Miami was driving. That had to be the highlight. I'll never forget we were so happy that Coach Mudra let the whole football team spend the night in Miami. It

141

Florida State snatched linebacker Joe Camps out of enemy territory—he played at Gainesville High School, near the campus of rival University of Florida. Camps played for three coaches at FSU and was captain of Bobby Bowden's first Seminoles team in 1976. He is a urologist and remains a mentor to many of FSU's African American players.

was back in the times when I guess they let you do that. We were so overjoyed.

Probably the highlight of my whole career was when we went to Tuscaloosa to play the University of Alabama [in 1974]. They were supposed to beat us. I think that was the year after Alabama won the national championship and we shut them out [through three quarters]. I played against Ozzie

Newsome and Calvin Culliver and Richard Todd. I still remember those names. We beat them physically. I had a great game that game. We confused that wishbone. We shut them down.

Probably the biggest disappointment I ever experienced was in that game. We had shut Alabama out for three straight quarters. We were deep in our end of the field, and our coaches decided instead of punting the ball out of the end zone, they would take a safety. At the time, a field goal would beat us, and, sure enough, they beat us 8–7, but we were leading the game 7–5. I thought, *Let's just punt the football. We had shut them out. Don't give them a chance to let a field goal beat us; [make] them score on us.* That had to be the biggest disappointment. We had physically beat them. I think we grew up that day. We knew we had talent enough. We were all young but started believing in ourselves.

Then, in came Coach Bowden, and we were able to recruit a few more skilled athletes. We had a 5–6 season [in 1976]. Probably the most memorable moment that year for me was we played in the Snow Bowl. We couldn't see anything. It was at North Texas State. It was a great victory for us [FSU won 21–20]. Here we are from Florida and we had no thermal underwear or anything, and I can remember the coaches scrambling around trying to find us some thermal underwear. We were throwing snowballs and having fun.

I sensed [a change]. The players were more disciplined; we were working harder. We had a better training table situation. Clearly, the resources were coming into the football program and things got a little bit better. We got strong. Coach Bowden was a real disciplinarian. He was very fundamentally sound in terms of not beating yourself. When you're playing out there a lot of times, it's the undisciplined aspects of the game, when you look at the film, that get you beat.

For instance, [he taught] that if you missed seven tackles in a ballgame, it ended up being a touchdown. Things like that we started paying attention to. People started believing in themselves, and the next year, Florida State went 10–2. You could see that team started to make that little turn. Once they did, Florida State was back to the glory years.

It was fun for me [after 1976] that, even though I wasn't playing, I felt like a winner. I knew we didn't have as many skilled athletes as some other schools and we were playing bigger teams. Sometimes the games we played were against competition that was better than us on their field because we needed to get the resources into the institution. But I never felt defeated.

143

I felt I was a winner. I felt like we lost a lot of the battles, but we didn't lose the war. I've held on to that for almost 30 years. I feel as much a part of the program, identify with it, because I played when I did.

To go on now and become a physician and be able to give back to the program in terms of the Seminole Boosters and being an ambassador for the university in the community and in the state, I still feel that winning attitude.

I became the president of the Seminole Boosters in 1997. I was the first black alumni to ever hold that position. To me, the boosters are the heart and soul of Florida State athletics. You see what the boosters have done. For instance, I'm proud to be one of the founders of the University Center Club. We were up in the Meadowlands when we played Kansas in the Kickoff Classic [in 1993], and we went to the Harvard Club. There were a bunch of us sitting around saying, "Gee, this would be a nice thing to have on Florida State's campus."

And there you see it [now]—the University Center and the ballrooms, the dining rooms, the game rooms, and all the memorabilia. You look at how, through the vision of [Seminole Boosters director] Andy Miller and several of the presidents we've had, you can see the growth of Florida State. I feel like I've been part of the growth of Florida State.

I have a lot of passion for the university because I have lived through an era when we were about to abolish the [football program]. I think some people now take that for granted. When you put yourself in my shoes and look at all of the Marked 10 and all the people who are involved now and are benefactors of the institutions, there's no way they can have an appreciation of where we are because when a bunch of folks could have quit, they chose not to do so.

I think of guys like George Langford, Godfrey Smith, and some old stalwarts—Stan Marshall, Bernie Sliger—people who never get recognition for their contributions. But to me, when I think of the spirit of being a Seminole, those are the warriors I think about. I like that term because it's the fight in Florida State that makes me passionate about being a Seminole.

When I see some of the kids who come along and don't take advantage of the fine facilities, I think, *If I had all this available to me, athletically, what would I be today?* In some ways, I'm glad I did what I did, because now in business and everything that I do, I approach it with the same tenacity, with the will to win and to be number one; to be the very best.

The one thing I appreciated the most about Coach Bowden, I can hear him now, he'd say, "Men, just do your best." I find myself telling my kids the same thing, and I really mean that. If you've felt like you haven't done your best, don't kid yourself. Doing your best accomplishes a lot. I even kid with some of my employees today when I say, "Have you given me a good day's work today?" If you can say, "Yes," I'm happy for you.

No matter what the circumstances are, we're playing to win. Being a surgeon now, the stamina, the discipline, the molding that I got early on with all the adversity [in football] has helped me to overcome adversity today. Even though I had a kid who had leukemia, my father was murdered in a shooting in Gainesville, I lost a brother-in-law in an electrocution, and my mother passed—we had so many difficult factors in life— [my football experiences] and belief in God and faith have helped me to cope and always believe I'm winning.

I'll go to my grave being a winner. I'm proud of Florida State. Sometimes, I hear certain people who are currently involved [with the university] feel like they understand and know Florida State. They don't know Florida State. They don't know where Florida State was. When you go back to that era and watch it today, had it not been for people who didn't quit back then, Florida State may not be where it is today. Certainly Coach Bowden, with his tenure here, has proven that.

Even in the tough years recently, where we sort of lost some of that shining armor, I look back at some of the coaches he's brought in now, like [offensive line coach] Rick Trickett, and I like his spirit. I like his saying, "People are going to dread seeing us come to town when they play Florida State." That's what we had all those great years, even when we were losing. Seminoles, they would battle. Florida State used to play you tough; we would battle. We had lost that edge, and I'm hoping that we've gained that back.

I went through that era. When I got here, Florida State was pretty good. They had gone to the Fiesta Bowl [after the 1971 season]. Then we started kind of that decline from the senior leadership, then I saw us get it back. When we got it back, we rode that ship a long time. We sort of lost that edge the last three or four years, and I think we're going to get it back again.

You hear this phrase, "Seminole Uprising." It means a lot to me. It's kind of a quiet spirit and a tenaciousness I feel; a fight in me that I feel when it comes to competition. You're getting ready to get it on.

I don't know that words can describe what it means to be a Seminole, other than the fact that every time I think about Florida State, I say, "Thank

God, I'm a Seminole. I don't want to be anything else." I don't want to be Oklahoma, I don't want to be a Hurricane, I don't want to be from Penn State.

If I had to do it all over again, I don't know that I would have changed a thing because so many times I think we compartmentalize our success in terms of wins and losses. But some of the things I learned through defeat made me a winner. I'm in the game of life for the long run, and I can look back and see how so much of that has helped me be where I am today. It's just a great feeling. I'm trying to instill that in my kids. I have two kids at Florida State, and I told them I would support them wherever they went to school but, "you know where I'd like you to go to school."

Dr. Joe Camps had the rare distinction of playing for three Florida State football coaches—Larry Jones, Darrell Mudra, and Bobby Bowden—from 1973 to 1976. A linebacker and captain of Bobby Bowden's first team in 1976, the Gainesville, Florida, native has made his home in Tallahassee. Past president of Seminole Boosters Inc. and cofounder of the Southeastern Urological Center, Camps remains active with Seminole Boosters and has been a mentor to many of the football program's African American players.

# WILLIE JONES
## DEFENSIVE END
### 1975–1978

I GREW UP IN HOMESTEAD, FLORIDA, and had a lot of opportunities coming out of high school. Ohio State, Texas A&M, Michigan, Alabama, Oklahoma, and Texas were recruiting me. I'd like to think I could have gone anywhere I wanted. But Florida State was intriguing at the time.

Darrell Mudra was the coach, and there was an opportunity to go in and play early. It was located in the state's capital, and I wanted to stay in the state.

I arrived at Florida State in 1975 and started the second half of the first game against Texas Tech. Florida State wasn't very talented at times. Randy Coffield started on the opposite side of me during my freshman season. He played in the NFL for several seasons after he left Florida State. But the other guys didn't have the big-time talent. The timing was right because I was a *Parade* All-American and one of the top recruits in Florida, so I was able to get on the field pretty quickly.

I don't remember a lot about Coach Mudra. I was a freshman who was kind of awe-stricken by the competition, the travel, and the academics that we had to endure. The head coach was the last thing on my mind at the time. I had a pretty tough position coach, Gene McDowell, who later became the head coach at Central Florida. He was a very hard-nosed guy. Our defensive coordinator, Pete Rodriguez, also was pretty tough. Those were the guys who were more visible to me.

We finished 3–8 during my freshman season in 1975. We lost our first game to Texas Tech 31–20 and then we beat Utah State 17–8 in Doak Campbell Stadium. We lost our next five games, against Iowa State [10–6], Georgia Tech [30–0], Virginia Tech [13–10], Florida [34–8], and Auburn [17–14]. We won at Clemson 43–7 late in the season, and it was good to get a win up in Death Valley. We lost to Miami 24–22 on homecoming and beat Houston 33–22 in our last game of the season.

Coach Mudra was known for coaching out of the press box, so maybe that's why I don't remember too much about him. The only thing I remember is the guy had an impeccable record before he got to Florida State. He wasn't very successful in the South, but all the other places he coached at, he was very successful. He was really dependent on his assistant coaches to lead the team. Like all great head coaches, he coached his coaches, and his coaches coached the players. The staff was very organized. I was only with Coach Mudra for one year. He left after my freshman season in 1975.

I wasn't really happy about the coaching change because I had signed to play with Coach Mudra. When I signed with Florida State, a lot of my friends thought I was crazy. Florida State was coming off seasons in which they finished 0–11 and 1–10. But I chose Florida State because I really liked Coach Mudra and his staff. Not to dispel the success that Coach Bowden has had—because I think Florida State has been very blessed to have him—but I think it also was blessed to have Coach Mudra. I don't know if Florida State had any other coach at the time, if its record would have been any better. We just didn't have the talent that other teams had at the time.

Florida State was probably among the bottom third of the college football teams in the country. By the time I graduated, the process of building a championship team at Florida State was just beginning. When I graduated, I was one of only five seniors on the team. The following season, Florida State had its only undefeated regular season, in 1979. You look at all the great years Florida State has had, that was the only undefeated season they've ever had.

For me, football was always a way to improve my life. It was a bridge to something better. It was an opportunity to get an education. I never really considered myself as a dominant pass rusher or great football player. It was just a chance to make life better for myself and my family.

When Coach Bowden got to Florida State, you could tell right away that he was an honest man. There was a transition period, but we started winning some games. We played our first three games of Coach Bowden's season on the road. We lost at Memphis State 21–12, then got beat at Miami 47–0. We played at Oklahoma, and they had a running back, Horace Ivory, who scored two touchdowns. We lost the game 24–9. We went home and played Kansas State and got a win, 20–10. We were down 10–0 in that game but rallied in the second half. I still remember how big their offensive linemen were.

We went and played at Boston College, which was nationally ranked, and upset them 28–9. That was a really big win for us, winning on the road for the first time. Then we played Florida in Tallahassee, and that was a great game. Florida was ranked No. 12 in the country, and we had a chance to win the game at the end. We had the ball at their 9-yard line but couldn't score. We lost the game 33–26. Even though we lost the game, it gave us confidence that we could beat teams like Florida. We were basically still trying to learn how to win games at that point.

We played another tough opponent, Auburn, the following week on the road. We lost 31–19, and their quarterback, Phil Gargis, ran for four touchdowns. Then we lost to Clemson at home, 15–12, after we led 9–0 at half-time. They scored a touchdown in the fourth quarter to beat us.

We finished the 1976 season with three straight victories. We beat Southern Miss 30–27 in a homecoming game that was really fun. Rudy Thomas, who was a senior and hadn't played a lot, ran for three touchdowns in the fourth quarter to help us win. Then we played at North Texas and won the game on a trick play. We scored a touchdown in the fourth quarter, and Larry Key, one of our running backs, threw a pass to Kurt Unglaub for a two-point conversion with about two minutes left. We won the game 21–20.

149

We beat Virginia Tech 28–21 in the last game of the 1976 season. Virginia Tech was driving for a touchdown late in the game, and they would have won if Roscoe Coles hadn't fumbled. Aaron Carter recovered the fumble at our 4-yard line. On the next play, Jimmy Jordan threw a 96-yard touchdown to Kurt Unglaub to win the game.

We finished the 1976 season with a 5–6 record. But winning those last three games was really important for our confidence. We were still a young football team, and Coach Bowden and his staff were just starting to sign recruiting classes that could build us into a winner. So we felt pretty good going into the 1977 season.

That 1977 season was a lot of fun. We opened the season by winning at Southern Miss 35–6 and Kansas State 18–10. We had a pretty good defense that season, with Ron Simmons and Scott Warren playing on the defensive line. Simmons blocked a punt in the Southern Miss game, and Warren picked it up and ran it in for a touchdown. Kansas State's touchdown came on a blocked punt, so our defense only gave up a field goal in that game.

We played Miami in Tallahassee and really should have won the game. We had a 17–10 lead going into the fourth quarter, but Miami scored three times in the fourth quarter, and we lost 23–17. We played at Oklahoma State the next week, and they had a great running back, Terry Miller, who was a Heisman Trophy candidate. But Larry Key, our running back, had a great game [Key ran for 127 yards and caught three passes for 72 yards and one touchdown], and we won the game 25–17. Oklahoma State fumbled a kickoff late in the game, we recovered it, and then Key caught a touchdown to win the game.

We beat Cincinnati 14–0, and they were supposed to have a really good defense. We played Auburn at home and beat them 24–3. It was the first time Florida State had beaten Auburn [and the first time FSU had beaten a Southeastern Conference opponent since 1972]. Larry Key had another great game [170 rushing yards and two touchdowns]. He wasn't a really big guy, but he was a really tough runner.

Against North Texas, I scored the first touchdown of my career. Their running back dropped the football in their end zone, and I recovered it for a touchdown. We were always taught to roll and cover the football, so it was good coaching, I guess. I didn't have to run far to score. We won the game 35–14. We went to Virginia Tech, and it was a rainy day. Virginia Tech was always tough, but we won the game 23–21.

We won our sixth game in a row, against Memphis State, 30–9. That was a fun game. Then we went and played at San Diego State. The coaches wanted us to have fun out there, but I think we had a little too much fun. They let us go down into Mexico, and most of us had never been there before. We went out there to work, but we lost the game 41–16. It was ugly.

But we ended the season with a big win, beating Florida 37–9 in Gainesville. Florida State hadn't beaten Florida in 10 years, so it was really special to win that game, especially over in Gainesville. Beating your in-state rival was always big, especially with the way we won that game. [Florida gained only 200 yards, was held without a touchdown for the first time since 1973, and Jones was named the defensive player of the game.]

We played Texas Tech in the Tangerine Bowl in Orlando. We won the game 40–17. Florida State hadn't been to a bowl game in quite a while [the

A feared pass rusher at Florida State, Willie Jones was named a second-team All-American by United Press International in 1979, as well as honorable mention All-American by the Associated Press and *The Sporting News*. Jones was a second-round pick of the Oakland Raiders in 1979 and played three seasons in the NFL.

Seminoles' last bowl appearance was in the 1971 Fiesta Bowl]. Larry Key ran a kickoff back for a touchdown early in the game, and we were just clicking on offense, defense, and special teams. We finished 10–2 that season and were ranked No. 14 in the country. It was quite a difference from my freshman season.

My senior season in 1978 opened with a game against Syracuse on the road. We ran them over, 28–0. We had a lot of young guys starting on defense, but we were really playing well. We played Oklahoma State in the second game and won 38–20. We beat Miami 31–21, and Simmons blocked another punt in that game, and we ran it back for a touchdown.

We lost to Houston 27–21 in Doak Campbell Stadium, but we really had the game won. We threw a touchdown late in the game, but they called it back because of a holding penalty. It was a pretty controversial ending. We beat Cincinnati 26–21, but the game was a lot tougher than we thought it would be. We always had tough games against Cincinnati. Then we went to Mississippi State and we just couldn't do anything right. They beat us 55–27. It was one of the worst beatings we ever took.

We went to Pittsburgh and played Pitt. We played a lot better in that game but lost 7–3. The defense played really well in that game, but we just couldn't score any points. Pittsburgh had a great defense, too. We won our last four games, against Southern Miss [38–16], Virginia Tech [24–14], Navy [38–6], and Florida [38–21].

We finished the 1978 season with an 8–3 season but didn't play in a bowl game because of politics. It was disappointing to leave as a senior without playing in a bowl game, but I felt like we put Florida State back on track.

After graduation, I was drafted by the Oakland Raiders in the second round of the 1979 NFL draft. I played three seasons in the NFL before I retired. After leaving the NFL, I got caught in the wilderness that a lot of professional athletes find after retiring. I had my problems, but I've been blessed to have so many people supporting me through the years. A lot of my teammates were there for me. Coaches were there for me. I feel truly blessed because of that.

Willie Jones, a native of Homestead, Florida, was a four-year starting defensive end for Florida State from 1975 to 1978. As a junior in 1977, he had 101 tackles, seven sacks, and three forced fumbles. He had 82 tackles, 10 sacks, three forced fumbles, and three fumble recoveries as a senior in 1978. Jones was named a second-team All-American by United Press International in 1979, as well as honorable mention All-American by the Associated Press and *Sporting News*. Jones was a second-round pick of the Oakland Raiders in 1979 and played three seasons in the NFL. He lives in Oviedo, Florida, where he operates a family-owned business and youth mentoring operation.

# KURT UNGLAUB
## WIDE RECEIVER
### 1976–1980

I WENT TO LEON HIGH SCHOOL IN TALLAHASSEE and decided to go to Florida State. We won the state championship during my junior season of high school and we were runners-up during my senior year. Wally Woodham and Jimmy Jordan, whom I later played with at Florida State, were the quarterbacks on that Leon High team.

I decided to go to Florida State because there was another wide receiver, Mike Shumann, who played at Leon High and went on to FSU. Mike talked me into going to Florida State because he thought I could go there and play early in my career.

I actually signed a national letter of intent with Tennessee. Back then, you could sign a couple of letters of intent. I was going to Tennessee but changed my mind based on Shumann's recommendation. He told me I could play a lot earlier there.

I was recruited by guys on Coach Darrell Mudra's staff at Florida State, but they left before I got to the varsity team. There was kind of a transition period there when Coach Bobby Bowden took over. The wide receivers coach under Mudra didn't really like me at all, but I was so committed because Shumann was there. I was barely 6′ tall, and speed wasn't my best attribute. But I wanted to play right away because I knew I wasn't going to be able to keep playing down the road.

Florida State had gone 0–11 the season before Mudra got there, so I thought they were only going to get better. With the reputation Coach Bowden had at West Virginia, I was pretty excited about it.

I started the first game of the 1976 season and started pretty much every game after that when I was healthy. I had a great time and made great friends. I made freshman All-American my first year, and we played against Oklahoma and Miami. I was an 18-year-old kid coming right out of high school and we were playing some big-time teams. In 1976 we played Oklahoma in the third game of the season, and catching a couple of passes against them was pretty neat.

We went 5–6 in 1976, and I was fortunate to have a good season. I caught two of the longest touchdowns in Florida State history, a 96-yarder and a 91-yarder. Both of them helped win the games, so I was pretty excited about that.

We played at North Texas late in the season, and there were about four inches of snow on the ground. It was a bunch of Florida boys trying to play in the snow. We didn't even think we were going to play the game. They put some cones out there and said, "Here, this is your field." We thought it was a lot of fun, and we ended up grinding it out and won the game 21–20. I caught four passes for 128 yards and a 91-yard touchdown, and caught a two-point conversion that won the North Texas game. We were riding on the bus back to the airport and were all singing Christmas carols. We had a blast.

We played Virginia Tech in the last game of the 1976 season. Late in the game, they were driving down the field to win the game, and their great tailback, Roscoe Coles, fumbled the football. On the very next play, Jimmy Jordan dropped back and threw it up for grabs. I jumped up with two defensive backs, they fell down, and I stayed on my feet. I scored a 96-yard touchdown, and we won the game 28–21.

We had a lot of younger guys, a lot of freshmen and sophomores, who were trying to make a name for themselves. We had a bunch of seniors who were trying to figure out how they could go out on as high of a note as they could. Winning those last three games and having a lot of fun in those last three games, based on what the seniors had gone through the previous three seasons, was pretty exciting. The seniors were great leaders. They'd already been through all the bad stuff.

In 1977 I got injured before the season started, but I ended up kind of hobbling myself back to the field. I caught a touchdown pass in the opener

Wide receiver Kurt Unglaub had two of the longest touchdown catches in FSU history as a freshman in 1976: a 91-yarder in a 21–20 win over North Texas State and a 96-yarder in a 28–21 win over Virginia Tech. The 96-yard touchdown still ranks as the second-longest touchdown pass in FSU history.

156

against Southern Miss [a 35–6 victory], but I didn't play at all in the Kansas State game [an 18–10 win]. I came back against Miami and caught another touchdown [in a 23–17 loss].

I kind of got healthy after that and finished out the season pretty strong. We beat Florida in Gainesville for the first time in a long time, winning 37–9 in the last game of the season. We hadn't beaten Florida in 10 years or something like that, so that was a big victory for Florida State. I caught the first touchdown against them, so that was pretty exciting. It was like winning the Super Bowl in the state of Florida. Being in that locker room, there was so much joy. We went home on the bus, and it pulled into Doak Campbell Stadium, and there were probably 20,000 people in there. It was just phenomenal. They closed the streets in Tallahassee, and it was like a midnight party.

We ended the 1977 season with a 9–2 record and wound up going to the Tangerine Bowl. It was really exciting to go to the Tangerine Bowl because it was the first time in a long time that Florida State had gone to a bowl game. We beat Texas Tech 40–17, and it was a lot of fun. We hadn't been to a bowl game since playing Arizona State in the Fiesta Bowl in 1971. The Tangerine Bowl wasn't a big bowl game back then, but we didn't care. We still had a lot of freshmen and sophomores guiding the ship, and it was a lot of fun.

We started off the 1978 season with high expectations and had a really good nucleus of young players. We ended up with an 8–3 record and beat Florida and beat Navy. We had some disappointing losses but still had a winning record. We really hadn't been on the bowl circuit so we didn't know how to play the bowl politics. We were invited to play in the All-American Bowl, but the Gator Bowl told us they'd invite us if we beat Florida. We beat Florida 38–21, and still didn't get invited to the Gator Bowl because they took someone else. We won eight games but ended up staying at home during bowl season.

I had great chemistry with Wally and Jimmy, who were my roommates. It was a confidence thing, and the game plans and routes we ran were very similar to what we did at Leon High School. It was more perfecting it rather than having to learn it all over again.

During my senior season in 1979, I started the first three games, but then I broke my foot. I had a really bad stress fracture, and it just ended up getting worse and worse. I sat down with Coach Bowden, and we talked about what would be the best thing to do. I could sit out three more games and kind of waste my senior year, or I could sit out the rest of the season and come back in 1980. So I took a redshirt season. We went undefeated during the 1979 regular season, and it was so difficult to watch, I couldn't even go to some of the games. I couldn't even watch the games on TV.

We beat Florida in the last game, 27–16, in Gainesville and got invited to play in the Orange Bowl. After my foot healed, I was able to participate in practices before the Orange Bowl but couldn't play in the game. We lost to Oklahoma 24–7 in the Orange Bowl. Sitting on the sideline watching all the guys I'd played with go through an undefeated season was difficult, but it built up my desire to get back on the field again.

I returned to the team in 1980, and it was definitely worth the wait. We had a great season with Rick Stockstill at quarterback, and we had better running backs. We were a little more balanced on offense, so we didn't throw the ball quite as much. The only game we lost that season was against Miami. I dropped a touchdown pass, and we lost 10–9. It was a disappointing loss. We won at Nebraska 18–14, and it was phenomenal. I remember holding for five field goals in that game. With Rohn Stark as the punter and Bill Capece as the kicker, I've never seen a better special teams performance than in that game.

We came back and beat Pittsburgh the next week, and they were ranked No. 3 in the country. I had a touchdown catch in that game that I'll never forget. That was when Pittsburgh had Dan Marino, Hugh Green, Mark May, and all those guys, and we beat them 36–22. That was one of the best teams

157

we'd played in Doak Campbell Stadium in a long time, and beating them was a lot of fun.

We beat Florida at the end of the 1980 season, 17–13. We beat Florida four times while I was at FSU, and we could have beaten them five times. During my freshman season, Jimmy Jordan and I were lining up to throw the last pass into the end zone, and Jimmy got sacked. When you played high school football in Florida, you kind of grew up with those guys playing Florida. It was a great rivalry.

Coach Bowden was kind of like my second father. He still helps me out today by speaking at some national sales meetings and at my church a couple of times. We're still pretty close. As a player, he always had confidence in me. He coached Fred Biletnikoff, and I was kind of a Biletnikoff-type of receiver. He always told me I was better than Biletnikoff, so he had a lot of confidence in me. My parents got divorced while I was in school, and he kind of took me under his wing and guided me through the process.

Kurt Unglaub, a native of Tallahassee, Florida, was a starting wide receiver for the Seminoles for four seasons, from 1976 to 1980. As a freshman in 1976, Unglaub led Florida State with 33 catches for 665 yards and four touchdowns. He had two of the longest touchdowns catches in FSU history that season: a 91-yarder in a 21–20 win over North Texas State and a 96-yarder in a 28–21 win over Virginia Tech. The 96-yard touchdown still ranks as the second-longest touchdown pass in FSU history. Unglaub played on FSU teams for five seasons—he missed all but three games of the 1979 season with a broken foot—and played on teams that played in the 1977 Tangerine Bowl, 1980 Orange Bowl, and 1981 Orange Bowl. He finished his career with 69 catches for 1,261 yards and 10 touchdowns. Unglaub has worked the last 25 years in technology and lives in Marietta, Georgia.

# JIMMY JORDAN
## QUARTERBACK
### 1976–1979

I GREW UP IN TALLAHASSEE and attended Leon High School. I had been recruited by Darrell Mudra, and, about half way through my recruitment, Coach Bowden took over. Wally Woodham, who was ahead of me one year at Leon High, had gone to Florida State and redshirted my freshman season, so we ended up being in the same graduating class at FSU.

I didn't play at all in high school until Wally graduated. I could have gone to Miami, Vanderbilt, or Rice; and LSU and Alabama were recruiting me a little bit. A lot of those teams were running veer offenses, and I was pretty much a pure pocket passer, so I didn't have a lot of options. I don't know what would have happened if I had gone to another college. I played as a true freshman in 1976 and played enough to letter. We played at Oklahoma in the third game, after losing our first two games to Memphis State and Miami, and Coach Bowden just decided to put a bunch of freshmen into the game against Oklahoma. I guess he just decided that he was going to take his lumps the first year, but then it would pay dividends down the road. He decided he was going to play for the future. It worked because we got better each season.

I played with Wally during my sophomore season in 1977. They tried to make it sound like we were different quarterbacks. They tried to say he was a short thrower and I was a long thrower, but I think they were just saying it for *Sports Illustrated*, which did a story on the two-headed quarterback. But Wally could throw the ball long, and I could throw it short.

A home-grown product from Tallahassee, Jimmy Jordan shared quarterback duties with his Leon High School teammate, Wally Woodham, at Florida State. Jordan led the Seminoles in passing in 1978 and 1979.

It was probably one of the best alternating quarterback deals ever because it worked out so well. The problem with playing in a two-quarterback system was, if you started the game slow and got yourself into a hole, you could dig yourself out of the hole if you played the whole game. But at FSU, as soon as I made a mistake, I was out of the game. As soon as Wally made a mistake, he was out of the game. You kind of had that possibility of being benched hanging over your head the whole time. It was added pressure because if you threw an interception, you always knew you were going to the bench.

But Wally and I always got along well and we're still friends today. I don't think you'll see a two-quarterback system that worked as well as we did together. It worked out really well for everybody involved. It was kind of hard on Coach Bowden, too. With the two-quarterback deal, you were splitting the team and splitting the town. There were fans for Wally and fans for me. I don't know if he ever wanted to do that again.

The two-quarterback system hurt me a lot when it came time to go to the NFL draft because I was having to split time with Wally at Florida State. Don't get me wrong, I had a great career at Florida State. But we were having to alternate the entire time we were there, and each of us probably would have been better if we were playing the entire time.

Beating Florida in 1977 was one of my greatest memories. Florida had beaten us nine times in a row, and they had 11 players drafted by NFL teams on that team. They were way better than us on paper. But we had a lot of guys on our team who weren't recruited by Florida, so we kind of had a point to make.

The year before, I came in at halftime against Florida after Jimmy Black was knocked out. They put me in as a true freshman. We were driving down the field to win the game from about the 7-yard line, and if I had made a throw in the end zone, we would have won the game. But I got a little bit of pressure and just made a bad throw. We lost the game 33–26, but it let Florida know that we were back.

We beat them 37–9 in Gainesville in 1977, and it's a game I'll never forget. We ended up beating them three out of four times while I was at Florida State. We really turned the tide in that series.

Another game I remember well is beating Texas Tech 40–17 in the 1977 Tangerine Bowl. They were a pretty good team, and we beat the dog out of them. We threw the ball all over the place. It was the first bowl game we'd won since the 1971 Fiesta Bowl.

We went 10–2 during my sophomore season in 1977 and 8–3 in 1978. Before Coach Bowden got there, they'd won four games in three seasons. In 1978 we beat Syracuse, Miami, Florida, and Navy, which had a really good team. We beat some good teams but still didn't get to play in a bowl game. It was weird. We just didn't have any respect from the writers, and they didn't think we were for real.

During my senior season in 1979, we finished undefeated in the regular season. We played Southern Mississippi the first game, and the only way we won was to return a punt for a touchdown in the last two minutes. To go undefeated, you've got to have a lot of luck involved. We played at LSU and it was a day game, for whatever reason, but it was still amazing to play in that place. We beat LSU 24–19, and I'll never forget how quiet that place was after we won.

We finished 11–0 during that 1979 season, beating Arizona State, Miami, LSU, South Carolina, and Florida, but we still didn't have any respect nationally. Even if we had beaten Oklahoma in the Orange Bowl [the Seminoles lost 24–7 to the Sooners], I still don't think we would have won the national championship with a 12–0 record. But to go undefeated against the schedule we played, that was pretty cool.

Coach Bowden was just such a good guy. He was just so personable and he never changed once he got there and started winning. He was just a great motivator. He's big into the history of the military and wars and he's just a great leader. He was always getting his players motivated to play. He wasn't a flashy kind of guy.

After college, I played with Ron Simmons and Paul Piurowski with the Tampa Bay Bandits of the USFL. Steve Spurrier was our coach, and he treated me right, that's for sure. I'm sure Florida State fans don't like to hear that, but the guy was awfully good to me. I don't have anything but good things to say about him.

Playing at FSU is something I'll never forget. I was able to stay at home, and my family and friends could see me play, which was pretty cool. I think what was the biggest achievement for me was coming from nothing when we started as a team in 1976 to going undefeated in 1979. When we got there, the team was terrible. But in four years, we had gone undefeated and played in a major bowl game. Not many people can say they went from the cellar to the top that quick.

Jimmy Jordan, a native of Tallahassee, Florida, was a four-year starting quarterback for the Seminoles, from 1976 to 1979. He split time for three seasons with Wally Woodham, who had preceded Jordan as the starting quarterback at Leon High School. As a freshman in 1976, Jordan threw a 96-yard touchdown to Kurt Unglaub against Virginia Tech, which was the longest pass play in FSU history and still ranks as the second-longest today. Jordan led the Seminoles in passing with 1,427 yards and 14 touchdowns in 1978 and 1,173 yards and 13 touchdowns in 1979. He helped guide FSU to a 10–2 record as a sophomore in 1977 and on 11–1 record as a senior in 1979. He played on two teams that played in bowl games: a 40–17 victory over Texas Tech in the 1977 Tangerine Bowl and a 24–7 loss to Oklahoma in the Orange Bowl during the 1979 season. Jordan completed 18 of 25 passes for 311 yards and two touchdowns against Texas Tech. Jordan works for the State of Florida and lives in Tallahassee.

# MONK BONASORTE

## SAFETY

## 1977–1980

I GREW UP IN PITTSBURGH AND, COMING out of high school, I got no bites as far as recruiting. I didn't even take an official visit, nothing. I got a letter that said if you wanted to pay $25 to register for school, send in your tapes and we'll try to get you in. I played two years of sandlot football, which was pretty organized.

My coach played in the Canadian Football League, and he was trying to help me get a scholarship. He kept calling people he knew, and Jack Stanton, one of the Florida State assistants, was from Pittsburgh. My coach would call him and call him and call him. I think Jack was so sick of hearing from the guy that he finally said, "Sure, come on down." So we drove down five days before school started in March and had no tapes and no film. I weighed about 210 pounds, and they got me in school, and I walked on the team.

They put me at defensive back, and I'd never played defensive back in my life. I'd never lined up back there, never did a backpedal, nothing. I'd been working out in Pittsburgh in January and February, and it was like 10 degrees or 20 degrees. I got down to Tallahassee in March, and it was 85 degrees. I was out of shape. At the end of spring, Coach Bowden told me, "I can't give you a scholarship. There are just too many players that are better than you." He told me he'd let me come back for two-a-days, but if I didn't do better, he couldn't give me a scholarship. I told him I couldn't do that because

163

I didn't have any money to pay for school. We'd had to cash out an insurance policy just to send me down there.

I went back to two-a-days and made a few plays, and three or four people got hurt. They kind of got stuck with me at that point. Then things kind of just fell into place. I was on the travel squad as a freshman in 1977 and started one game. Two guys got hurt, one guy got disciplined, and a couple of guys got moved to different positions. It was just pure luck that it happened. I'd never played defensive back in my life.

The next year, I went home and got in better shape and kind of figured out the game. I got back to FSU as a sophomore and started as a safety. There were eight sophomores who started on defense that season. We started every game together after that. To be playing major college football, for a kid from the Steel City and kind of a ghetto boy who never thought he'd have an opportunity to do that, it was pretty amazing.

We opened the 1978 season at Syracuse, and they had quarterback Billy Hurley, who they were touting for the Heisman Trophy. They had tailback Joe Morris and wide receiver Art Monk, who were two great players. At that time, you didn't know how good they were until after their pro careers. We got up there, and they had a pretty decent team. Reggie Herring and Scott Warren knocked Bill Hurley out of the game midway through the second quarter, and we won the game 28–0. It was our first road victory, and, with eight sophomores starting, it was quite a victory. My family is from Pittsburgh, so I had quite a few people making the trip to the game.

We beat Oklahoma State in Tallahassee, 38–20, and they had some pretty good players. They were some big boys. Oklahoma State scored on a fumble recovery in the end zone, and they had a one-yard run and a six-yard run. Our defenses were pretty good at the time. Willie Jones was a great defensive lineman at the time. We went down and played Miami in the Orange Bowl and won 31–21. They had O.J. Anderson at tailback and, man, was he good. Ron Simmons blocked a kick, and we scored on that, and Bobby Butler intercepted a pass, which set up another touchdown.

We came home and were losing to Houston 27–7 at halftime. They were big and ran that wishbone offense. We came back and scored 14 points in the third quarter. We actually won the game with about two minutes left in the game, but they called it back and threw a penalty flag against us. They called holding on one of our offensive linemen, after we'd thrown a touchdown pass that would have put us ahead 28–27. We ended up losing the game 27–21.

We played Cincinnati, and every time we played them it was the same score. They weren't that good back then, we just couldn't beat them. It was always a struggle, but we won the game 26–21. Then we went to Mississippi State and just got clobbered 55–27. They just kicked our rears. They threw five touchdown passes. We just couldn't do anything. They were running reverses and throwing bombs.

The next week we went to Pittsburgh. When I even thought about going to Florida State, I thought, *Just get me to my sophomore year and let me be on the travel squad when we go to Pittsburgh.* We'd just gotten our rears handed to us by Mississippi State and were feeling pretty bad. Pittsburgh had a pretty good team. We lost 7–3 after Mark Lyles fumbled on about the 20-yard line going into the end zone. It would have given us the lead if we'd scored. You don't want to say you played well in a loss, but I guess I can say it 30 years later. It was probably the best game I ever had. I had 17 or 18 tackles, two caused fumbles, and a couple of pass deflections.

I was a local boy, and my brother had played for Pittsburgh in the early 1970s. I remember sitting in the stadium, and they'd be announcing names like Hugh Green and Tony Dorsett a little funny. They started announcing my name over the loud speaker because I was a local boy. I had 58 people in the stands. I was a ghetto boy, and my guys would bring beer into the stadium and sneak it past the security guys because everybody knew each other. I used to work out in that stadium in the summer with some of their players. I knew their coach, Jackie Sherrill, really well. Just to be home and playing in that stadium was strange. To get on a plane and fly home and stay in a hotel was kind of strange. I spent the night at home after the game because I was in a wedding that day and flew back to Tallahassee on Monday. That made the trip even sweeter.

We beat Southern Miss 38–16 in Hattiesburg, and that was always a tough game. It was always a night game, and they had some pretty decent players who were always junior college transfers. Then we played Virginia Tech in Tallahassee and won 24–14. Virginia Tech was a pretty disciplined team and was more of a grind-it-out team. It was always a good rivalry because we played them almost every year.

Navy had a pretty good football team in 1978 and they were nationally ranked when we played them. But they were so out of shape. They were throwing up on the field because it was still 75 degrees in Tallahassee in November. They didn't have a chance, and we beat them pretty bad 38–6.

I got hit in the knee and got hurt. I had surgery that Monday to repair two inside ligaments on my leg. At that point, my doctor told me I might never play again. I already ran the 40-yard dash in 4.8 seconds.

I didn't get to play in the Florida game at the end of the 1978 season. I was on the bench trying to help out Gary Henry, who was making his first start at safety. When we finished 10–2 in 1977, we played Texas Tech in the Tangerine Bowl and won 40–17. After we finished the 1978 season with an 8–3 record, we were told we had another opportunity to go to the Tangerine Bowl, but we wanted to go to the Peach Bowl. The Peach Bowl was afraid of us because we had to play Florida, and they didn't want to give us an opportunity. Since we told the Tangerine Bowl no, we ended up not going anywhere because everyone else had extended all their opportunities. It was pretty disappointing because we'd finished 8–3 and most of our games were pretty close, except the Mississippi State game. We still had a pretty dang good football team but ended up not going anywhere.

We thought we were going to be pretty good in 1979 because eight sophomores had started on defense in 1978. We thought we had the horses we needed on defense, and we had Jimmy Jordan and Wally Woodham coming back at quarterback. We knew we could score some points.

We opened the 1979 season against Southern Mississippi, and they weren't nearly as good as they'd been in the past. But we were losing in the fourth quarter at home 14–3. I'd always been the blocking return guy, but we called a block. I got completely wide open and blocked the kick, and we ended up scoring off of that. Then Gary Henry returned the next punt for a touchdown, and we ended up beating a Southern Miss team that wasn't very good 17–14.

Then we played Arizona State in Tampa, and it was pouring down rain. They had Mark Malone at quarterback, but we beat them pretty good 31–3. I had two interceptions in that game. We went back and played Miami at home and won 40–23. I had two interceptions in that game. We had Ron Simmons on the line, Paul Piurowski and Reggie Herring at linebacker, and a bunch of other great players on defense. When people don't have a lot of time to throw the football, and people are throwing Hail Marys because you're ahead, it's a lot easier for me to intercept passes. A defensive back is only as good as his defensive line. If I don't have a good defensive line, and if I've got to cover people for a long period of time, I'm in trouble. It was just a perfect scenario for what we had.

Monk Bonasorte was an unrecruited walk-on from Pittsburgh who became a three-year starter and All-American free safety for Florida State, from 1977 to 1980. A ball-hawking free safety, he had 15 career interceptions during his four-year career at Florida State, a record that stood for 11 seasons. He now is executive director of the FSU Varsity Club.

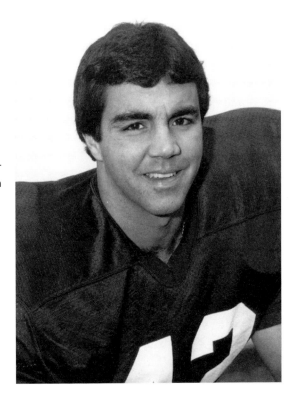

167

We played Virginia Tech, and it was rainy and misty in Blacksburg, but we beat them 17–10. We went on the road to play Louisville and beat them 27–0. We came back home to play Mississippi State, and they were running the dang wishbone. Against the wishbone, you just played as tight as you could on the line, and didn't worry about the pass. We had Bobby Butler covering the receiver man–to–man. You just played run, and I had another one of those games with 15 tackles. My responsibility was to line up over the center, four or five yards behind the linebackers, and let the linebackers take blocks. I either had the pitch or quarterback on the option. That was a physical game. I got hit in the second or third quarter and got knocked out. I played another quarter, and finally came to my senses and didn't really know where the hell I was. They took me off the field, and I spent about two days in the hospital. When I looked at the film, I played a lot better not knowing what I was doing than when I did know what I was doing.

We played LSU, and that was the first game in playing them three straight years on the road. That was one of the most intimidating stadiums I'd ever played in, but we won the game 24–19. I had two interceptions and a recovered fumble in that game. Then we went to Cincinnati and had the same exact score we'd had against them the year before, 26–21. We were losing in the fourth quarter, but Jackie Flowers caught a touchdown in the corner of the end zone to put us ahead with very little time left in the game. It was a close call. I don't know if he was out of bounds or not. It was a close call against a team we should have beaten pretty badly.

Then we went home and played South Carolina and running back George Rogers, the Heisman Trophy winner. He had one run for 80 yards and broke a couple of tackles and scored. But otherwise, we held him under 100 yards and won the game 27–7. The Memphis State game was just a fun game. We won 66–17, and everybody got to play. Then we went to Gainesville and beat Florida 27–16.

We had an undefeated season and were kind of like the BYU, Boise State, or Colorado State of today. No one knew who the heck we were. We didn't go to a bowl game the year before that. We'd gone to the Tangerine Bowl in 1977, but had records of 5–6, 3–8, 1–10, and 0–11 in the four seasons before that.

But we went undefeated in 1979, and it was an exciting time in Tallahassee. We'd go on the road to play, and when we got home there would be hundreds of people at the airport. People loved us. The expectations were so much different. It was a game, and it was fun. It was a game, not a business. It was fun to be with Coach Bowden. It was fun to see the excitement from the fans and the love from the community. The one thing that was so different then than it is now is we did everything together as a team—everything. We'd go to places together and all lived in the same places. We didn't have a lot of great talent, like Florida State has had in the past, but we were so much of a team. We ate together, hung out together, and went to the pool together. It was such a unique experience.

We went to the Orange Bowl after the 1979 season and played Oklahoma. I think we were just kind of in awe and really didn't understand how we got to where we were and how we were undefeated. Oklahoma had David Overstreet, Billy Sims, and J.C. Watts. Barry Switzer was their coach. You had Oklahoma and the wishbone. I think we overprepared ourselves. We worked really hard during two-a-days before we went down there. I think people thought it was good enough to be in a major bowl game on national television. We weren't in that class yet and weren't at that level yet. But I think after playing that game, even though we lost 24–7, we realized we could be at that level and could be in that class. We were determined to get to that level next year.

We opened the 1980 season on the road and had a new quarterback, Rick Stockstill. We opened at Louisiana State, and I think we threw the ball about four times in that game. We were determined to win that game defensively. We had eight sophomores starting in 1978, and now you had eight seniors starting in 1980. We were unified and knew what each other did. Our defensive backs could look at each other and switch coverages on the run, just by knowing where people lined up. Everybody played together.

We beat LSU 16–0 and shut them out on the road. We played Louisville and shut them out 52–0. We played East Carolina and won 63–7. Now, those were fun games where we just dominated. Then we went to Miami. It was a brutally hot game in the Orange Bowl. They went ahead late in the first half, and I'll never forget how they scored. I'm not crying about it, but they threw a bomb out of the end zone. It didn't hit in the end zone—it hit the net behind the end zone. But they still called pass interference on one of our guys, and it was a spot foul so they put the ball at the 1-yard line. They scored to go ahead 7–0 at the half.

We scored late in the game and trailed 10–9, and Coach Bowden decided to go for the two-point conversion because that's the way we were. If we'd tied the game, we'd still be undefeated for the last season and a half. But we went for two, and Jim Burt jumped up and knocked the pass down. We lost 10–9. It was kind of devastating with the way we lost. We didn't score a lot of points, but we played pretty well defensively.

Our reward was to go play Nebraska—at Nebraska. I thought LSU was the most intimidating place to play. You drive through corn field country through Nebraska for 30 or 40 minutes, and get to the stadium and everybody is dressed in red and white. We were there three or four hours before the game, and the place was packed. They were the loudest fans I'd ever heard. It was an unbelievable atmosphere. It was a great game. Bill Capece kicked four field goals and helped us with field position on kickoffs.

The most amazing thing about Nebraska fans was after that game, when we walked off the field, the whole corner section of the stadium gave us a standing ovation. After the game, they came down and asked us all for autographs. They told us they just loved and enjoyed great football. For a school like that, for them to give us a standing ovation, it was an incredible feeling.

In five games, we'd given up 31 points, and none in the fourth quarter. Now, we had to get ready to go home and play Pittsburgh. They had Dan Marino, Hugh Green, Rickey Jackson, Mark May, and a bunch of other guys who were selected in the first round of the NFL draft. When Jackie Sherrill spoke at Florida State a couple of years ago, he said it was the best college football team he'd ever coached. When Dan Marino was inducted into the Pro Football Hall of Fame, he said the 1980 Pitt team was the best team he ever played on. He said, "We could have beaten Georgia and Notre Dame in the same day, but we lost to Florida State."

We played Pitt in Tallahassee and won 36–22. The summer before, I was working out in Pittsburgh and got a telephone call from a reporter in Jacksonville. He was asking me what I thought about playing Pittsburgh and Dan Marino, being a kid from Pittsburgh. I said, "Listen, it's July and we don't play Pitt until October. I don't care about Pitt. We've got to play it one game at a time." The next day in the newspaper, the writer wrote, "Bonasorte doesn't care about Pitt. Marino isn't the best quarterback in the country. Bonasorte's going to have his boys ready."

We used to own a family bar in Pittsburgh, and Jackie Sherrill would always come in there and eat and see my parents and my brother. I used to work out at Pitt's stadium during the summer. But one day, Sherrill dropped the newspaper in front of me and said, "Boy, don't come up here anymore." I said, "Come on, Jackie, you know I didn't say that." He looked at me and said, "Boy, don't write a check your butt can't cash." The war was on. People in Tallahassee found about it, and they were holding signs at the Pitt game that said, "Bonasorte, Cash the Check!" We beat them 36–22, and I think they probably had the best defense in the country.

Then we beat Boston College at home 41–7. We played Memphis State again and won 24–3. Playing Tulsa was kind of a joke, and we won 45–2. We played Virginia Tech at home and won 31–7, and I got my last interception in that game. I broke the record for career interceptions against Virginia Tech.

We finished the regular season playing Florida at home, and they had Cris Collinsworth and Tyrone Young, two guys who were about 6'6". We won the game 17–13. We went into the bowl game without giving up a point in the fourth quarter the whole season. Pitt led the country in allowing the fewest yards, and we were second. We led the country in scoring defense, allowing only 7.8 points per game. We only had two guys drafted off that defense: Bobby Butler and Ron Simmons. Keith Jones and I weren't very fast, and Reggie Herring never went to the NFL. But we probably had one of the best defenses Florida State ever had. When you give up 85 points in 11 games, that's pretty strong.

Once again, the bowl bids were handed out pretty early. We had one loss, losing to Miami by one point, and Notre Dame didn't have a loss. The Sugar Bowl took Notre Dame to play undefeated Georgia. Before that game, Notre Dame got killed by Southern Cal, and we beat Florida. We moved up to No. 2 in the country, and we should have played Georgia for the national championship. Instead, the Sugar Bowl took Notre Dame because of its name and tradition. Georgia beat Notre Dame in the Sugar Bowl, and we lost to Oklahoma 18–17 on a two-point play at the end of the Orange Bowl. We had a couple of chances to win the game earlier, but we dropped a couple of interceptions and fumbled.

But the bottom line was if we'd kicked the extra point against Miami earlier in the year, and hadn't gone for two and the win, we would have finished 10–0–1 and played Georgia without the controversy. That's not the way we wanted it, though. We had something to prove against Oklahoma because they ran for about 300 yards against us when we played them in the Orange Bowl the year before. We stopped the option running in the 1981 Orange Bowl, and they actually beat us with some passing plays at the end. The next day, both teams went to a party, and Barry Switzer said he'd never seen a team that could stop their running game. We came to play that game.

Everyone is going to take claim to where they put Florida State on the map. But if you look at where Florida State was going 0–11 in 1973 and 1–10 in 1974, and then going undefeated and playing in the Orange Bowl five years later, that's quite an achievement. Most of Florida State's notoriety has come from playing on ESPN and television all the time. We didn't have all that, but we put that program where people could see us and we became visible with what we were able to do.

I remember sitting with Coach Bowden when he told me he couldn't offer me a scholarship. He never really dealt with the defense because he was always working with the offense. But every time we went into that locker room, he said, "Defense, if they don't score, we win." I think the most important reason I love the school so much and why I'm here is because of the way Coach Bowden treated his players. He has done more for me in my personal life than he could ever do for me as a player. He has made more boys

171

into men and done more for so many people. It's not his wins and losses that make him one of the best coaches in the country. It's what he does for you as a person.

Monk Bonasorte, a native of Pittsburgh, went from an unrecruited walk-on to a three-year starter for Florida State from 1977 to 1980. Bonasorte had 72 tackles and three interceptions as a sophomore in 1978. He finished fourth in the country and broke the school's single-season record with eight interceptions and was named third-team All-American by the Associated Press. He had four interceptions as a senior in 1980, earning honorable mention All-America status, and left FSU holding the career record with 15 interceptions, a mark that stood for 11 seasons. Bonasorte briefly played pro football and was an assistant coach in the United States Football League. He lives in Tallahassee and is executive director of the FSU Varsity Club.

# REGGIE HERRING

## LINEBACKER

### 1977–1980

IWAS AN ASTRONAUT BOY FROM TITUSVILLE Astronaut High School. Jim Gladden, off of Coach Bobby Bowden's staff, recruited me to Florida State. I was part of Coach Bowden's second recruiting class at Florida State. I had scholarship offers from Alabama, Florida, and South Carolina. Those were my four schools. I was born in South Carolina, lived in the state of Florida, and my dad wanted me to go to Alabama.

I think the biggest thing was that Florida State was in-state, it was close to home, and they weren't really an established program. The University of Florida was the most important school in the state at the time. I visited Florida during the summertime before my senior season of high school, and I just never really felt comfortable there. Coach Gladden and Coach Bowden had a lot to do with me going to Florida State. Coach Bowden is down home, and the idea he was selling at the time, that they were going to be good and were on the rise, sounded good to me. Of course, Coach Gladden had signed a teammate of mine from Titusville Astronaut High, Scott Warren, who was a great player.

Bear Bryant came to recruit me and went through the high school and all that stuff, and South Carolina was my birthplace. But at the end of the day, I just felt most comfortable at Florida State. I really got along well with Coach Gladden. Coach Bowden was very personable and was a father figure. It was just a comfortable fit for me.

Linebacker Reggie Herring was a three-year starter at Florida State, from 1978 to 1980 and led the Seminoles in tackles in each of those seasons. He had a career-high 170 tackles as a senior in 1980.

I went to Florida State in 1977, and guys like Paul Piurowski, Bobby Butler, Monk Bonasorte, Ron Simmons, and Rick Stockstill made up our crew. We all came in as freshmen in 1977, and I will say this: I did graduate before all those rascals. Keith Jones and I were the only players in our recruiting class to graduate in four years. Rick redshirted as a sophomore and stayed for another year, and Paul and I both played side by side and played together for three years.

The teams that made back-to-back trips to the Orange Bowl in 1979 and 1980, had eight of us who were sophomores in 1978. We started for the next three years—it was a buildup and it was a team thing. There was a lot of chemistry. We all started together as sophomores, and for the next three seasons it was basically the same guys.

That was a close-knit bunch, and it was ground-raising level. We beat teams that had more talent than us, but I think we epitomized what it means to be a team. The offense and defense were very close, and I'd like to think we were the group that set Florida State off and got it going in the direction to what it is today. Or at least we were a piece of that foundation that got the ball rolling to what it is today.

We were probably the crew that was too dumb to know we weren't supposed to be good, and too tough to know we weren't supposed to beat teams, as well. We thought it was the toughest thing we'd ever gone through. Going through the off-season conditioning program and the mat drills and all that other stuff was hard. We used to sit in our dorm rooms and have butterflies because we knew how hard we were going to be worked in those mat drills. There would be a trash can in every corner for guys to throw up. They made an investment in us in 1978, and it ended up being a weird season. We didn't go to a bowl game even though we finished 8–3. The 1979 and 1980 seasons were two seasons in which nobody expected us to do much, but we did it anyway. Those were probably the two years that got people's eyebrows raised around the country as to, "Hey, who are these guys?"

The University of Florida had been the dominant team in the state for a long time. Miami was floundering, and Florida State was somewhat floundering. But all of a sudden, here we come on the scene and go 11–0 in 1979 and go to the Orange Bowl. Then go 10–1 in 1980 and go back to the Orange Bowl. We beat Nebraska at Nebraska in 1980, and the next week we beat Dan Marino and Pittsburgh. That is when you knew something special was going on with this crowd. We started beating those top-five teams, whereas five years before that, I don't even know if Florida State was on the map.

The magic was very simple. There were no gimmicks about it. The fact was we had a very hard-nosed defensive coordinator in Jack Stanton, and we had great assistant coaches, such as Gene McDowell, Bill Shaw, and Jim Gladden. Coach Bowden was running the offensive scheme, and George Henshaw was the offensive coordinator. There was a blue-chip, had-a-chip-on-your-shoulder mentality. We had a couple of really good players, such as Bobby

175

Butler and Ron Simmons, but around them were a bunch of just football players. I guess we were all highly recruited but not to the point where you had Notre Dame, Michigan, Southern Cal, and everybody else after us. We were just football players. They took some guys and put together a team and built some chemistry and pride. We just refused to be beaten by anyone. We felt we had something to prove, and it just seemed to come together.

I was a backup safety and special teams guy in 1977. Paul and I both went as safeties, and Paul was immediately moved to linebacker. I followed suit the summer after my freshman season. We both started at linebacker in the first game against Syracuse in 1978. We had Keith Jones and Monk Bonasorte at safeties, and Bobby Butler and Ivory Joe Hunter at cornerback. We had Ron Simmons and Scott Warren on the defensive line. We were pretty salty.

Bobby Butler and Ron Simmons were big-time players, but we had a special chemistry, and we'd been put to the woodshed as far as hard work. We just had a bunch of tough guys who liked to compete. We didn't have a bunch of All-Americans on our roster. As a coach looking back at it 26 years later, I'd say we were a blue-collar team with a chip on our shoulders and we just refused to lose. We just had a confidence about us. Nobody knew about us, except us.

We opened the 1978 season at Syracuse, and it was "Bill Hurley Day" at Syracuse. We broke his ribs, and Scott Warren and I knocked him out on the sideline and put him out for the rest of the season. You never want to see anyone get hurt, but that was a pretty good trophy. It was all clean and it was all fair. That was my first start, and I'd never played linebacker before. It wasn't very hard to adjust—just go to the football and knock people out. That was something I already knew how to do. It was my calling. They just got me out of the secondary and put me in the right place.

We lost to Houston early in the season 27–21, and we just didn't play well. We lost at Pittsburgh 7–3, and it was very disheartening because we'd played well on defense. The only touchdown Pittsburgh got was controversial. It was a question of whether the receiver went out of bounds on his own or was pushed out of bounds because he came back in and caught a long touchdown. We got ambushed at Mississippi State 55–27. Their quarterback, John Bond, was the SEC player of the week after he played us and he threw about four or five bombs on us. We just got shellacked.

We won eight games in 1978 and didn't play in a bowl game. But it set the stage for the next two seasons. You have to understand the bowls and the politics back then. We turned down some lesser bowls because we thought we were going to the Gator Bowl, and the Gator Bowl people kind of led us to believe that we were going there. But at the last second, someone else became available, so the Gator Bowl took them, and we were left with nothing. That was the dirty politics of bowl games back then. Everybody was behind the scenes wheeling and dealing. Compared to what it is today, it was a free-for-all.

We lost one regular season game in two seasons, 10–9 to Miami in 1980. It could have been perfect back-to-back seasons. Coach Bowden never was much for ties, so he was going to play for the win at the end. Their big nose guard knocked down a two-point try, and we didn't get it. The only way they got the touchdown was on a pass interference penalty when we collided with them on a Hail Mary right before halftime. They snuck it over with no time left right before the horn blew. We lost 10–9. It proved to be what was to come of the series. It set the stage for the traditional Miami–Florida State game, and the rest is history.

We were getting ready to play at Nebraska the next week. We were getting on the bus after the Miami game and had just lost. We still knew that we had a special team and were really good. That game hurt us, but it didn't break us. I saw Coach Gene McDowell, my position coach, sitting on the front of the bus. I looked right at him and said, "Coach, don't worry. We'll beat Nebraska next week."

When we went to Nebraska, there wasn't a bit of fear or any lack of confidence. Nobody in that stadium or the country knew what was about to happen, except us. We just rolled up our sleeves and went jaw to jaw with them and got after them. We just flat whipped them on their home field 18–14. Nebraska didn't lose at home back then. Oklahoma was probably the only team that beat them. Nebraska probably didn't even know who Florida State was before that game. It wasn't a fluke. We physically got after them and played their style of football.

It was very dramatic at the end. The quarterback sprinted out from about the 8-yard line to beat us, and Paul Piurowski chased him down and caused a fumble. Garry Futch pounced on it, and we were all right there. The celebration began. When we got back to Tallahassee, the whole town was shut down. That Tennessee Street was blocked off and the party was on. You couldn't even get home after we landed at the airport because of the cars and the people. They shut down Tallahassee. It was a proud moment for all of us. It was a game that told us and everyone else that we belonged.

We had to get ready to play Pittsburgh. We got a little taste of what it was like against Nebraska. Winning at Lincoln, Nebraska, gave us the confidence to beat Pitt. Pitt had 11 draft picks that year. They had Mark May, a future Hall of Famer, at tackle. They had Hugh Green. They had Dan Marino. They were just a powerhouse. They were rolling, coming into our place. But we had a special confidence that we weren't afraid of anyone. We felt like we were going to win any game we went into, and we won 36–22.

We played Florida late in the season. They had Cris Collinsworth, who I played with in high school, and another gazelle at receiver. Wayne Peace was their quarterback, and they were starting to get their thing rolling. I think the biggest thing we hung our hat on was we never lost to Florida. We were 4–0 against the Gators and went to two Orange Bowls.

We finished the 1980 season with a 10–1 record, but we didn't get to play Georgia for the national championship in the Sugar Bowl. They took Notre Dame to play Georgia, even though we were ranked second in the country. You remember all the dramatic times in your life. Coach Bowden had a deeper wisdom about him than we did. All we knew is Georgia was No. 1, and we were No. 2 and wanted to play them. It just seemed like a natural, regional rival. Why wouldn't they? We were all sitting in the club room waiting for the bowl games to call in and issue the invitations. I remember when they announced we were going to play Oklahoma in the Orange Bowl, I can honestly say it was a disappointment to the players. Why wouldn't they pit No. 1 and No. 2?

But Coach Bowden found a way to put a positive spin on it. He said everything was going to be okay because Notre Dame was going to beat Georgia, and we were going to beat Oklahoma and win the national championship. The only problem was the Sugar Bowl was played before the Orange Bowl. Getting on the bus to go to the Orange Bowl, we already knew Georgia had won, and that was disheartening. But we had too many seniors and too much of the right stuff as a group to fold the tents. We beat the snuff out of Oklahoma, except on the scoreboard. They won 18–17 on a two-point play at the end. We dropped some interceptions at the end and gave J.C. Watts just enough room to wiggle in for the score.

We didn't do enough to get it done in the Orange Bowl. But who knows what would have happened if we'd known going into that game that we were playing for the national championship? At the end of the day, maybe if we had just beaten Miami and had been 11–0, they would have had to have put us up against Georgia. But it was a great experience and it was very positive. It was a major feat for a school like Florida State to go to back-to-back Orange Bowls back then. They were like BCS bowl games, and there were only four New Year's Day bowl games. I do think it was those two seasons that got the ball rolling.

To me, believe it or not, people don't know Coach Bowden's competitive drive and his audacity. He was a great father figure for me. He was a great leader. He lived a great, Christian, inspirational life. But he was so demanding of his players and demanding of his coaches. He was tough but fair. He had a special aura about him and instilled confidence in us. When he spoke, you listened and you didn't want to let him down. You just didn't want to disappoint him. I don't care whether it's academics or athletics, Coach Bowden and his coaches have given Florida State a national identity.

We were just a great chemistry football team. I can't stress that enough. It was about coaches and players coming together for a common bond, working hard and doing it the old-fashioned way. We didn't have the best players in the country, but we had players who were good enough. The coaches molded them together and built a team that competed at the highest level. They took us to the limit and got every bit of talent and spirit and fight you could get out of a player.

To me, that's the epitome of the college football experience. We had worked so hard and sacrificed so much that we weren't going to give in and weren't going to give up. We believed we had worked harder and were tougher than any other team in the country and had earned that right to be one of the best. When nobody else gave us that right, we just went and took it. It was a special team.

> Reggie Herring, a native of Titusville, Florida, was a three-year starting linebacker for Florida State from 1978 to 1980. He led the Seminoles in tackles in each of those three seasons, including a career-high 170 stops and six sacks in 1980. Herring helped lead the Seminoles to an 11–1 record in 1979 and 10–2 record in 1980, and they finished each of those seasons playing Oklahoma in the Orange Bowl. In 2007 Herring entered his 25th season coaching college football, the last two as the defensive coordinator at the University of Arkansas. He also has coached at Oklahoma State, Auburn, Texas Christian, Clemson, and North Carolina State, as well as two seasons as linebackers coach for the NFL's Houston Texans.

# KEITH JONES
## DEFENSIVE BACK
### 1977–1980

I DID NOT GROW UP A FLORIDA STATE FAN. I did not grow up a college foot-ball fan of anyone. I focused mostly on my education in high school, which sounds a little ironic coming from as small a rural high school in Wildwood, Florida, as I did.

I was first contacted and recruited by the Naval Academy. The academies, at least at that time, could contact you as a junior because you had to go through the appointment process. That was my first introduction to any type of contact at the college level. I ended up going through that process, having the two-day physical, a meeting with the counselor and the psychologist; having to write the letters to the representatives and congressmen.

It wasn't until the spring of 1977—my junior year going into my senior year—that I was first contacted by [FSU assistant coach] Jim Gladden. After that, Florida, Georgia Tech, Alabama, and a few other schools became inter-ested, and the recruiting "thing" started in the fall. I'm sure it's much differ-ent today than it was back then because contacts were limited. You could only make one phone call a week; text-messaging had not yet been invented.

I knew that Florida was heavily after Cris Collinsworth. Cris was a quar-terback at that time, which is what I played. I knew Alabama wanted me to play quarterback. They had signed a little kid the year before named Stead-man Sheely who hadn't quite made his name known yet. I figured by the time I was through with my senior campaign and getting the you-know-what kicked out of me, that I wanted to move to the defensive side, and Florida State was really the only school that recruited me as a defensive back. That's kind of what solidified the deal.

The other point that closed the door was when I came up here for my visit, Coach Bowden and Coach Gladden arranged for Dean Ray Solomon from the College of Business to come meet with my father and me. Dean Solomon had just been promoted to that position. Prior to that he was chair of the Risk and Insurance Department. Risk and insurance was what I wanted to major in, so that deal was closed pretty easily and pretty quickly by having the ability to meet the dean who came from the field and discipline that I wanted to major in.

What was interesting, and you hear it said even today, 30 years after the fact, is it was like a family. Jim went out of his way to develop a relationship with my mom and dad, and Daddy and Coach Gladden stayed in contact until probably just a couple years before my father's death last year. I went to Coach Gladden's house. I saw Julie, who is now a doctor, grow up. That family atmosphere that you hear so much about was present even then. Jim wasn't my segment coach. I didn't meet my segment coach until I came up for my one-day orientation the summer before I reported to camp.

My defensive coordinator/segment coach was Jack Stanton, and I figured really early that he and I were not going to be bosom buddies. Having said that, I don't mean it negatively. He was a coach and I was a player, and that was the only relationship we were going to have until I graduated. After I graduated, he became a friend. He was the best I've ever seen at being professional in his dealings with the players.

Now, there were times we hated him. Oh, my goodness. But that was a different era. We went out to practice every day scared to death. We weren't worried about getting hit by a coach, but we might end up doing 47 million gassers. We may be demoted to fourth team. It evidently is much different today than it was then because we were scared of him. That never changed, even after I was a three-year starter with my position solidified, I was scared to death that I was going to get demoted every practice.

We were actually the first full recruiting class in terms of Bobby [Bowden] being involved because he came late. You've got to remember in those days you could sign a conference letter of intent the Saturday after your last high school football game, then the national letter the first of February. Florida State honored the Southeastern Conference letters, so once I signed with Florida State, everybody else backed off, and I signed in November. You consummated it, if you will, with your national letter in February.

So when Coach Bowden got here that first year, he came in late December/ early January of 1976. Much of the signing class had already been done. Right, wrong, or indifferent, we call ourselves the first "full" recruiting class.

Things were different—Coach Bowden's office was about 8′ by 12′, and three of the walls were concrete block with no paint. We had one helmet, practice and game, so Friday night before the game, the managers would spray paint it and put the decal on it. My practice pants my freshman year would not fit me. I had to tape them. We just didn't have any more. We had one pair of cleats. When we played on Astroturf, we had to borrow cleats from some other school, depending on who wasn't playing on Astroturf.

We did not get what I call the uniform we're used to seeing until my senior year. We had two helmets—a practice helmet and a game helmet— and we had the gold pants and the garnet jersey folks would be familiar with now. We didn't think anything of it; we didn't know any better.

My freshman year, I never dressed for a game. It was an interesting time. In 1977 you had some holdover senior kids—Larry Key, Louie Richardson, Aaron Carter, Jimmy Heggins. These were kids who had won three or four ballgames coming into Coach Bowden's first year in 1976 and went 5–6, and three of those six losses were by less than a touchdown.

182

So now they come into the 1977 season, they're seniors, they had a small taste of success, and we just took off. The wide open, gambler style was what Bobby had to put in and use for two reasons: you had a group of seniors who didn't know how to win, and you've got all these young kids.

In 1976 they went out to Oklahoma and got completely blown off the field. The next game they started eight freshmen and seven sophomores, along with that core group of seniors [juniors then]. To translate that into 1977, you've got a bunch of sophomores starting, a few juniors, and the core seniors led by Larry Key.

I did not dress a single game my freshman year until the bowl game, and there were four freshmen who were allowed to go—I was fortunate to be one of the four. I remember putting on my uniform for the Tangerine Bowl down in Orlando and Coach [Bob] Harbison came up to us four freshmen and said, "You boys have to stay in the locker room during warm-ups because you don't know what to do. You don't know where to go, you don't know where to line up." So I put my uniform on and I didn't ever go out for the

Keith Jones was a star safety for the Seminoles on teams that had a 4–0 record against rival Florida. Jones was a two-time Academic All-American and had been recruited to attend the U.S. Naval Academy. Jones has worked the last several years as a television color-commentator for FSU football games and does radio commentary for Seminoles basketball games.

ballgame until the kick. Of course, I didn't get into the game, but that was the first time I had ever put on the uniform.

We opened the 1978 season at Syracuse. I was the number-two free safety, and one of our cornerbacks turned an ankle. We moved the number-one safety, who ended up getting hurt a couple games later, so I ended up starting that game. The first time I ever ended up dressing for a ballgame [to play] was when we were starting at Syracuse. Coach Stanton came up to me—we were about to go out for the kick—and said, "You're starting." I was scared to death. They had a quarterback—I can't recall his name [Bill Hurley]—but he was being touted for the Heisman, and Reggie Herring and Scott Warren nailed him on the sideline. It was a legal hit, and he was out for the rest of the year. We ended up winning that ballgame.

We got back home, looked at the tape, and Stanton switched me and Monk Bonasorte; moved me to strong safety and Monk to free safety, and that's where we stayed for the rest of our careers. Evidently, I didn't do well at the free-safety spot, and of course Monk went on to become an All-American. That was probably only the third time I had been on an airplane. For my recruiting trips—I drove to Gainesville, drove to Tallahassee, drove to Tuscaloosa—I had very little experience of staying in a hotel. Everything was brand new.

We played Auburn, we played Pittsburgh, later on we played at Nebraska. Miami became very good later on the in the 1970s and through their time.

Florida was the school we had not won against simply because the way things worked out, and we ended up sweeping them. We beat them all four years. Mine was the first class that never lost to the Gators. That was huge at the time. Of course, it would be huge now, too.

But we didn't have a clue what we were doing in terms of the big picture. We went out every day and worked, we played every game, and we literally didn't have enough worldly experience to understand what we were a part of until we got through with it because it had never been done at Florida State before.

My personal most memorable game was the 1980 Florida game. It was my senior year, we played in Doak Campbell Stadium, and it was on national TV. I had two interceptions in the second half. We won the ballgame. We finished that year number one in the country against the score [scoring defense] and number two in total defense, and I led the team with interceptions that year.

You always remember your last home game because it's Senior Day, your parents are there, and you're given special attention. To be able to have won the game and then to have had a couple of interceptions—selfishly and personally—that had to be the game that stands out for me.

As a program, as part of the program, of course the 1980 Nebraska game is one everybody probably points to [as FSU's arrival on the national stage]. I had an interception in the second half of that one. But the Florida game for a multitude of reasons stands out—it was the only game my mom went to in person. She wouldn't come to the games, but because they invited her to be a part of Senior Day, she came. Of course, my daddy was at every game, every time. My momma would listen to the game with [radio announcer Gene] Deckerhoff on the radio, or watch it on TV when we were fortunate enough.

My mom got banned from high school games. My daddy wouldn't let her go. My sophomore or junior year I threw an interception, fumbled, or something, and somebody said something about me. She hit him over the head with her pocketbook, so Daddy wouldn't bring her anymore.

The greatest impression of Coach Bowden was his life; how he lived his life. You didn't hear him curse. Every Sunday during the middle of two-a-days, we went to a church. We went to a Catholic church one time, First Baptist one time; we went to a predominantly black church one time. He was always supportive of the Fellowship of Christian Athletes, which I was involved in. He was married, had six children; everything from a totally outward appearance was admirable. And mind you, I had one conversation with him one time in his office, and anybody who says they spent a lot of time in Coach Bowden's office either had a lot of problems or were in trouble, because your head coach just doesn't interact with you that much.

I had my one meeting and went in and told him I was going to quit. The only two questions he asked me were, "Have you prayed about it?" and, "Where do you go to church?" He didn't talk to me about playing time or how I got along or didn't get along with Stanton. He asked me about me.

So the number-one thing I remember most was him, his lifestyle and persona. What I've come to appreciate after the fact is that he is a genuinely good person. That is not an act. That is not just something that is in front of the players. There are several things you know about Coach Bowden when you play for him. He'll never lie to you. He's not going to tell you you're going to start as a freshman unless you're going to start as a freshman. He'll tell you you've got to pay your dues. And you'll get three strikes. The first one, he might even overlook it. The second one, you will be disciplined. The third one, you will be gone.

People wonder, for example, with the Laveranues Coles versus Peter Warrick situation—they both did the same thing. Why was Laveranues let go and Peter wasn't? Was it because [Warrick] was a Heisman Trophy candidate? No. It was because Laveranues already had his two strikes. Pete didn't have his. Ask Randy Moss. He's the only one I know who came in here and Coach Bowden said you've already got two strikes. You don't get anymore, and the first time he messed up, he was gone.

People wonder about Coach Bowden playing favorites and not being disciplined and not controlling his players. That's just an absolute myth because you never hear about a Florida State player getting in trouble a second time, and there are a lot of players walking around with one and two strikes, and you never know what they did the first time.

The last thing about Bobby, he is a funny and humorous individual. He's serious when it comes to football—and don't mess with him on game day—but after the fact, he's one of the funniest guys I've ever been around in my life. He could be a stand-up comedian if he chose to, and sometimes when he does his speaking engagements, he probably is.

I came from a small, rural community. I was the first in my family to get a four-year degree. My dad had a two-year degree and my mom had a registered nursing degree. Getting a degree and going back to that environment, in my thought process, I wasn't going to have the same opportunities.

I didn't want to go to Atlanta, New York, or L.A. because I was from a small town. I wanted to stay somewhere or be somewhere where there was an element of that rural philosophy or pace. Candidly, Tallahassee just fit. It had enough of the small town to help with my insecurities about the big city, but it had enough of the opportunity that I could ply my wares, so to speak, and not be restricted by population or demographics. I just fell in love with the city. I got married my junior year in college, which was highly unusual at that time, to a girl who was from Tallahassee. It just fit.

A lot of people talk about, "Well, maybe I should have done this, or should have gone away." I'm not one of those. I'm right where I was intended to be. I wouldn't change anything about that process.

When I graduated in June of 1981, I ran away from the program, as most non-NFL players do, because you've been busting your you-know-what for four years, you're not making the money—at that time, hundreds of thousands, today, millions of dollars—that the elite athletes are. I spent two or three years where I'd come to a ballgame but I wasn't interested in staying plugged in. After about a two- or three-year period, I was 25 years old and I wanted to be doing something [in the program]. I never really wanted to coach; that wasn't something that intrigued me. So what could I do to get plugged back into the program? I had no experience, but fortunately [then FSU athletics director] Hootie Ingram sat down and listened to me.

There was a change on the Seminole Football Network broadcast crew. Bob Shackleford passed away, and so I wanted my name put in that mix. Now, appropriately and understandably, Vic Prinzi was chosen and had a marvelous career [providing color] with Deckerhoff on the football side. But because I had expressed that interest early, and then a couple of years later when the College Football Association got off the ground—Hootie was very involved in the CFA—I was fortunate enough that Hootie favored me. In 1988 when Sunshine Network—now Sun Sports—signed on and started paying money, I evolved into that position. In 2007 it will be year 20.

It's a little bit of work now, as opposed to being pure fun, but when the Marching Chiefs are out there, when Osceola rides Renegade and that spear hits, it's probably more emotional now than when I was playing. Because when you're playing, you're so focused. Now I'm focused from the standpoint that I don't want to embarrass myself on the air, but I get to be a fan. Game day is an absolute blast for me.

Keith Jones, a native of Wildwood, Florida, was a three-year starting safety for Florida State from 1977 to 1980. He played on Seminole teams that compiled a 39–8 record, including a 4–0 record against rival Florida. A two-time Academic All-American, Jones led FSU with five interceptions as a senior in 1980. Jones won an Emmy for his football color commentary work with Sun Sports' FSU rebroadcasts, and also serves as the basketball radio color partner of Gene Deckerhoff. He lives in Tallahassee, Florida.

# *The*
# EIGHTIES

# RICK STOCKSTILL

## QUARTERBACK

### 1977–1981

I REALLY GREW UP IN GEORGETOWN, KENTUCKY, and then we moved to Fernandina Beach, Florida, going into the summer of my junior year of high school. Florida State was basically the only school recruiting me. Clemson recruited me a little bit, but then they went through a coaching change. Red Parker got fired and Charley Pell came in, and I kind of got lost in the shuffle. I got a bunch of letters and all of that stuff, but when it came down to it, my only option was really Florida State.

I was getting phone calls and people were coming to see me, but Florida State was really where I wanted to go. I went to football camp there during the summer before my senior season of high school. Being around Coach Bowden and all those guys, it was kind of my dream to go to Florida State.

I got to Tallahassee in 1977, and back then, freshmen could not redshirt. You played a junior varsity schedule, and I got in one or two plays with the varsity team in the Tangerine Bowl at the end of the 1977 season. Then I redshirted the following season in 1978. Jimmy Jordan and Wally Woodham were the quarterbacks the first three seasons I was there. In 1979 I played on a lot of special teams and mopped up a lot of games.

The 1977 freshman class was Coach Bowden's first full class. We had Bobby Butler, Ron Simmons, Reggie Herring, Ken Lanier, Rohn Stark, Paul Piurowski, and Monk Bonasorte. We were scout team and we played on Mondays. We played LSU, and they'd been beaten by Kentucky the Saturday before. All their players came out to the JV game with decals all over their helmets, so I think their coach got mad and made all the varsity players play in the JV game. We played Miami, Florida, and Auburn. I think we were so young and maybe naïve to really look it and say, "Hey, we've got a chance to be pretty good."

The 1979 season was probably a big move for Florida State because we went undefeated. I'm not saying this just because I was the quarterback the following year, but I think 1980 was the season that really gave us the most credibility. We beat Nebraska at Nebraska, when the Cornhuskers were ranked No. 3 in the country. We beat Pittsburgh at home, when the Panthers were ranked No. 4 in the country. We got beat by Oklahoma by one point in the last minute of the game in the Orange Bowl. I think that gave us some credibility on a national scene. Although we went undefeated in 1979, we were still playing Louisville, Southern Miss, Cincinnati and those type of schools. I just think 1980 was really the year that got it started. In 1981 we beat Notre Dame at Notre Dame and Ohio State at Ohio State.

I made my first start against LSU in Baton Rouge in 1980. It was pouring down rain and, weather-wise, it wasn't what you want as a quarterback. I wasn't nervous. I'd been at Florida State for three years and was going into my fourth season. I'd been in the stadiums before, although I hadn't played a whole bunch. I was just confident, and Coach Bowden and the other coaches made us feel confident.

191

I've always said this about Coach Bowden: he had the ability to make an average player play like a good player, and the ability to make a good player play like a great player. From the way he prepared us and motivated us, I was confident and prepared. We didn't throw the football a whole bunch because of the weather, but we did what we had to do to win the game. Our defense threw a shutout and we won 16–0. We didn't turn the ball over, which is hard to do in weather like that. We didn't put our defense in bad field position, and our defense made a lot of plays and kept them out of the end zone. To go to Baton Rouge as a season opener and win—no matter who you are—I thought that was a heck of a win for us.

We went back home and played Louisville. I remember Coach Bowden saying after the game that he wanted to see if we could throw the ball. We didn't throw much the first game. We threw it around a little bit, and I had four touchdown passes and beat those guys pretty good 52–0. It was a good way to come back home. Those games were a lot of fun, not only for fans, but for the players, quarterbacks, and receivers, getting to throw the football around like that.

We blew out East Carolina 63–7 and then went to Miami to play. We'd gotten down to our third- or fourth-team center. John Madden got hurt, and we were down to our third-team guy, and we had a bunch of fumbled snaps. I don't know if we ever lost one, but I know we had a bunch of fumbled snaps. Right before the half, they threw about a 50-yard pass into the end zone, and the officials called pass interference. They put the ball on the 1-yard line, and they scored to go up 7–0 at the half. It was back and forth in the third and fourth quarter, and not a lot was going on.

We got the ball back with about two minutes left for our last drive. We drove down the field, and I hit Sam Childers for an 11-yard touchdown. We called timeout and, back then, ties were never a consideration for Coach Bowden, probably more so because of his personality and the fact we weren't in a conference. Kicking the extra point and tying was never an option. We went for a two-point conversion, and we were going to run a little drag route to Phil Williams. As he flashed across the middle, I had a throwing lane there. But Jim Burt, their nose guard, ended up knocking the pass down. We went for the onside kick but didn't get it.

I just remember being in the locker room and feeling all the pain and the hurt. That was my first loss as a starting quarterback. To this day, I don't handle losing very well. It hurts me to lose, and I hurt after that game like all of us did. It was two really good defenses playing, and we had a chance to win the game at the end but didn't get it done. Having been in this business as a coach, that's all you can ask of your players. We had a chance to win the game but didn't do it, despite our effort and competitiveness and passion for the game. I think our coaches were disappointed we lost but probably proud of the way we fought and competed in the game.

We had to come back and get ready to play at Nebraska. Coach Bowden was one of the best motivators I've ever been around. He didn't allow us to dwell on the Miami game. I was young, and it was my fifth game, so I was anxious to play another one. We had a 3–1 record, and our goals were still intact. We still had a chance to get to a bowl game, and we were not intimidated by going out to Nebraska. I guess we didn't know any better. I guess it goes back to Coach Bowden. We thought we were supposed to win the game and beat Nebraska. It wasn't like we were going out there in awe of them, in any sense of the imagination.

I think we just went to Nebraska with a lot of confidence. We were down 14–0, and then Bill Capece kicked a field goal right before halftime. When we got the field goal right before the half, it gave us a little life. We went in the locker room and we had hope. You could see in everybody's eyes, and see the way everyone was talking, that we could beat these guys. We came out in the second half and got another field goal. Then it was a one touchdown game. We got back in the thing. We had confidence that they weren't invincible.

Sam Platt scored late in the third quarter, then Capece kicked two more field goals to put us ahead 18–14. Nebraska was driving late in the game, and Jeff Quinn, their quarterback, was driving them for the win. But Paul Piurowski chased him down and knocked the ball loose. You were just hoping somebody got there and recovered it, and Garry Futch recovered it.

When Gary came up with it, it was like the opening of the old *Wide World of Sports*: the thrill of victory and the agony of defeat. We were feeling the thrill of victory in winning at Nebraska. The week before had been the agony of defeat. We were so close to winning at Miami and just came up short. It was so much fun to be part of something that was so special, winning at Nebraska. Coach Bowden says all the time that win at Nebraska was probably the best victory in his coaching career. I believe that's the win that put Florida State on the map and put Coach Bowden's stamp on the program. Prior to that, we'd beaten some good teams, but Nebraska was a powerhouse. That's one of the elite programs in the country of all-time.

193

After beating Nebraska, we had to come back and play Pittsburgh, which moved up to No. 4 in the country after Nebraska lost. You go through Pitt's roster, both on offense and defense, and everybody who started on both sides of the football eventually made an NFL roster. They had great defensive backs, Hugh Green and Rickey Jackson on the edge, and Sal Sunseri at linebacker. On offense, they had Mark May on the line and Dan Marino at quarterback. They had a team full of NFL players.

They could have already been in the NFL, but they weren't going to beat us that night. We came into Doak Campbell Stadium with a ton of confidence and a ton of belief. We had a great game plan, especially offensively. George Henshaw put a great plan together. We threw the ball well. We ran the ball well. We played great defense, and got turnovers. We kicked the ball well. That was probably as complete of a game that any team could play. We threw three touchdowns passes and had a couple of rushing touchdowns. We kicked field goals. We punted well. We made plays all over the field. We won 36–22, and it was probably as good of a game that an entire team could play, when your offense, defense, and special teams come together.

We finished the 1980 season by beating Boston College 41–7, Memphis State 24–3, Tulsa 45–2, and Virginia Tech 31–7. When you look at that stretch, we probably weren't a whole lot better than Virginia Tech and Boston College. But we were so confident. It wasn't being cocky and it wasn't an arrogant confidence. We were just so confident in everything we were doing. We were still practicing hard, and everything we were doing was still the same. Our heads were still able to fit inside our helmets, and we weren't cocky. We were still working and doing everything we had to do. It was an electrifying time for Florida State football in Tallahassee.

We took a six-game winning streak into the Florida game, the last game of the regular season. We'd beaten them three years in a row, but we were behind 13–3 at halftime. They moved that game for TV, so there was, like, a four-week layoff between our last game and the Florida game. I remember everybody making a big deal about it. Everybody was worried about that having an effect on our timing and rhythm. We took the first drive down the field and kicked a field goal, and looked like a dadgum well-oiled machine. But after that, we kind of sputtered.

We went into the locker room down 13–3, but I remember very, very vividly that there was no panic. There was no panic from Coach Bowden. There was no panic from the players. We'd been there before. We were down 14–3 at Nebraska and won the game. We'd worked too hard to lose. I think the biggest thing was that you could see a calm, and we weren't worried. We were a very mature team by that point.

So we went out in the second half and cranked it up on both sides of the ball. I hit Hardis Johnson for two touchdowns in the second half, one on a post and one on a square in. We played well the second half and won 17–13.

We went into the bowl games after the 1980 season ranked No. 2, and Georgia was No. 1. We were disappointed we didn't get a chance to play Georgia in the Sugar Bowl. We played Oklahoma in the Orange Bowl. But we thought we had a chance to win the national championship if Georgia lost and we won. I don't know if there had ever been a co-champion before then, but I've always thought if we had beaten Oklahoma, we'd at least be co–national champs with Georgia because we'd have beaten Nebraska,

After graduation, Florida State quarterback Rick Stockstill went into coaching. He was a longtime assistant at Central Florida, Clemson, East Carolina, and South Carolina. Stockstill was named coach at Middle Tennessee State after the 2005 season and led the Red Raiders to a 7–6 record and a bowl game in his first season.

Pittsburgh, LSU, Florida, and then Oklahoma. You beat all those guys, and you lose one game by one point early in the year, I don't know how you can't be national champs.

But when Georgia beat Notre Dame, we didn't go out and say, "We don't have anything to play for now." Oklahoma's defense was really, really good. They were really physical and really big. We had a hard time with their speed. Defensively, we did a pretty good job of shutting them down for 58 minutes. We had chances on the last drive. Garry Futch had a chance to intercept a pass that got knocked out of J.C. Watts's hands, but he tried to run before he caught it. Garry made that big play at Nebraska, so maybe the football gods were looking down, telling him, "Hey, we gave you that good fortune at Nebraska. We're not going to give you two games this year." It was a great game.

To lose two games that year, both by one point in the same stadium, you're disappointed and you're hurt as an 18-year-old or 19-year-old. But when you're 45, you look back at it and think, *Wow, what an amazing run. What an amazing run we had in 1980.*

Going into the 1981 season, we were a very young team. We lost most of the offensive line and most of the guys on defense. We were breaking in a new team. Nebraska beat us 34–14. We went to Ohio State and won 36–27. The next week we went to Notre Dame and beat them 19–13. Then we had to go to Pittsburgh, and they beat us 42–14. We had to go back to LSU. We won 38–14.

We won three out of the five games, but I really believe at that point we ran out of gas. If you look at it today, I don't care if you say Southern California, Texas, or whoever—if you say you're going to play Nebraska, Ohio State, Notre Dame, Pittsburgh, and LSU, five weeks in a row and all on the road—nobody plays that kind of schedule. But that's what we had to do back then at Florida State. I believe we ran out of gas those last three games of the year. We beat Western Carolina 56–31 but then we lost to Miami 27–19, Southern Miss 58–14, and Florida 35–3. We finished the season with a 6–5 record.

When you look back at it now, I don't believe there was anybody we had at quarterback, running back, or receiver who could play now. Maybe Dennis McKinnon could because he played in the NFL for a while. We weren't the most talented guys out there. Phil Williams, one of our receivers, couldn't break a 4.9 in the 40-yard dash. But he was a great route runner and caught the ball. Hardis Johnson made nice catches, and Kurt Unglaub was a great route runner. He wasn't very big and wasn't very fast, but he had good hands.

We were a blue-collar team that cared about each other, both on and off the field. We worked hard and competed and just believed in ourselves and our coaches. Everything that a team is supposed to stand for, I think we did. We're really close to this day. Twenty-five years later, we still stay in contact. I don't think we were the most talented team out there, but I do believe nobody was closer or cared for each other more than we did.

After my senior season, I played in two all-star games, the East-West Shrine Bowl and the Japan Bowl. I only needed to do my internship to graduate, but because I'd played in those all-star games, they said I'd missed too much school and couldn't do my internship that spring. I didn't think it was too fair, but I was happy I got to stay in college a little longer. I worked that summer and came back in the fall and graduated in December 1982.

I thought I wanted to coach but wasn't really sure. I was interviewing with Jostens, the ring company, and had about four or five interviews with them and thought that's what I was going to do. But Monk Bonasorte, who was one of Florida State's graduate assistants at the time, called me and said Larry Little had been looking for me. Little was the head coach at Bethune-Cookman and wanted to offer me a job. I went to Daytona Beach, Florida, and interviewed for the quarterbacks coach job. That's how I got into the coaching profession.

197

I was an assistant coach at Bethune-Cookman, Central Florida, Clemson, East Carolina, and South Carolina for several years. I've been very fortunate in this profession, with where I've coached and who I've coached with. I really thought the last three of four years that I was ready to be a head coach. A lot of young coaches, as soon as they get into it, they say, "Hey, I'm ready to be a head coach." But I really felt confident the last three for four years that I was ready. When I got the opportunity at Middle Tennessee, I didn't feel overwhelmed. I haven't felt that I'm not prepared for this.

I go back so much to the Florida State beginnings because this place is so, so similar to Florida State when I first got there. We've got a 30,000-seat stadium. Florida State had a 35,000-seat stadium. FSU had to go on the road to play Nebraska, Pittsburgh, Notre Dame, and all those big boys. Here, we're playing Oklahoma, Louisville, South Carolina, Maryland, LSU, and Virginia. We're playing all these guys on the road, like we did at FSU. We've only been a Division I program for seven years. When I first got to Florida State, they were thinking about dropping football because they went through that stretch where they weren't winning any games.

I'm really trying to build this program, and I use so many things I learned from Coach Bowden, like how he dealt with the players. I never saw the staff meetings and all of that, but I saw how he dealt with the players and how he built the program to what it is today. I really use a lot of my Florida State upbringing here at Middle Tennessee.

Rick Stockstill, a native of Fernandina Beach, Florida, was a starting quarter-back for Florida State for two seasons, in 1980 and 1981. He led the Seminoles to a 10–2 record as a junior in 1980. Florida State won at Nebraska 18–14 that season, a victory that is still considered the most important in school history, and also beat No. 4 Pittsburgh 36–22 in Tallahassee. The Seminoles finished 6–5 in 1981 and beat Ohio State, Notre Dame, and Louisiana State on the road. After graduation from FSU in 1982, Stockstill became an assistant coach at Bethune-Cookman College in Daytona Beach, Florida. He spent the next two decades as an assistant at Central Florida, Clemson, East Carolina, and South Carolina. Stockstill was named head coach at Middle Tennessee State. In his first season, he guided the Blue Raiders to a 7–6 record and their first bowl appearance in the Motor City Bowl. He was named the 2006 Sun Belt Conference Coach of the Year.

# PHIL WILLIAMS

## WIDE RECEIVER

### 1978–1981

MY FATHER WAS A METHODIST PREACHER, so we moved around quite a bit, mainly in Middle Georgia and South Georgia. I went to Warner Robins High School in Georgia and played for coach Robert Davis. We won the high school national championship during my senior season at Warner Robins. We had James Brooks [later a star running back at Auburn and in the NFL], Ron Simmons [an All-American nose guard at Florida State], and Jimmy Womack [later a star fullback at Georgia].

I had some small college scholarship offers, but my only big offers were from Navy and Air Force. Gene McDowell, who was recruiting me for Florida State, came into the school and said, "Hey, we had a guy that wasn't very big and wasn't very fast, but he turned out to be a heck of a receiver. His name was Fred Biletnikoff." He offered me to walk-on, and the only other major college that had offered me a chance to walk-on was Auburn. But Florida State was just a lot more positive about it.

I got to Florida State in 1977 and was there for one week. In my whole career, I had caught everything. If there was one thing I could do, it was get up and catch the ball. But during that first week of two-a-days, I was so nervous that I was dropping about every third ball that came my way. A lot of people who walk on in college just want to say they were a part of the team. I was there to either play or move on. Because I was doing so poorly and was so homesick, I quit the team after a week.

Phil Williams was an invited walk-on to Florida State's football team, but left school only a few weeks after enrolling in 1977 because he was home sick. After convincing Coach Bobby Bowden to give him a second chance, Williams returned to the team the following season and quickly became one of the team's top wide receivers. Williams was an Academic All-American and works as a sports agent in Atlanta. His clients include several former FSU football players.

I went home and went to Georgia Southern, which didn't have a football team back then. I knew I had made a mistake. So I wrote Coach Bobby Bowden at Florida State and mailed him a letter from rural Georgia. Three days later, I got a return letter back from him, inviting me back on the team for winter workouts. It said something like, "You know, if you'd stayed, you would have a good chance to be playing already. But I understand how those things work out. I'd love to have you back in January, getting ready for next season." It stunned me. I thought he'd welcome me back, but I didn't think he'd be that positive about it.

I went back to winter workouts and went through spring training. When I went back to the team, there were 18 receivers on the team, and I was number 18 because I'd quit the year before. But halfway through the first practice, I was second-team and was never less than second-team after that. When spring training was over, I went to see Coach Bowden. He didn't tell me I had a scholarship, but he said he was going to save me one in the fall. He said, "How's that?" I said, "I don't know, Coach, with me having to pay the out-of-state tuition." So he told me to come back in two weeks and he'd have an answer. I went back to his office two weeks later and he had a scholarship for me. It was a big day for me.

I ended up being part of the 1978 freshman class. Rohn Stark, the punter, was part of that class, and we became good friends. I remember during my sophomore or junior season, every receiver was hurt, so I was running first-team, second-team, and third-team. I was just dying. Coach Bowden always used to say, "Get water when you need it." Rohn Stark was just sitting over there punting a little bit, and he was my buddy, right? I said, "Go get me some water." He felt like he was all put out that he had to go get me a little cup of water.

201

In 1978 and 1979 Jimmy Jordan and Wally Woodham were our quarterbacks. We had a great group of wide receivers, with Jackie Flowers, Sam Platt, Kurt Unglaub, and me. We opened the 1978 season at Syracuse, and that was before the Carrier Dome was built. It was my first college game, and the field up there where Jim Brown and Art Monk played was as bad as any field I'd ever played on in high school. There were holes in the field. You had to be careful you didn't sprain your ankle.

I was in the receiver rotation, and at the end of the first half, they actually ran a play to me in the end zone. I was running a curl, and we were always taught to come back to the football. I was coming back, but Jimmy was holding onto it. I kind of pulled up to stay in the end zone, and Jimmy threw it late. Bill Hurley [who also was the Syracuse quarterback] stepped in front of me and picked it off. George Haffner, the offensive coordinator, was so mad at me I didn't play the next two weeks against Oklahoma State and Miami [the Seminoles beat the Cowboys 38–20 and beat the Hurricanes 31–21]. I had to sit a couple of games and earn my way back.

I came back for the Houston game, and we were behind 21–0. We ended up losing 27–21. We beat Cincinnati 26–21 the following week, and then when we went to play Mississippi State in Starkville. They screwed up and put my name down as a starter. They had my name opposite Mardye McDole [an All-American receiver for the Bulldogs], and I remember thinking, *Wow!* [McDole had 175 receiving yards in the Bulldogs' 55–27 victory].

During the Southern Miss game late in the season [a 38–16 victory], Coach Bowden pulled me aside and said, "You're starting this game." I was like, "What's going on here?" I ended up catching two or three passes against Hanford Dixon [an All-American cornerback and later a Pro Bowl cornerback for the Cleveland Browns]. Two weeks later Navy came to town, and they had a converted nose tackle playing cornerback. He jumped on my back after a catch and just drilled my shoulder into the ground. I've been tossing and turning at night ever since because of that, and that's the truth. I had a separated shoulder and didn't get to play in the Florida game at the end of the season [a 38–21 victory].

We finished undefeated during the 1979 regular season. It was a great season. We opened against Southern Miss in Tallahassee, and we blocked a punt late in the fourth quarter, and Gary Henry ran it back for a touchdown. We won the game 17–14. The following week, we played Arizona State in Tampa. Before the game, I remember all they were talking about was how tough of a coach Frank Kush was, and how Arizona State was used to playing in the heat and was in better shape than anybody. It rained before the game, and they were dying in the humidity. We won the game 31–3.

We beat Miami 40–23 in Tallahassee. It was the second year in a row we beat them. We went to Blacksburg and played Virginia Tech. Games weren't televised much back then, but that game was televised. They showed all of our pictures on television, and that was neat. We won 27–0 at Louisville, and our leading receiver only had two catches in the game. That happened to our offense sometimes. We were ranked in the top 10 and played Mississippi State in Tallahassee and won 17–6. I had one catch in that game and pulled my hamstring during the first quarter. I wasn't supposed to play at LSU the next week because I hadn't practiced the whole week and could hardly run. But against LSU, Sam Platt caught a touchdown and was high stepping in the end zone and sprained his ankle. The coaches looked at me and said, "Phil, you've got to play." I couldn't play. I was out there and was like, "Don't throw me the ball!" The cornerback was looking at me and saying, "You're sorry, man." I was so ticked off. At least we won the game 24–19.

We played at Cincinnati the next week, and I had a big play in that game. We were down 21–7 in the fourth quarter. We had fourth down and five, and Coach Bowden knew he could depend on me. The play was "Cadillac X Drag." That meant I was running a drag route across the middle. If I didn't catch it, the game was over. As I started to run the play in from the sideline, Coach Bowden still had his hand on my face mask. He snatched my head back, nearly breaking my neck, and screamed at me with the biggest eyes I'd ever seen. He screamed, "Don't drop it!" Fortunately, I caught the pass for an eight-yard gain, and we won the game 26–21.

We played South Carolina at home the next week, and both teams were ranked. That was a big game for me because they had a coach who lived in Warner Robins. He was after Ron Simmons, James Brooks, and Jimmy Womack, and I wanted him to be after me. I saw him before the game and even went up to him after the game and said, "Remember me?" They had George Rogers, who was a great running back.

The Orange Bowl gave us an invitation to play Oklahoma right before we played Memphis State. We went out and won 66–17. We finished the season by beating Florida 27–16 in Gainesville. That win wrapped up a perfect regular season, but we weren't looking at it like that. We were a "Johnny come lately" that was just scrapping and fighting to win ballgames. We didn't feel like we were big-time. We just took one game at a time. Other than that game being Florida, I don't remember there being any other special feeling about that game. We didn't know how good we were, but we were trying to be as good as we could be.

During practices for the Orange Bowl, Coach Bowden made an announcement one night that I'd been named an academic All-American. Ken Lanier, one of our huge offensive linemen, turned and looked at me and said, "Dang, Phil, I didn't know you were smart." I always took pride in the fact that no one knew I was smart.

Oklahoma spanked us in the Orange Bowl 24–7. They whipped us pretty good. I ran a drag in that game, and Wally Woodham threw it. It was way over my head, and I jumped to catch the ball. I remember thinking, *Why did I jump?* George Cumby knocked me out. I remember waking up, and he was holding me up. I was hanging like a rag doll, went to the sideline, and the stadium was shaking. I was spitting up blood and couldn't think for the rest of the night. That was it for me.

We might have been the best team in the country in 1980. We opened the season at LSU and won 16–0 in Death Valley. We had a smart, scrappy, tough defense. We were still working out the wrinkles on offense [Williams was the leading receiver in the game with 13 yards]. We blew out Louisville the next week 52–0, and [quarterback] Rick Stockstill threw four touchdowns. Then we beat East Carolina 63–7 and really had the offense rolling.

We went down to Miami the following week. We lost 10–9 when we failed to get a two-point conversion at the end. The pass was supposed to go to me, but their nose guard jumped up and it hit him in the face mask. Losing at Miami might have been the best thing that ever happened to us. I've never been around a team like that. All week long, there was a crispness in the air. Not only were we playing Nebraska, but it was something new for Florida State. If we'd beaten Miami, I don't know if it would have been like that.

Nebraska went ahead 14–0, and we kicked a field goal near the end of the half. It kind of gave us confidence that we could win the game and play with Nebraska. Late in the game, I caught a pass from Stockstill to the 6-yard line, and then Sam Platt ran it into the end zone for a touchdown. Later, Stockstill threw me an out-and-up down the right sideline for a 40-yard gain. Then we kicked a field goal to go up 18–14. That field goal was key because now they had to score a touchdown to beat us. Nebraska was driving down the field, and they called interference against us, and the Nebraska fans were yelling at the refs, "Don't give it to us!" That's what it looked like was happening. When Paul Piurowski sacked their quarterback, and Garry Futch recovered a fumble, they could have penalized me for dancing on the field. It was such an unbelievable win for a school that was still trying to make it. Even though we'd been undefeated the year before, I didn't feel like we'd made it yet. Beating Nebraska at Nebraska meant we had arrived. Playing a part of it was beyond words. I remember my dad coming into the locker room, and I don't know if my dad had even ever met my coach, but they were hugging. It was an unbelievable feeling.

We had to come right back and play fifth-ranked Pittsburgh. They had Dan Marino, Hugh Green, Rickey Jackson, and Mark May. They were loaded. It was easy to refocus because we were that kind of team. Nowadays, Florida State might have to worry about that kind of thing, but we were just a bunch of hungry guys, fighting our butts off. Even though they had a roster full of NFL draft picks, we won the game 36–22.

After beating Nebraska and Pittsburgh, we were ranked seventh in the country and played Boston College at home. We won that game 41–7. Then we beat Memphis State 24–3 and Tulsa 45–2. Our defense was just dominant at that point. We beat Virginia Tech 31–7 and then got ready to play Florida. We trailed Florida 13–3 going into the third quarter but came back and won 17–13.

We finished the season 10–1, and we felt terrible. It was one of the injustices in college sports. We should have played Georgia in the Sugar Bowl for the national championship, but the Sugar Bowl chose Notre Dame. It was all about money and Notre Dame's popularity. We were clearly the better team than Notre Dame. There was no question about it. It made it easier for Georgia. They played the Sugar Bowl [the Bulldogs beat the Fighting Irish 17–10] before we played Oklahoma in the Orange Bowl.

Once we knew our chances of winning the national championship were gone, it deflated us a little bit. We still should have beaten Oklahoma, but it deflated us some. Oklahoma was very talented on defense. We missed a long field goal at the end of the game. It was a very deflating loss. J.C. Watts did great at the end of the game, and I guess we weren't meant to win the game because they got a two-point conversion at the end on our best player, Bobby Butler.

During our senior season in 1981, we were pretty young, but I was still pretty pumped about the season. But we played five games—at Nebraska, at Ohio State, at Notre Dame, at Pittsburgh, and at LSU—and they were calling it "Octoberfest" in Tallahassee. Coach Bowden killed us during that stretch because those games were so difficult. I was like a walking zombie for a few weeks. We were dead. We went 3–2 stretch during that stretch, but we were dead.

I went into Coach Bowden's office during my senior season and told him, "Coach, you've called five deep passes to me during my entire career here, and four of them were completions. That's 80 percent!" We started the season against Louisville and won 17–0. I ran my rear off in that game, and they didn't throw a single pass my way. I went into Coach Bowden's office Monday, crying, "You've got to throw me the ball!" Every receiver is selfish, I guarantee it.

We beat Memphis State 10–5. Then we started Octoberfest and lost at Nebraska 34–14. They scored two touchdowns in less than a minute, and

Roger Craig was a beast. Eric Riley, a freshman safety on our team, was a friend of mine, and I'll always remember that Craig hit him, knocked him on his back, stepped on his chest, and kept going for a 94-yard touchdown. Nebraska was hyped about winning that game after we beat them the year before.

Then we played at Ohio State, and my grandfather had died that week. I didn't practice the entire week. My dad was at the game, and I was very close to him. We won that game 36–27, and I remember looking up into the stands for my dad, and I was crying. He had already left the game. It was good to win after having lost to Nebraska.

Notre Dame wasn't as good that year. But it was still a big deal just being at Notre Dame. In some ways, it was similar to going to Nebraska the year before, just the aura of the place and the football tradition. It was exciting for me because they asked me to lead the pregame devotion. Just playing at Notre Dame, we had to win. We won the game 19–13. Notre Dame wasn't that good back then, so that took a little bit away from it because we didn't feel like we were playing a good team. But it was still a tremendous achievement to go up to Notre Dame and win the game.

We had to play at Pittsburgh the next week, and Marino and all those guys were back on the team. They beat us 42–14, and had 500 yards offense. Our defense wasn't as good as it used to be. Simmons and a lot of those guys had graduated. Pitt has an east-west stadium, instead of north-south. I was wide open for what would have been a 92-yard touchdown. Our quarterback threw the pass, and I knew nobody was near me and all the defensive players were running toward me. But I lost the ball in the sun and couldn't see it. Then at the last split-second, I saw something blurry to my left. I dove, and the ball somehow stuck to my fingers, but I fell to the ground. It was the best catch I ever made, but the coaches were like, "What are you doing?"

We won back-to-back games against LSU [38–14] and Western Carolina [56–31] after finishing Octoberfest. Then we started being zombies. We lost to Miami 27–19 after we were ahead in the first half. Then Southern Miss ate us up 58–14 and destroyed us. We ended the season with a 35–3 loss at Florida. We finished the season with a 6–5 record. It was pretty horrible. Through that Octoberfest, it was still exciting. But after that, we just fell apart. I attributed it more to the fact that we practiced so hard and worked so hard and had been on the road for so long. I've never been a part of a team that was so exhausted, mentally and physically.

I can never say anything bad about Coach Bowden. I felt like a nobody, a walk-on freshman receiver. I got crushed on a sideline route one time and popped right back up. Coach Bowden came running down the field and said, "That's what I'm looking for, Phil Williams!" Willie Jones was the star on that team, but Bobby Bowden always treated me with the same respect. He was a fair man, and he respected you. Nobody is perfect, but he is a very fair, ethical man.

Phil Williams was a starting wide receiver for Florida State from 1979 to 1981. He led the Seminoles in receiving yards with 413 in 1981. He was named an Academic All-American in 1980 and was the first Florida State player to receive an NCAA postgraduate scholarship. Williams received an accounting degree from Florida State and now works as a sports agent in Atlanta, representing former Florida State players Brad Johnson, Amp Lee, Pat Carter, and Orpheus Roye, among others.

# ALPHONSO CARREKER
## DEFENSIVE LINEMAN
### 1980–1983

I WAS FROM COLUMBUS, OHIO, and Ken Lanier, an offensive lineman at Florida State, had played at the same high school. I wouldn't say that opened the door for me to go to Florida State, though, because I knew of Kenny but really didn't know Kenny. He was a senior at Marion Franklin High School when I was in the ninth grade, so there was quite an age difference between us. When I came down to Florida State to visit, of course, we spent some time together.

The biggest reason I went to Florida State was that I played tight end in high school and wanted to go to a college that threw the football a lot. Of course, that wasn't the way it played out when I got to Florida State. I was also recruited by Michigan and Indiana, which were recruiting me pretty heavily, and there was some genuine interest from Ohio State.

I don't know how much Ohio State was really after me because I was more of a basketball prototype than a football player. Woody Hayes, the Ohio State coach, visited my high school, along with Archie Griffin and Greg Bell and all those guys. I did visit Arizona, believe it or not, and visited West Virginia. I really liked Morgantown and almost went to school there.

I got recruited pretty heavily in basketball, too, but it was more by historically black universities. It wasn't any Big Ten Conference schools, but I had opportunities to visit a lot of them. But by the time basketball season started, I'd already made up my mind to play football. I played center and power forward in basketball in high school, but being only 6'6", I didn't think much was going to be attainable in college.

I arrived at Florida State in 1980 and was moved to defense on a technicality. My first week or two there in training camp, we lost two or three major defensive linemen. A couple of starters and a backup went down, so they gave me the opportunity to make the traveling squad if I moved to the defensive line. The first couple of days I was out there, I practiced at tight end. We had Sam Childers, who was starting at the time, and Zeke Mowatt was behind him. Those guys were ahead of me the first couple of practices because they knew what they were doing. I didn't think they were better athletes than me, but I never really got a chance to show my skills as a tight end.

I moved over to defense to make the traveling squad. When you're trying to make the transition from high school to college, you kind of go with the flow as far as where the coach is putting you for the betterment of the team. I never got a chance to go back and at least have a chance at catching the ball in a practice setting. I was upset about it. Back then, black athletes were trying to transition themselves into what were predominantly white schools. You didn't question things.

209

I'd played both ways in high school and was the punter, field goal kicker, and kick returner. I don't think I came off the field. I'd played some defensive line, so it wasn't that big of an adjustment. The technique was a big adjustment, though. When I came out of high school, technique wasn't that big of a factor. In college, we learned formations and tendencies. When you were in high school, they might have tried to teach you those things, but as long as you were aggressive and hustled, you were going to be a starter. But in college, we got quizzed on techniques and tendencies and those sorts of things.

Jack Stanton, our defensive line coach at Florida State, was a big, big disciplinarian. I think the first year or so I was there, you might not have appreciated the little things he taught you. But when you went to the pros or got into another professional setting, you appreciated certain things he taught you. We were disciplined and we knew what things were going on. If a meeting was at 7:30 in the morning, you were there at 6:45 in the morning. The coaches under Bobby Bowden—Jack Stanton, Jim Gladden, Bill Shaw, and Gene McDowell—were disciplinarians.

Bill Shaw took a special interest in me. With the way I hustled as a freshman, I got to split time with a senior, Greg Futch, who I thought was a pretty good defensive lineman. Mark Macek was playing at the other end in 1980. I learned a lot from all those seniors. We had Ron Simmons, Paul Piurowski, and Reggie Herring. I didn't think they were the most talented players, but they were well disciplined and well coached. Jack Stanton was the guy who was responsible for producing those great defenses of the past.

In the time and era we played, Jack Stanton was one of the best defensive coaches in the game. We were ranked No. 2 in the country in defense in 1980, and it was all a credit to Jack Stanton. He was the best. He made you so effortlessly flawless. Every little thing you did wrong, he pinpointed it and put it on a pedestal. You got to the point where you made less mistakes because they were so out there for everyone to see. You didn't want to be wrong. You hustled to the ball every time.

When you watch these guys nowadays, I don't think they could have played with us. Not because they don't have the talent, but because I don't think they could have dealt with the discipline during my era. It's almost like the kids today, with the way they're raised and the things that are given to them, they don't have the respect for their elders. We were heads above all that because things weren't tolerated like they are now. That's what made you gain the respect of your coaches, because nothing was tolerated. The game is just played totally different now.

I was a little bit different from the average athlete, even in high school. I didn't start playing basketball and football until the ninth grade of high school, and that's only because I was the biggest kid on the block. It was always just a fun thing for me. When I got to college, the rivalry between Florida and Florida State—it was just another team for me. I really didn't know anything about it. I was out there to have fun.

During my sophomore season, we played Nebraska, Notre Dame, Ohio State, LSU, and Pittsburgh on the road. It was just fun to me, and I didn't look at the significance of the game or that they'd never played a game of that magnitude. None of that really ever crossed my mind. Sometimes, until we played somebody or they told us who we were playing, I didn't know who the next opponent actually was going to be. I was just out there to have fun; that was my thing. I guess I just wasn't the average football Joe. Some guys knew what LSU did 10 years prior to us playing them. But I couldn't tell you who coached who and who played for who. I wasn't a football fan.

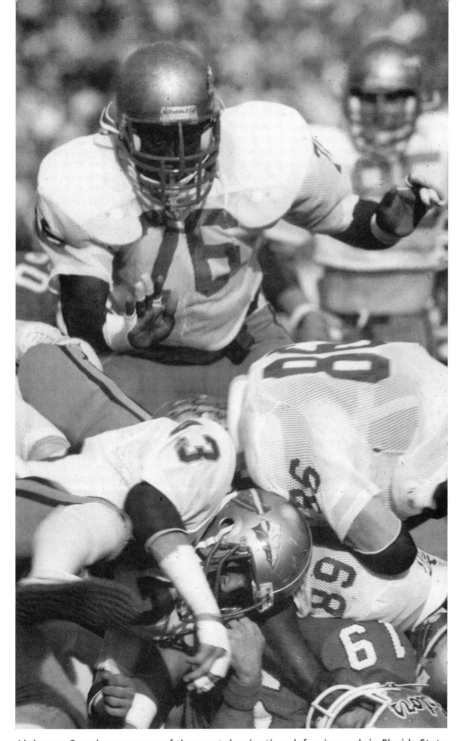

Alphonso Carreker was one of the most dominating defensive ends in Florida State history, finishing his college career with 20 sacks and 19 tackles for loss. He later played in Super Bowl XXIV with the Denver Broncos.

I didn't watch it on TV or all of that. It was just me. I never cared much about it.

It was very exciting to go back to Ohio State during my sophomore season in 1981. Before we went up there, my mom was telling me about the things that were being written in the newspapers in Columbus. It was like, "Who's Carreker? We didn't try to recruit him." The newspapers guys were asking how Ken Lanier got out of Columbus, and now here's another FSU starter coming back to play Ohio State. The first year we played Ohio State, that team was built on size and strength. They outmuscled us and were bigger than us, but by the time it was third or fourth down, they weren't ready for us. We were just way above what they had.

It was a thrill to win [36–27], and it was almost like I got a chance to go back and slap those guys in the face. I wanted to get back at the coaches and organization for saying, "We didn't want this guy anyway." From Christmas to February, before we signed our national letters of intent, I always had an Ohio State guy at my high school. For them to say they didn't want me anyway, that was ridiculous. But that's the way the game was played; they were always looking to play head games.

We beat them two years in a row, and it was rewarding. The second year we went up there was even more impressive. We just dominated them in the second half [and won 34–17], and Ricky Williams just ran all over them. They weren't expecting him to go up there and do what he did.

We played Nebraska, Ohio State, Notre Dame, Pittsburgh, and LSU, all on the road and all in a row. We won all those games expect Nebraska and Pittsburgh, and nobody expected us to win any of those games. We were heavy underdogs in all of those games. We had a quarterback, Rick Stockstill, who had mostly played on the scout team, and had a running back corps which had mostly played on the junior varsity squad the year before.

We had a lot of new players on defense, and our scheme was based on speed. We didn't have a lot of big guys back then. I was 6'6″ and probably 250 pounds. I was still built to play tight end. I wasn't built to play defensive end. But our defense was based on penetrating and creating havoc in the backfield, and we were so smart that we always created a turnover. I think Florida State has kind of gotten away from that.

Ron Simmons left after my freshman season, and I got a lot of double-teams. Chuck Amato came in during my junior season, and they tried to put me in a position where I was over the guard, center or tackle. They tried to put me in a position where I could use my quickness off the ball and get engaged with something in the backfield. The adjustments were to double-team me a lot, especially when I played defensive end on the tight end side. We'd make adjustments where they'd put me out over the tight end, where we would have a third linebacker. It was almost a 3–3 defense. It kind of caught a lot of teams off-guard, especially when we played at Arizona State [during Carreker's senior season in 1983]. They had an all-world tight end, who was creating havoc all over the place. They put me on him and said, "Don't let him off the ball and don't let him block you." They put me in a lot of positions where I created havoc and the offensive line usually didn't expect it.

Back in the day, it was a different ballgame. Nowadays, they've got defensive linemen who weigh 315 pounds. Back then, if you were 260 or 265 pounds, you were overweight. The technique we played was quickness. We beat people off the ball and didn't wait to see what they were going to do. If you got a 2′ surge or a 3′ surge, you had interrupted the offense. They've got these big guys now who are there just to hold people and let the linebackers make plays. We didn't do that; that wasn't Florida State's philosophy on defense.

213

Before my senior season, the school had a marketing campaign where they started calling me "the Secretary of Defense." I don't know where it came from. It wasn't something just Florida State came up with. Nobody called me that until my senior year. Reggie White got the same name at Tennessee and a couple of other guys had the same name. It was almost like a slogan to me, more than a name.

One thing I always appreciated about Coach Bowden more than anything else was when I was there, I always felt like I could go talk to him, whether it was related to football or not. He always made himself available to me, no matter what it was. There were times when I had things on my mind, and I went and talked to him. His leadership skills were very good. He led his assistant coaches, and that leadership came back down to us. It was something I'd never seen before, and I was always impressed by it. I always thought he was very good with the media and crowd. Whatever we said together on the field, you could always tell he had our back. Whenever something happened that you needed support with, he showed support with the way he talked to the media. He not only preached support, but he lived it. You can't get any better than that.

Any guys who played at Florida State from 1977 to the end of my era, they've got to feel like they laid the foundation. You've got to understand where that school came from. When I got there and until I left, a school that was labeled an independent was playing one of the toughest schedules in the country each and every year. We took on all comers as an underdog and won a high percentage of games. Absolutely we laid the foundation because we put the school on the map. After that, the school had more opportunities with the shoe and equipment companies. Back then, Florida State was a rising star. It was starting to be a force to be reckoned with.

I was drafted by the Green Bay Packers in the first round of the 1984 NFL draft. To me, Green Bay was not something I was accustomed to. When I went to Green Bay, it was kind of a culture shock to me. Although my mind was on my business and football, I was extremely bored there. When I first went to Green Bay, it was in a place like where the Oakland Raiders are now. Players went there to just prolong their longevity. They'd either played 12 years or they were a problem child. [Oakland Raiders owner] Al Davis will sign anybody now, and that's how the Green Bay Packers were back then.

Forrest Gregg was in his first year as coach, and he couldn't come in and change that cancer that was there. It was definitely a cancer. It was almost like the Arizona Cardinals now. They got a first-round draft choice every year and couldn't turn that team around. Something had to change that whole situation around. I just wasn't comfortable living in Green Bay. By my third season there, it was terrible. Coaches were fighting with each other, and coaches and players were fighting. The organization was in turmoil, players were getting caught with this and that, and it was one thing after the other. Being a young buck, the only thing I wanted to do was get out of there. Football really wasn't important to me at that point.

I signed with the Denver Broncos in 1989, and it was a completely different beast. Dan Reeves was a completely different kind of coach, and Denver was a city that was really alive. You were going to a team that was full of life and had John Elway, a fantastic quarterback and the comeback kid, who was in his prime. You had a swarming speed defense that I thought I was tailor-made for. It was a like brand new start. It was a fresh start, and we started winning and believed we were part of something great.

We got to a Super Bowl and we got beat by San Francisco. It was ugly [Joe Montana led the 49ers to a 55–10 victory], but playing the game was fun again. It was almost like being at Florida State again.

Alphonso Carreker, a native of Columbus, Ohio, was a three-year starting defensive end for the Seminoles from 1981 to 1983. Carreker had eight quarterback sacks in 1982 and was named honorable mention All-American by the Associated Press. He had 12 tackles for loss in 1983 and again was named honorable mention All-American by the Associated Press. Carreker finished his FSU career with 20 career sacks, ninth-most in school history, and 19 tackles for loss. He was inducted into the FSU Sports Hall of Fame in 1990. Carreker was a first-round draft choice of the Green Bay Packers in the 1984 NFL draft and played five seasons there. He signed with the Denver Broncos in 1989 and helped lead the team to Super Bowl XXIV in 1990. Carreker retired from the NFL after the 1991 season after suffering a series of knee injuries. He is a mortgage broker and lives in Marietta, Georgia.

# TOM McCORMICK

## CENTER

## 1980–1983

IWENT TO BAY HIGH SCHOOL IN PANAMA CITY, Florida. I was being recruited by Florida State and Southern Mississippi to be a walk-on, and I'd heard from a few Ivy League schools. My brother had gone to Johns Hopkins University, and I was considering going to Cornell. But I always wanted to play Division I football, and Bill Shaw, who was the defensive line coach at Florida State at the time, offered me an opportunity to be an invited walk-on. That meant nothing more than your room and board being paid for when you came in for two-a-days.

I jumped at that opportunity, like the genius that I am. Even living in Panama City, I was never much of a Florida State football fan. That wasn't during Florida State's heyday, and my parents were both from up north. I don't even think I knew there was a football team in Tallahassee until I was in junior high. I thought I was a pretty good football player, but I went to a small high school in a fairly small town. I was probably the biggest player on a poor high school football team. I played about every position in high school except the offensive line. I made the all-county team but didn't make any all-state teams or anything else.

I got to Florida State in 1980. I went there as a defensive end and a fullback. But I ended up being a defensive end during my freshman season. I played in some games in a scrub role and got on some special teams. We had a great defense in 1980, and that's why I was a scrub. I primarily played on the scout team.

Going into the spring before my sophomore season in 1981, I moved to the offensive line. I didn't think a whole lot about moving to the offensive line. I'd played a couple of different positions on offense but had never played on the line.

At the time, I had a girlfriend going to Auburn and considered transferring there. I even went up there and made a visit and talked casually to Coach Pat Dye. He offered me the same scenario, going up there as a walk-on and getting a chance to earn a scholarship. But my dad would have nothing to do with it. He was one of the people that thought if you had made a commitment, by God, you're going to see that commitment through.

I'm glad I did. I went back that spring and earned a starting position, earned a scholarship, and started for three years. George Henshaw was our offensive line coach, and he was great. He was definitely a player's coach and ran a wide-open offense. He left, and they brought in Wayne McDuffie for my senior year, and there was a big difference between those two. Henshaw thought football should be fun. He'd work you hard, but we always had a ball. During my sophomore and junior seasons, we ran a wide-open offense and our defense struggled. It just never seemed to be a big deal to us if it was third-and-10 or third-and-20. If the other team scored, it was like, "Okay, let's go score again."

217

The spring before my senior season was when McDuffie showed up. He was the exact opposite of Henshaw. He didn't give a damn about having a relationship with you, and, by God, it was three yards and a cloud of dust or the highway. His philosophy was the offensive line were the first players on the practice field and the last ones off the field. I think he had a philosophy that he'd run you until someone puked or you fell out. He'd run us after practice until one of the two those things happened. I had a lot of respect for him. I didn't care for him personally, but I thought he was a damn good coach. He was just 180 degrees different from what George Henshaw was.

During the spring of the 1981 season, Bob Merson and I ended up competing for the starting center job. I ended up beating Bob out, but during the first few games that season, we ended up rotating series or quarters. I'd start the game, he'd come in for a quarter, and then I'd go back in for a quarter. After about three games, we lost one of our starting guards, and they moved Bob over to guard, and I started the rest of the year at center.

The 1981 season was the year of Octoberfest. We beat Louisville 17–0 and Memphis State 10–5 to start the season, then we hit the road for five straight

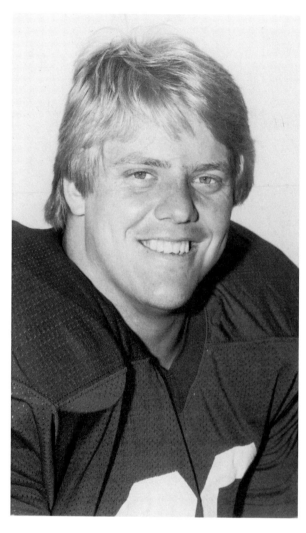

Tom McCormick went from a walk-on to a three-year starting center at Florida State. He is widely regarded among the best offensive linemen to play at Florida State and excelled because of his hustle and technique. McCormick was one of the team's captains during his junior and senior seasons, and he played on teams that appeared in two bowl games.

weeks against nationally ranked teams. We went to Nebraska the first week and had beaten the Cornhuskers in Lincoln the year before, during my freshman season. Nebraska is a great place to play, whether you're a visitor or not. We thought we had a good chance going into the game and we kept it close until halftime. Then Nebraska just blew it wide open and won the game 34–14. That was kind of a reality shock.

We went to Ohio State from there and won 36–27. Art Schlichter was Ohio State's quarterback, and Rick Stockstill was our quarterback. We had 496 yards on offense, and they had 496 yards on offense. We went up 36–21 in the third quarter. It was Stockstill's only season as a starter, and Coach Bowden kind of let him open the offense a little bit, and he had a really good game. Our defense had a couple of nice stops, and we had a 99-yard drive to score toward the end of the game. We ran a fake kick, Kelly Lowrey scored, and we blocked a punt, and Ron Hester ran it in for a touchdown. To be able to go into Ohio State and win was a thrill. Both Nebraska and Ohio State were great places to play football.

We went to Notre Dame and growing up as a good Catholic boy, I always wanted to go to Notre Dame. I thought that was what I always wanted to do until I got there. I was really disappointed when we got there because I thought they treated visiting teams like dirt. Their facilities were small, and I don't even know if they turned the air-conditioning on in the locker room. It was kind of like, "You guys should feel privileged to be here." But that was a thrilling game for me because I'd grown up a Notre Dame fan. We had a lead at halftime, and Coach Bowden walked in. Half our team was probably from Ohio and the Midwest, and Jarvis Coursey stood up and screamed, "Let's go out and beat these Yankees!" I was looking around, thinking half the team was from north of the Mason-Dixon line. We had a ball and won the game 19–13.

219

We played against Pittsburgh and Dan Marino the next week, and that didn't go very well. They had Bill Fralic, and their offensive line basically picked our defensive line up and moved them down the field. Nebraska kind of did the same thing, but Pitt was just loaded. They had a lot of talent and beat us 42–14. The thing I remember most about Pittsburgh was their fans were probably the opposite of Nebraska fans. Nebraska was a great place to play, and they treated you well; Pittsburgh was the opposite of that. It was a very tough town. I always liked the challenge, but they just out-classed us that game.

We went to Baton Rouge and played LSU in a night game. I always liked playing in Baton Rouge. It was a bunch of drunk fans who had all day to drink. The louder they got, the faster they shut up when you scored. Every year we played there, I enjoyed it. Even when I was a senior in high school, I drove over to Baton Rouge to see Florida State play LSU. We won that game 38–14.

We went home and played Western Carolina and won 56–31, but I think we were done by then. We lost to Miami at home 27–19. We had a chance to win the game. We played Southern Mississippi soon thereafter, and that game was just a complete loss. They whipped us 58–14, and then we lost at Florida 35–3. Those five weeks on the road just killed us.

We finished the 1981 season with a 6–5 record, but I don't think you could find too many teams in the country that could play that kind of schedule right now. Considering the number of people we'd lost from the year before, especially from our defense, and going on the road five straight weeks and playing the teams we played, I think we had a good year. We got beat by Nebraska and Pitt, but we were competitive for a fair part of the game. I think when we came back, we were spent, and most everybody was relieved the season was almost over. Everybody was just burnt out.

During my junior season in 1982, we played Pittsburgh in Tallahassee. Marino was still the quarterback, and the score was tied 17–17 at halftime. It was a hot day in Tallahassee, and by the time halftime came around, their defense was worn out. Although we weren't completely man-handling them, we could basically do what we wanted to do. When we got back from halftime, it had rained and the temperature had probably dropped 20 degrees. It was storming like crazy, and we couldn't control the ball as well as Marino could in those weather conditions, so they won the game 37–17.

We came back and beat Southern Miss 24–17 and then went back up to Ohio State and won again 34–17. We beat Southern Illinois 59–8 and East Carolina 56–17, and then got ready to play Miami in the Orange Bowl. That was a great game. It was on national television, and our defense played a heck of a game. They made several key stops on short yardage and goal line. Our offense did what it had to do, and we won the game 24–7. That was a great win. We were rotating quarterbacks, Kelly Lowrey and Blair Williams, and they were rotating in and out.

We beat South Carolina 56–26 and Louisville 49–14 and took a seven-game winning streak to LSU. We lost to LSU 55–21 in a game that decided which team was going to the Orange Bowl and which team was going to the Gator Bowl. It was one of the those games where the game was close at halftime, and then we came out in the second half and we couldn't do anything right and they couldn't do anything wrong. We were disappointed and lost to Florida 13–10 two weeks later. We had plenty of chances to score in that game but never could put it in the end zone. They kicked a field goal at the end to win the game.

We played West Virginia in the Gator Bowl and won 31–12. It was built up in the press because Coach Bowden had coached at West Virginia. We weren't even supposed to be in the game with them because they had all these All-Americans. Jeff Hostetler was their quarterback, and they had an All-American defensive end who was going to play opposite my roommate, Jimbo Thompson. If Jimbo was soaking wet, he was 6'6" and 225 pounds.

The talk was they were just going to push us all over the field. It was Henshaw's last season, and his mindset was they worked our butts off at the Orange Bowl two years earlier, and we weren't playing for the national championship, so we were going to have fun. I can remember practicing for that bowl game, and the offensive linemen were running pass routes and doing other fun stuff. We were going to do what we had to do but were going to have fun as well. We had a couple of dinners with the West Virginia players before the game, and those guys were beaten up and bruised. They were working their rears off, and we were just as relaxed and laid back as we could be. It really showed in the game.

We went into the 1983 season and switched to a freeze option offense. The biggest difference was that, with the blocking schemes we had before then, you didn't have to have the big, massive offensive line to push around. McDuffie's philosophy was much different than that. But Florida State hadn't recruited linemen to be able to do that. We played bigger teams, and it was tough. Our offensive line wasn't very big, and we were undersized across the line.

We opened the 1983 season against East Carolina, and it was a wild game. Our defense really struggled in 1982 and 1983. If you look at some of the scores, it was like whoever had the ball last was going to win. We had the ball last against East Carolina, and Kelly Lowrey threw a touchdown pass to Tom Wheeler to win the game with about 4:30 to go. We went to LSU and won 40–35 the next week. It was kind of remarkable that Florida State played at LSU five years in a row and won four of them. There aren't many teams in the country that have done that.

We were ranked in the top 10 in the country and lost at Tulane 34–28. That was really a disheartening loss after the way we'd started the season. It kind of led to some of the heartbreaks that happened later in the year. We lost at Auburn 27–24. Rosie Snipes had a long touchdown run that was called back in that game. I think if you look at the film of that game today, you'll still see that he never stepped out of bounds. We still had a chance to come back at the end of the game. We were driving and threw an interception. We were playing against Bo Jackson, and I always wanted to beat him. I was pretty disappointed in his performance in that game. He took himself out of the game, and that wasn't what I expected. I thought we outplayed them, and the offensive line played great in that game, and it was heartbreaking to lose. Plus, my girlfriend was still in school there, and that made it worse.

We went back to Pittsburgh, and Marino was gone. They still had a great defense and a big offensive line. We lost the game 17–16. We beat Cincinnati 43–17, Louisville 51–7, and Arizona State 29–26. The Arizona State game was a great game. Kelly Lowrey, our quarterback, got hurt. We got the ball on our 17-yard line with a little bit over one minute left, and our backup quarterback, Bob Davis, drove us the length of the field to win the game. He threw a 10-yard touchdown to Jessie Hester with six seconds left. Arizona State's defense was so worn down you could just block them with one hand, and Bob just got really hot. Other than some of the bigger victories over Notre Dame, LSU, and Ohio State that we'd had earlier in my career, that is still one of my favorite games.

We beat South Carolina 45–30 in Tallahassee. They called their defense the "Fire Ants." We'd beaten them in Columbia 56–26 the year before. It was the same team and a different coach in 1983, and they were a lot better when they came to Tallahassee. They about beat us to death. We won the game, but they wore us out. They were a completely different football team. We had almost 500 yards, but their attitude was completely different from one year to the next.

Miami came to Tallahassee the next week, and we had our chances to win the ballgame but didn't. We just couldn't score when we had a chance. Miami won the game 17–16. We went to Gainesville the last week of the season and got pounded 53–14. We just couldn't do anything right, and they pushed us all over the field.

I finished my FSU career playing North Carolina in the Peach Bowl in Atlanta. It was freezing cold weather, and I think there was a wind chill below zero. Of course, coming from Tallahassee, we weren't prepared for those kind of conditions. If the ground wasn't frozen solid, it was pretty close to it. The managers went out and bought all the biggest size panty hose they could buy, and my dad went out and bought all the batting gloves he could buy. He passed him out to all the offensive linemen because it was cold. We won the game 28–3.

After graduation, I went to training camp with the Seattle Seahawks. I got waived by them and went to camp with Tampa Bay. I got hurt trying to play for Tampa in the United States Football League and broke both my ankles.

I signed a free-agent contract with the Minnesota Vikings, and they sent me to an orthopedic surgeon, who told me never to run again. So I went back to school and retired from football. I got my engineering degree and worked as a graduate assistant for Coach McDuffie for a couple of years.

Coach Bowden was always consistent and fair. He wanted practices to be hard, so games seemed easy and fun. I always thought he was just a very real and excellent motivator. He was then and I think he still is now.

What we did for Florida State had been unparalleled. Playing the schedule we played, and beating Nebraska on the road and beating Ohio State and Notre Dame, that put Florida State on the map. There aren't too many teams in the country that can say they've done that. We set the standard. Guys were watching Florida State on TV, realizing they could go to FSU and play on TV and play the big-name teams we were playing. There's a lot to be said for that.

Tom McCormick, a native of Panama City, Florida, went from being a walk-on to a three-year starting center at Florida State. He is widely regarded among the best offensive linemen to play at Florida State and excelled because of his hustle and technique. McCormick was one of the team's captains during his junior and senior seasons, and he played on teams that appeared in two bowl games: the 1982 Gator Bowl and the 1983 Peach Bowl. McCormick was named honorable mention All-American by the Associated Press in three straight seasons, from 1981 to 1983. He had a brief career in the NFL before returning to Florida State to finish an engineering degree. McCormick works in the construction business and lives in Katy, Texas.

# GREG ALLEN
## RUNNING BACK
### 1981–1984

IGREW UP IN MILTON, FLORIDA, which is near Pensacola in the panhandle. I was recruited by Billy Sexton to Florida State and visited there. I also was considering Auburn and Florida, and I got letters from all sorts of schools. But Florida State was close to home and it was close enough for my mother to come see me play, which was really important to me.

I had no idea I'd play as a freshman in 1981. I just knew I had to be ready to play. The guys ahead of me, Ricky Williams, Cedric Jones, Billy Allen, and Tony Smith, had stayed in Tallahassee the summer before I got there, so they had a head start on me. It took a while for me to move up the depth chart. That season, we had five tailbacks come in as freshmen. The first few games of the 1981 season, I was mostly playing on special teams, and they were giving me a little bit of spot duty at tailback.

That was the season we played at Nebraska, Ohio State, Notre Dame, and Pittsburgh. It was quite an experience going to play at those kinds of schools. It was something different and something I'd never seen before. All I remember at Nebraska was seeing that sea of red when we walked in the stadium. I'd only played in front of about 1,000 people in high school. We won a couple of championships in high school, so there were quite a few people at those games. But it was nothing like the crowds we saw in college. We'd beaten Nebraska the year before I got to Florida State, so they were looking for payback. They got it, too, when they beat us 34–14.

We won at Ohio State 36–27 and actually beat them two years in a row up there. Then we played at Notre Dame, which was a great experience because that was really one of the great traditional programs. It was a prestigious school and was known for its football, but anybody can be beaten at any given time. That wasn't one of Notre Dame's best teams, and we won the game 19–13. We played at Pittsburgh the following week, and Dan Marino was their quarterback. We lost the game 42–14.

Ricky Williams was hurt in the Pittsburgh game, and I had a pretty good week of practice before the LSU game. Coach Bowden told me I was going to start at LSU. I was a little bit nervous because one of our fullbacks, Darish Davis, was really teasing me the whole week, trying to make me scared or whatever. I was a little bit scared, but once I got in the game and settled down, I was okay. I just tried to play like I'd been practicing. The blocking was great, and the offensive line really made some great blocks. I just read the blocks and ran to the hole. The first time I got the ball, I busted out into the open and really surprised myself. [Allen ran for 202 yards and one touchdown on 31 carries in FSU's 38–14 win at LSU.]

We played Western Carolina the following week. They scored the game's first touchdown and kicked off to us. I ran the kickoff back 95 yards for a touchdown. I guess I was still hyped up from the LSU game, and I remember I was pretty tired at the end of that run. [Allen also ran for a school-record 322 yards and one touchdown on 32 carries in the Seminoles' 56–31 victory over the Catamounts.] I'd played two games and had run for more than 500 yards, and it was a little bit surprising. The only thing I was thinking was, *What am I going to do the next week to try and top that?* It put a little bit of pressure on me.

225

We lost to Miami 27–19 the following week. I ran for 109 yards in that game and was the first person to run for 100 yards against that Miami defense. We lost to Southern Miss 58–14, and they had a great quarterback. They really surprised us. They were running an option offense, and we hadn't really seen it before. We lost at Florida 35–3. We never had much luck against the Gators. It was tough down in the swamp. I don't know if that five-game road trip at the beginning of the season wore us out. All of that traveling can wear you down.

We finished with a 6–5 record during my freshman season. I wasn't really pleased with the record, but I was excited I got a chance to play and could help out the team as much as I could. Coming into my sophomore year,

Former Florida State tailback Greg Allen couldn't have asked for a better college debut—he ran for a combined 524 yards against Louisiana State and Western Carolina. His 322 rushing yards against the Catamounts is still the highest single-game total in FSU history.

I didn't know what people were looking for from me. There was a little pressure, I made sure to do everything I could to be ready to go.

Coach Bowden used to call us into the locker rooms and compare us to the opponents. He'd come in and say, "Greg, everything this guy does, I want you to do it." Coach Bowden was a great motivator and really had a lot of confidence in us.

My sophomore year began with us beating Cincinnati 38–31, and then we played Pittsburgh again in Tallahassee. They were ranked No. 2 in the country, and Marino was still their quarterback. We had them on the ropes early in the game, and they were really struggling with the humidity. But then it started raining and the field was just a mess. They handled the wet conditions better than we did and pulled it out 37–17.

We went back out to Southern Miss and got a little payback. We won the game 24–17. Of course, they didn't have the quarterback they had the year before, either. We played at Ohio State again and won the game 34–17. I was kind of sharing carries with Ricky Williams, and we were switching in and out of the game. [Allen ran for 104 yards against Ohio State; Williams ran for 77 yards against the Buckeyes.] We were running the option offense that season. It worked, though. I scored on an option play in that game. I liked the offense.

227

We beat Southern Illinois 59–8, and then we beat East Carolina 56–17. We played Miami in the Orange Bowl, and both teams were ranked. We won the game 24–7. We always had good luck in the Orange Bowl; they always beat us at our place. We went up to South Carolina and won 56–26. I had a good game in that one. [Allen ran for 46 yards and four touchdowns against the Gamecocks, then ran for 173 yards and four touchdowns in a 49–14 win over Louisville.] They always seemed to give me the ball at the goal line. When we got to the goal line, that's when they put me in there.

We went to LSU again, and the winner of the game was going to get invited to play in the Orange Bowl. LSU was waiting for us this time and they won the game 55–21. We lost the next week to Florida 13–10, in Doak Campbell Stadium. I never had any luck against the Gators. In each of my four years at FSU, they beat us.

We finished the regular season with an 8–3 record and played West Virginia in the Gator Bowl. It was a great game. It was raining in Jacksonville, but we had a great game plan and won the game. Billy Allen ran back a kickoff 95 yards for a touchdown, and I was named Most Valuable Player in the game, which was exciting. [Allen ran for 138 yards and two touchdowns in the Seminoles' 31–12 victory over the Mountaineers.] It was the end of the season, and we wanted to end the year on a good note. We were able to do that and won the game.

We opened my junior season against East Carolina at home and won 47–46. It was a wild game, and our defense couldn't stop them. As soon as we scored, we'd have to go right back on the field again. We never really had a chance to rest. [Allen ran for 154 yards and two touchdowns on 33 carries against the Pirates.] We played LSU on the road the following week, and both of us were ranked in the top 15. There was a lot of hype before that game. It was another shootout, but we won the game 40–35. LSU had Dalton Hilliard, who had a big game in the Orange Bowl the season before. I ran for 201 yards and a touchdown, so I was feeling pretty good.

We went to Tulane the next week and played them in New Orleans. I took a pitchout in that game and was running behind Jamie Dukes. One of their guys undercut Jamie and ran into me. My shoe got caught in the turf, and I hyperextended my knee. They returned an interception for a touchdown and blocked a punt for a touchdown, so we had a really big hole from the beginning. I think we had too much fun on Bourbon Street and too much of New Orleans. They came to play and beat us 34–28.

I didn't play the next week at Auburn, and Roosevelt Snipes had a great game there. We lost the game 27–24. I came back and played against Pittsburgh the following week. We played up there, and Marino had graduated, thank goodness. But they still beat us 17–16 in what was really a close game. We beat Cincinnati 43–17 and beat Louisville 51–7. We went out to Arizona State and won 29–26. We won the game when Jessie Hester caught a touchdown at the end. It was kind of dry and hot out there.

We played at South Carolina and won 45–30. Cletis Jones, one of our fullbacks, fumbled into the end zone, and I recovered it for a touchdown to tie the game in the first half. We lost to Miami at home 17–16—we could just never beat them in Tallahassee. Then we lost again at Florida 53–14. That game was one of the worst beatings we took. We beat North Carolina 28–3 in the Peach Bowl in Atlanta. It was a cold day, and I didn't play that much in that game. I think I had a pulled hamstring.

We won our first four games in my senior season. We beat East Carolina 48–17 and won at Kansas 42–16. Eric Thomas was our quarterback, and we were still running the ball a lot because he was an option quarterback in high school. We beat Miami 38–3 in the Orange Bowl. We took a 24–0 lead early in the game and really jumped on them after that. We beat Temple 44–27 at home. Then we played at Memphis, and they kicked a field goal at the end of the game for a 17–17 tie. Nothing was clicking for us. The receivers weren't catching the ball, and we weren't throwing it really well, and we kept them in the game with our mistakes.

We went back home and played Auburn. They scored a fluke touchdown, when the football popped up in the air and their guy grabbed it and ran it in for a touchdown. They ended up winning the game 42–41. We beat Tulane 27–6 and played much better that time. Then we won at Arizona State 52–44 in what was just another wild shootout. Our games against them were always really high-scoring. There just wasn't a lot of defense in those games. I had an 81-yard touchdown on a counter play in that game. I broke out to the outside and had one defender to beat. I was running right behind him, and he turned around to get in position to tackle me. When he turned around, I stepped to the other side and ran right by him. That was a great run. I've still got that one on videotape because that was a nationally televised game.

But that Arizona State game also was the game where I blew out my knee. I came off the field late in the game, and they put somebody else in there for me. I put back on my gear and ran a pitch to the outside and slipped. Nobody hit me, I just slipped. I got up, and my knee felt a little funny. It didn't hurt, but it just felt a little funny. I ran one more play, and when I got to the sideline, my knee had swollen up. It got really tight, so they kept me out the rest of the game. I had torn cartilage in my knee on a freak play that I had been running for four years.

229

I tried to play against South Carolina the next week, and they let me start to test the knee and see how I'd do. My knee was wrapped up pretty heavily, and it just didn't work out. That was the end of my season. I didn't play against Tennessee-Chattanooga or Florida at the end of the season, and didn't play against Georgia in the Citrus Bowl. It was really difficult to watch. At that point, my family was telling me to sit out so I could get better. I thought I had a chance at the pros.

I was drafted by the Cleveland Browns in the second round of the 1985 NFL draft. The knee injury probably ruined my chances of being drafted in the first round, but those things happen. I guess that was just the way God wanted things to happen. I played one season for the Browns and went through preseason with them the next season. I finished the 1986 season with the Tampa Bay Buccaneers and went to camp the following year with the Indianapolis Colts. My knee just never got better.

I had a great time playing at FSU. We all got along, and I made a lot of friends. Darryl Gray was my roommate, and we were like brothers. We're still very, very close and still stay in touch. It was a great time to be at Florida State.

Greg Allen, a native of Milton, Florida, was a starting tailback for the Seminoles for four seasons, from 1981 to 1984. As a freshman in 1981, Allen led Florida State with 888 rushing yards and three touchdowns. In his first two starts at FSU, against LSU and Western Carolina, Allen ran for 524 combined yards. His 322 rushing yards against Western Carolina is still an FSU single-game record, and his 223 yards against Arizona State in 1984 is the third-most in school history. In fact, Allen has four of the 10 highest single-game rushing totals and still holds 13 single-season and career records at FSU. Allen had 1,134 rushing yards as a junior in 1983, the fourth-highest total at FSU, and was named a consensus All-American. His 3,769 career rushing yards are second-most in school history, behind only Warrick Dunn. Allen had 16 100-yard games in his career and set a school record by scoring 126 points and 21 touchdowns as a sophomore in 1982. Allen was a second-round choice of the Cleveland Browns in the 1985 NFL draft and played two seasons in the NFL, after suffering a knee injury late in his college career. He owns a construction company and lives in Milton, Florida.

# JAMIE DUKES
## GUARD
## 1982–1985

I GRADUATED FROM EVANS HIGH SCHOOL in Orlando and was recruited to Florida State by Jim Gladden, an assistant coach there. Florida, Miami, Ohio State, South Carolina, Georgia, and Georgia Tech were recruiting me as well. My mother made the decision. She liked Coach Bowden because he was a Southern Baptist and a man of cloth, so to speak. I grew up in the church, and she felt that was the best place for me.

I ended up starting the first game of my freshman season in 1982 and started every game during the four years. When I got there, they had some injuries on the offensive line. George Henshaw was my offensive line coach. They needed defensive linemen, too, and I played a little bit of defensive tackle and nose tackle, too. It became a question of where I could play sooner, and the offensive line was the best place to do that.

I started at guard in 1982, and Kelly Lowrey and Blair Williams were rotating at quarterback. Kelly was an interesting guy. He had a lot of moxie and savvy, but he was a gambler, so we turned the ball over a little bit. Bob Davis was a backup and a drop-back passer. Kelly was kind of a linebacker playing quarterback. He was Jared Lorenzen before Jared Lorenzen. He was a big guy and was tough to bring down.

We opened the 1982 season against Cincinnati and won the game 38–31. We won at Ohio State 34–17, and Ohio State had a lot of great players. I'd been recruited by Ohio State. They had Mike Tomczak at quarterback and

231

Tim Spencer was the running back. There was a lot of talent on that team, and it was my first time playing in front of 80,000 people. It was something else. We played Pittsburgh in the second game and lost 37–17. Dan Marino was Pittsburgh's quarterback, and they had about 20 guys drafted into the NFL off that team.

Later that season, we played Miami down in the Orange Bowl, and both teams were nationally ranked. We had a guy named Orson Mobley, and he caught a pass on a play that Coach Bowden called a "Gator" pass. It was kind of a fake screen with the tight end going across the middle. Orson was a big tight end, probably 6'6" and 250 pounds, and that was really the play that opened the game up. He scored a 24-yard touchdown at the beginning of the fourth quarter and kind of broke the game open. We won the game 24–7.

We played at South Carolina the following week and won 56–26. South Carolina had a good team the year they had the "Fire Ant" defense, but we used to just wear them out. Those games were always track meets.

We beat Louisville 49–14, and then we went and played at LSU. I'll never forget that. It was the game for the Orange Bowl, with the winner being invited to play in the Orange Bowl. Needless to say, we ended up going to the Gator Bowl. They whipped us 55–21. Imagine being at LSU at night with the Orange Bowl on the line. They bombed us eight ways to Sunday. They had a lot of great players and about 15 or 16 guys who got drafted into the NFL. Every time they scored, the fans would throw oranges at us. They would just come raining down on us on the field. Looking at the score, you can imagine how many times we got pelted by oranges. Basically, we were covered in orange juice by the end of the game.

We played Florida in the last regular season game in 1982, and Florida just had more talent that us. That's basically what it boiled down to. They beat us 13–10. They had 22 guys drafted by NFL teams off that team. Their second- and third-team running backs were John L. Williams and Neal Anderson. They had James Jones and Lorenzo Hampton in the backfield. That's just the backfield. They had Lomas Brown, a great tackle, and Wayne Peace was the quarterback and a Heisman Trophy candidate. They were just absolutely loaded on offense. On defense, Alonzo Johnson was a backup linebacker, and the starting linebacker was some guy named Wilber Marshall. They were just loaded across the board with talent.

After losing our last two games of the season, we played West Virginia in the 1982 Gator Bowl. Florida State had gone to the Orange Bowl twice

during the late 1970s, but then they had a season where they didn't go to a
bowl game at all. It was kind of a lean season, and we were retooling. To be
able to go out and get the first bowl victory [since the 1977 Tangerine Bowl]
was special. That started that run of 14 straight years of winning or tying a
bowl game. That Gator Bowl victory started that streak. West Virginia had
Jeff Hostetler at quarterback and Darryl Talley at linebacker. It was certainly
a chance to show our wares against a good team, and we won the game
31–12. It was good to win after struggling in those last couple of games.

We opened the 1983 season against East Carolina and won 47–46. Then
we beat LSU 40–35. We had a lot of shootouts and could score with the best
of them, but we just couldn't stop anybody. The LSU game was a day game,
and it was really kind of redemption for us. We let one off the hook the year
before, and we remembered being pounded by those oranges the year before.
It was really hot, and they were still pretty loaded with talent. We jumped
on them early and won the game.

We went to Tulane and lost 34–28 in New Orleans. We had a 21–14 lead
and let a win get away from us. We lost at Auburn 27–24, and they had about
20 guys who went to the NFL off the team. David Rocker was playing there,
and Bo Jackson was in the backfield. We lost at Pittsburgh 17–16, and Bill
Fralic was on that team. They had another big offensive line, but they were
still trying to get settled at quarterback after Marino left. They still had a
good, stingy defense.

We went home and beat Cincinnati 43–17 and beat Louisville 51–7. We
went and played at Arizona State, and I lost 20 pounds during the game. It
was dry as a bone out there in the desert. Bob Davis came into the game in
the fourth quarter and threw the game-winning touchdown to Jessie Hester
with six seconds left. It was a go route, and they had blitzed us the whole
game. Bob didn't have his contact in and couldn't see really well, but he took
us down the field, at least that's the urban legend. We thought we'd found
ourselves a quarterback. It was a great game and an absolute shootout. We
won the game 29–26.

We beat South Carolina 45–30 and then lost to Miami 17–16. They kicked
a field goal at the end to win the game. We couldn't beat Miami at home but
always beat them on the road. We went to Florida and got walloped 53–14,
and they were just completely loaded with talent again.

In 1984 we finished 7–3–2 and went to another bowl game. We went to
this freeze option offense that Art Baker, the new offensive coordinator,

233

brought with him. Eric Thomas was our quarterback, but we just couldn't throw the ball. We had great wide receivers, but we just couldn't throw the ball on a consistent basis. Thomas wasn't a great athlete, but he could run and could make the reads on the option. It was a huge change for the offensive line. You had to change your stance because we were run-oriented. We were running quite a bit because I was pulling one way or the other. About 80 percent of the offense was being run behind me. We ran the ball and put up points, but we couldn't take advantage of the long ball and the play-action pass.

We opened the 1984 season and beat East Carolina 48–17 and then Kansas 42–16. Cletis Jones had a big game against Kansas. He had always been a blocking fullback, but that game was his defining moment. He was one guy we really never got into the game plan enough because he was just a specimen. There was something about the offense where it just didn't fit him.

We went down to the Orange Bowl to play Miami, and they were ranked fourth in the country. We blew them out 38–3, and Jessie Hester had a big day. He scored a long touchdown off a reverse in that game. We beat Temple 44–27, and you know your defense is a little bit suspect when Temple scores that many points against you. We went to Memphis State, and the game ended in a 17–17 tie. They had a great defense and always played great defense. They had two shutdown cornerbacks who went to the NFL, and they played the 46 defense that Buddy Ryan took to the NFL.

We lost to Auburn 42–41, and they had an onside kick that one of their guys returned for a touchdown. He was a walk-on and told his wife he was going to score a touchdown for her. He ended up doing it against us when he caught a line drive and ran right down the field on the opening kickoff of the second half. Brent Fullwood scored on a touchdown run at the end to beat us.

We beat Tulane 27–6 and won at Arizona State 52–44 in a game that was just another shootout. South Carolina had that "Fire Ant" defense in 1984, and we lost up there 38–26. We beat Tennessee-Chattanooga 37–0 and then lost to Florida 27–17 in Doak Campbell Stadium. We played Georgia in the Citrus Bowl, and Kevin Butler almost kicked a 70-yard field goal at the end of the game to win it. He just barely missed.

We finished the 1984 season with a 7–3–2 record, but we thought we were close to turning it around. Going into my senior season in 1985, we thought we had a chance to be pretty good. Everybody really liked Danny McManus

234

at quarterback because he could throw the ball. Unfortunately, McManus got nailed in the Memphis State game, got a concussion, and was never the same. Kirk Coker replaced him, and then Chip Ferguson came into the lineup a couple of weeks later. McManus was our guy on offense, and we just never really got it back after he was hurt.

Despite being a consensus All-American as a senior at Florida State in 1985, Jamie Dukes wasn't selected in the 1986 NFL draft. He signed with the Atlanta Falcons as a free agent and played 10 seasons in the NFL. He lives in Atlanta and is a television analyst for the NFL Network.

We went to Nebraska the second week of the season before McManus was hurt. Nobody really gave us a chance to win that game. Florida State had won there in 1980 and, by winning in 1985, Florida State was the only team in NCAA history with a winning record in Lincoln. It was, like, 125 degrees on the field on the artificial turf—it was amazingly hot. I remember having to soak my shoes in ice water because it was so hot on the field. Tom Rathman, their big fullback, ran for a 60-yard touchdown in the first few minutes. We were all thinking, *Oh, you know what!*

McManus got hurt the next week against Memphis State, but we won the game 19–10. We beat Kansas 24–20 the following week, but then we got drilled by Auburn 59–27. Auburn literally scored 28 points in five minutes during the fourth quarter. McManus got hit in that game and got a little punchy, and he was calling some weird plays in the huddle. We were trying to help him out, but it just didn't work. We were all hoping McManus would come back, but it never happened. Chip Ferguson had a courageous effort, but he was still green. We knew we needed McManus to take us to the next level.

We beat Tulsa 76–14 and North Carolina 20–10, but then we lost to Miami 35–27. Michael Irvin had a huge game against us in Tallahassee, and Vinny Testaverde was the quarterback. Vinny was so big, our defense couldn't bring him down. We won easily against South Carolina 56–14, and that was a little payback for the "Fire Ant" issue the year before. That was the "Raid" game. We beat Western Carolina 50–10, and then ended the year losing to Florida 38–14. We just never had anything for Florida.

We beat Oklahoma State 34–23 in the Gator Bowl. I remember Oklahoma State's starting tailback was a guy named Thurman Thomas, and his backup was a guy named Barry Sanders. We really took them to the woodshed offensively, and Chip Ferguson probably had his best game as a college player. That game really set up Chip for the following season.

That season, they had brought in Deion Sanders, Sammie Smith, Peter Tom Willis, and Brad Johnson as freshmen. We knew that was the best recruiting class they'd brought in for a while. It was by far the best recruiting class. Supposedly, our recruiting class was supposed to be good, but these guys were better athletes. Deion's class was incredibly talented. So we knew Florida State had a pretty bright future.

I always respected the way Coach Bowden handled himself. He had so many high school All-Americans with big egos coming in there, and I thought he was fair to everyone who walked in there. You would hear the grumblings, and a player would be upset because he couldn't beat out the All-American who was in front of him. I just remember how good of a man Coach Bowden was and what a fair man he was.

After graduation, I went into the NFL draft when teams thought centers were supposed to be 6′3″, guards were supposed to be 6′4″, and tackles were supposed to be 6′5″ or taller. I had a bunch of teams that were trying to sign me, but they all kept telling me they couldn't draft me because I was shorter than 6′. I was the shortest offensive lineman in the NFL for five or six years. I'd played against all the great players and played well and had all the credentials, but my height was the issue. But I moved to center during my second season in the NFL and played in the league for 10 years.

Jamie Dukes, a native of Orlando, Florida, started every game at guard after he arrived at Florida State in 1982. He was one of only four offensive linemen in FSU history to start every game as a freshman. Dukes was named a freshman All-American by *Football News* in 1982 and was an honorable mention All-American as a sophomore and junior. As a senior in 1985, Dukes was a consensus All-American. He helped lead FSU teams to four bowl games: the 1982 Gator Bowl, 1983 Peach Bowl, 1984 Citrus Bowl, and 1985 Gator Bowl. Undrafted by NFL teams in 1986 because of concerns about his height, Dukes signed as a free agent with the Atlanta Falcons and played 10 years of pro football. He lives in Atlanta and is an analyst for NFL Network.

# DANNY McMANUS

## QUARTERBACK

## 1983–1987

IWENT TO HIGH SCHOOL AT SOUTH BROWARD High School in Hollywood,
Florida, and Florida State was down there playing Miami during the 1982
season. Coach Bowden and some of the coaches came to look at one the linebackers on my high school team. During that game, I ended up having a
pretty good game throwing the football, so I wound up making my way onto
their recruiting list.

My college choices basically came down to Florida State and Pittsburgh. I
actually had to tell my older brother, Jerry, who was coaching defensive backs
at Pitt, that I wasn't going there. He was okay. He said, "You've got to do
what you've got to do. Don't come to Pitt just because I'm going to be here.
You got to pick the school that's going to work for you." As soon as I got on
the Florida State campus, I had a feeling that's where I was going to go to
school. I took my first visit to Florida State, and the other schools I visited
never matched up with Florida State.

I got to Florida State in 1983 and ended up taking a redshirt season. Bob
Davis and Kelly Lowrey were the starting quarterbacks, and I basically spent
that season learning behind them. I did the same thing during my redshirt
freshman season in 1984, playing behind Kirk Coker and Eric Thomas. That
was the season they installed the freeze option offense, after Art Baker came
in as the offensive coordinator. To be honest, I was looking around for
another school at that point. I investigated Central Florida and a small school

in Alabama. I just wanted to find a place that was throwing the football. I was looking to see what else was out there.

But Baker was only there for one season, and Mark Richt came back to Florida State from East Carolina in 1985. He was a graduate assistant when I first got there, and he came back as the quarterbacks coach under Wayne McDuffie. I started the 1985 season, but then I got knocked out in the third or fourth game, and Chip Ferguson came in and started the rest of the season. I took a pretty good shot in the Nebraska game [a 17–13 win], and then we came home and played Memphis State [a 19–10 victory], and I took another pretty good shot to the head.

That second hit to the head was it for the season. I ended up having a pretty good case of vertigo, and it put me on the sideline all that year. I participated briefly in spring practice the next year. It lingered for quite a while. There were times I was sitting in the dorm room, and the room would just start spinning. I'd look down, and things would be very much out of focus. It took quite a while to get things back to normal. It was a different feeling each day waking up, you didn't know if you were going to make it through the day with nothing happening, or if it was going to be one of those days where everything was going to happen. It was a tough deal.

We ended up finishing 9–3 in 1985 and beat Oklahoma State 34–23 in the Gator Bowl. I didn't even dress out for the Gator Bowl. During the spring of 1986 I worked in a couple of practices and got in the spring game. Things started to feel back to normal. I was a little bit more familiar with what was going on and didn't have the dizzy spells anymore. I stayed in Tallahassee the summer before the 1986 season and really wanted to get back to where I was before.

In 1986 Chip Ferguson started the season as the starter, but then I came back and won the job again after we almost beat Michigan up there. I came in, in the fourth quarter of the Michigan game, and we were down 20–10. I threw a touchdown, and we put some points on the board, and then got a two-point conversion to cut their lead to two points. But we never got the ball back to get anything going, and we lost the game 20–18. Being at Michigan Stadium on Friday afternoon and seeing all the stands empty, and then seeing it Saturday morning all filled up, was quite an experience for a guy who usually played in front of about 1,500 people in high school. It was pretty neat. I really realized then I was a part of big-time football.

After the Michigan game, Coach Bowden told me, "You're back. You're back to what we recruited." I think he had confidence in me and knew that the whole plan was going to start coming together. He knew the talented players who were coming, and he thought I was going to be a guy that was good enough to lead them.

After losing at Michigan, we blew out Tulane 54–21 and beat Wichita State 59–3 [McManus threw three touchdowns in the game]. We beat Louisville 54–18, and things were really going well. Sammie Smith was running the ball really well. Things started to gel as the season went on, and I happened to come in at the right time.

We won three games in a row and played at Miami, which was ranked No. 1 in the country. We were playing against Vinny Testaverde. It was a hot day, and those guys were throwing the ball over the place and were scoring points. Injuries started nailing us, and they ended up beating us pretty good 41–23. During the Miami game, I banged my thumb on a helmet and didn't play against South Carolina the next week. Chip Ferguson started that game [a 45–28 victory]. I came back and played against Southern Miss [a 49–13 victory], and then we lost to Florida 17–13 in the last game of the season. We played Indiana in the All-American Bowl and won 27–13.

I came out of the All-American Bowl and was the starter in the spring of 1987 and started the season. Chip Ferguson and Peter Tom Willis were playing behind me. We beat Texas Tech 40–16, East Carolina 44–3, and Memphis State 41–24 to start the season. Then we beat Michigan State 31–3 and we had a 4–0 record going into the Miami game. Things were going pretty good on offense. We were putting points on the board, and the defense was getting the ball for us. Everything was setting up for that Miami game.

We were down 26–19 in the final two minutes of the fourth quarter, playing Miami at Doak Campbell Stadium. We were trying to get the ball down the field. The play before, Dexter Carter made a great leaping catch on a halfback flat, then up route. He went up and caught the ball and got us in great position. We had all-go routes on the next play, and I saw Ronald Lewis going down the sideline. I threw it up, and I'm not sure if he was in bounds, but there was a police officer sitting right there who threw his arms up. The official saw that and he put his arms up as well. I think we might have gotten some home cooking there.

The score was 26–25, so we decided to go for a two-point conversion and the win. The play was a slant, with the tight end going into the flat, and then he was going to roll it up to the top corner. I just got focused on the tight

A pair of concussions derailed quarterback Danny McManus's college football career, but he played in the Canadian Football League from 1990 to 2006. He helped three teams win Grey Cup championships in the CFL: the Winnipeg Blue Bombers in 1990, British Columbia Lions in 1994, and Hamilton Tiger-Cats in 1999.

end going up to the corner and threw it up there, but the pass got knocked down. If I'd stayed with the slant route, Ronald Lewis would have been standing in the back of the end zone wide open.

We came back and beat Southern Miss 61–10, and it was their homecoming game. Things were going well that day really quick. We beat Louisville 32–9 and Tulane 73–14 at home. Deion Sanders ran a punt back for a touchdown against Tulane. We knew he was going to be a great player because we saw it in practice every day. We saw what he could do every day; other people just saw it on Saturdays.

With players like Deion Sanders, Edgar Bennett, Sammie Smith, and Pat Carter, I think the coaches saw the talent first. I think the players were like, "Hey, we just came off the All-American Bowl. What kind of club do we really have?" But I think the club kind of gelled as the season went on, and we all realized that we could play with the big guys. We realized we had a chance to do something really special, and we had a chance to not only put Florida State among the best teams in the country, but also a chance to maybe even be No. 1 at the end.

We closed the 1987 season by beating Auburn 34–6, Furman 41–10, and Florida 28–14, which was the only time I beat them. It was at their place, and it was the only time I'd beaten Florida in my five years there. It was good to finally get them.

We played Nebraska in the 1988 Fiesta Bowl and won 31–28. To be playing Nebraska and to be kicking off New Year's Day—because it was an 11:00 kickoff out in Tempe, Arizona—the whole atmosphere was really neat. Usually, we were at home watching these games on TV, and now we had a chance to play in the game. We were playing against a team like Nebraska, which always has been one of the best teams in the country. It was really special for all of us, especially with the way the game ended. We had a fourth down and 15, and we scored the winning touchdown on a 15-yard pass to Ronald Lewis near the end of the game. We won the game and finished 11–1. We were ranked No. 2 in the country, and it was a great year.

You never know what would have happened as far as being drafted in the NFL if I'd played all those years at FSU. But I might not have played 17 years in the Canadian Football League, either. Coach Bowden always told his players, "If you give everything you have to Florida State, good things will happen to you." I think all of us at the quarterback position were very fortunate to have great careers, not only in football, but outside of the game, too.

I started playing in Canada with the Winnipeg Blue Bombers in 1990. We won the 1990 Grey Cup when I was with the Blue Bombers, and I won another Grey Cup in 1994 with the British Columbia Lions. I won another Grey Cup with the Hamilton Tiger-Cats in 1999. I never would have imagined I'd play 17 years in the CFL. I thought it was going to be two or three years, then I'd get on with my sports marketing career and see if I could possibly become an agent. I never thought I'd keep playing football for 17 years. But I've had great offensive linemen. It's a passing league up there, and I've been very fortunate to have some outstanding offensive linemen, whose number-one desire was to keep me dry and keep me on my feet. That's the number-one reason I've played so long, and I feel very fortunate.

Danny McManus, a native of Dania, Florida, was a starting quarterback in parts of three seasons for the Seminoles, from 1983 to 1987. He was the team's starting quarterback in 1985 but suffered a pair of concussions that sidelined him for much of the season. He came back in 1986 and was named the team's most outstanding offensive player, throwing for 872 yards and seven touchdowns. In 1987 McManus led the Seminoles to an 11–1 record, including a 31–28 victory over Nebraska in the Fiesta Bowl. He threw for 375 yards and three touchdowns against the Cornhuskers and was named the bowl game's Most Valuable Player. He finished his senior season with 1,964 passing yards and 14 touchdowns. McManus was drafted in the 11th round of the 1988 NFL draft by the Kansas City Chiefs, but later found his home in the Canadian Football League. He has helped three teams win Grey Cup championships: the Winnipeg Blue Bombers in 1990, British Columbia Lions in 1994, and Hamilton Tiger-Cats in 1999. He was named Most Outstanding Player in the CFL and Most Valuable Player in the Grey Cup in 1999. He is one of only three players in CFL history with more than 50,000 passing yards. McManus played last season with the CFL's Calgary Stampeders and lives in Vince, Florida, during the off-season.

# PETER TOM WILLIS

## QUARTERBACK
### 1985–1989

FLORIDA STATE HAD THOSE TWO GOOD YEARS where they played against Oklahoma in the Orange Bowl two years in a row. Ron Simmons was there, and they had some great players, and then it dropped back down again, falling into just a Top 25 team, ranked in the 15 to 20 range.

Then, all of a sudden, starting in 1987, people started wanting to come to Florida State to play football. Coach Bowden has always been a tremendous recruiter, but I also think people wanted to come there because there was so much competition on the field. That's the key for any program. If you look at any great program, the most competition you'll see is in practice, and that's the way it was. When every afternoon you are out there scrimmaging against your defense, and they are probably as good or better than anybody you are going to see on Saturdays, you can't help but get better.

We were in the top five in the country from 1987 until 2000, that's 14 straight years. It has to do with the number of kids you are recruiting and the kinds of kids you are recruiting. When you are having to compete at the highest level just to get on the field to play, it makes a big difference. Quite honestly, I think that is one of the problems Florida State has had over the past six years. They don't have the depth of talent and the competition. You have guys that are slated in and they are not having to fight for a job at their position every day.

Now, somebody like Deion Sanders didn't have to fight for his position, but, with his pride, he competed as hard as anybody in practice. That's what great teams and great programs are all about.

The 1987 season was the start of the run, Deion's sophomore year, and Danny McManus was the quarterback. We were a top-five team and we were No. 1 until we lost to Miami in the middle of the year. One thing Coach Bowden has always done a great job of is he plays the younger guys. He doesn't necessarily take away from the veterans, usually if it is close he will play the veterans, but he is not afraid to play younger guys. That keeps guys coming in there and, by the time they are ready to start, they can play at a high level and are used to playing there. It is very rare that you had a guy come in cold and expect him to play; he had already been playing for a year or so.

We were beating Miami 14–10, but they were playing well. We had a third down and 11 late in the game, and I had to scramble out of the pocket. Right before I was going to step out of bounds, I saw Dexter Carter down the middle of the field and kind of lofted the pass up to him. He made a great catch, and we ended up scoring a touchdown. We could have given them the ball with pretty good field position in the fourth quarter. My senior year, people said that was the turning point of the season.

245

I remember in 1987 we could have kicked an extra point and tied them and been No. 1 at the end of the year. We lost the game 26–25, and Miami went on to win the national championship.

I didn't start until my senior year, though there was a good moment in 1988 when Chip Ferguson was hurt. We went up to South Carolina and beat them 59–0. It was a pretty big deal for me. We played great offensively, and it was a special deal for me. It was an important game because South Carolina, I think, had lost one game and we had lost one game, and whoever won that game was going to a major bowl. But Chip had played well for us, and he came back and played well. Coach Bowden had always said you weren't going to lose your job being injured.

I got my shot the next year. I was not going to transfer. I thought about it, I'm not going to lie. But if you go to a university worth playing for, nobody is just going to give you a job. I always felt I was as good as whoever was playing, and if I had transferred maybe I would have felt I wasn't good enough for Florida State. I never felt that. What you should do is relish the opportunity to compete and realize that is going to make you a better player.

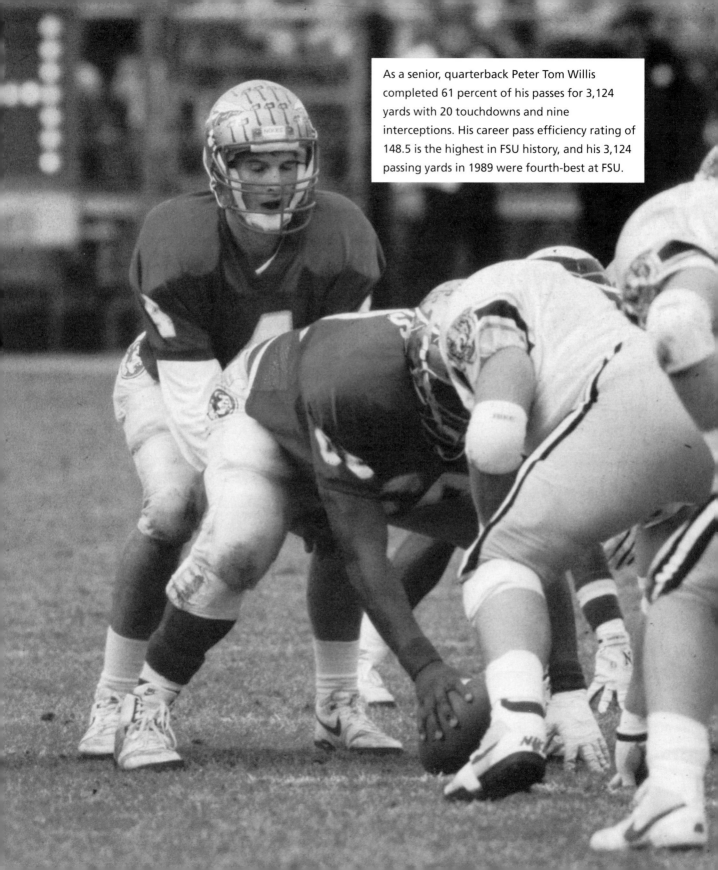

As a senior, quarterback Peter Tom Willis completed 61 percent of his passes for 3,124 yards with 20 touchdowns and nine interceptions. His career pass efficiency rating of 148.5 is the highest in FSU history, and his 3,124 passing yards in 1989 were fourth-best at FSU.

That's what happened at Florida State in the mid-1980s. You can look at every position at Florida State, and that's what happened. If more kids would relish the opportunity to compete instead of wanting something given to them, they would be better off.

During my senior season in 1989, we lost our first two games [against Southern Mississippi and Clemson] and then won 10 in a row. We were playing the toughest schedule in the country that year, so it was great to have a guy like Bobby Bowden around. He settled everybody down.

We started out losing to Southern Miss 30–26, and nobody understood why we lost at the time, but they had a guy named Brett Favre playing quarterback for them. Then we lost to Clemson 34–23 at home. We didn't play bad in either game—a play here, a play there.

Then we played LSU on the road and beat them 31–21. The turning point of that season was LSU. We were down two touchdowns and came back in the fourth quarter to beat them. Tommy Hodson was the quarterback, and playing in Baton Rouge is one of the toughest environments in college football. It kept our season going. You never know what might have happened if we started 0–3. But we got on a roll and started believing.

Then we beat Tulane 59–9 and beat Syracuse 41–10 up there. Syracuse was a good program back them. We beat Virginia Tech 41–7, Auburn 22–14, and Miami 24–10. The only year we beat Miami was in 1989, so that was a special year. The day we beat them my senior year, I still tell people that's the loudest I have ever heard Doak Campbell Stadium. Back then, it held only 60,000 people, instead of 80,000. I still remember the hair on my arms standing up. They were loud before the game started and they never sat down.

I still remember their first play from scrimmage. Gino Torretta threw an interception, and on our first play from scrimmage, we ran a toss sweep to Dexter Carter. He ran 37 yards for a touchdown. The other big play I remember is we had the ball on our own 1-yard line—and this is typical Coach Bowden—and he calls a bomb. I threw a 59-yard pass out of our own end zone to Ronald Lewis. That was a turning point, too. I think we ended up scoring points on that drive.

We beat South Carolina 35–10 and Memphis State 57–20. We closed the regular season by beating Florida 24–17 over at their place.

We played Nebraska in the Fiesta Bowl in 1989. When we got to the bowl game, we felt we good. We just didn't think we could be beat, and that's not being cocky. When you get on a roll and beat the teams we beat, I think we

247

all had confidence. I think at that point we were throwing and catching the ball so well. It felt like we were going to have success throwing the football.

Nebraska tried to play a little too much man-to-man coverage, and we ate them up. It was one of those games where Nebraska had some turnovers, and we took care of the football really well. It was kind of close in the first quarter, then we just exploded. We started out slow, and then I think we scored three touchdowns in the second quarter. It was a great end to the season.

We had lost a lot of great players from the year before, Deion Sanders and Sammie Smith, and some of our better players and leader-type players. I think in those situations, where you lose some of the better players, you tend to play a little safe, and that's what we did the first couple of games. We just decided to let it go and play loose, like we had in the past. We played well the rest of the year.

For all of us who were fifth-year seniors, it was great to beat them. When you stepped on the field, you knew their athletes were going to be as good as your athletes.

I still remember when I was a freshman, a kid from a small town in Alabama, and Coach Bowden came into our meeting to coach us on how he wanted to throw the deep ball. He thought we were throwing the ball too much on a line and he wanted us to put some air under it so the receiver could run under it. I got excited when he came in there because he was going to coach us up.

He got on the chalkboard and says, "Dadgumit, boys!" Then he starts drawing these stick figures as football players and he puts the face mask on them and everything. He draws the receiver and the defensive back as stick men, and then he shows these dotted lines on how he wants the ball to come down into his hands. Some coaches might be hard to understand, but our head coach was drawing stick men up on the board.

Coach Bowden is a great coach, and everybody knows that. He is a great man and is respected, and we're all proud he is our coach. To a lot of people who are really close to the program, he is our second father.

Peter Tom Willis, a native of Morris, Alabama, played quarterback at Florida State from 1986 to 1989. As a senior, he led the Seminoles to a 10–2 record and No. 3 national ranking. Florida State beat five nationally ranked opponents that season: Louisiana State, Syracuse, Auburn, Miami, and Nebraska. Willis completed 61 percent of his passes for 3,124 yards with 20 touchdowns and nine interceptions. He threw for 482 yards in a 57–20 victory over Memphis State on November 18, 1989, the fifth-most yards in a game by an FSU quarterback, and set a school record with six touchdown passes. Willis's career pass efficiency rating of 148.5 is the highest in FSU history, and his 3,124 passing yards in 1989 is fourth-best at FSU. Willis was drafted by the Chicago Bears in the third round of the 1990 NFL draft and played four seasons with the Bears. He also played for the Tampa Bay Storm of the Arena Football League. Willis was inducted into the FSU Sports Hall of Fame in 1998 and has worked as the school's radio color commentator for football games since 1999.

# DEXTER CARTER
## RUNNING BACK
### 1986–1989

I GREW UP IN BAXLEY, GEORGIA, and attended Appling County High School. I was recruited by South Carolina, Georgia, and Clemson, but they all wanted me to move to wide receiver. Florida State was the only big school that was recruiting me to play running back.

I'd played running back since I was eight years old. After I had 1,800 rushing yards during my junior season of high school, all those other schools came into the picture during my senior season. But I had already decided where I was going to school because I had attended Bobby Bowden's football camp during the summer after my junior year of high school. I knew it was a done deal as soon as I got to Tallahassee.

Prior to my going to Florida State, we had a guy from Appling County who played football at South Carolina and played with the Cleveland Browns. But I was the first one to really hit it big. After I left Baxley, there was a guy who grew up on my street, Carl Simpson, who played defensive tackle at Florida State and later for the Chicago Bears. They ended up renaming our street "NFL Drive," which was pretty cool.

We ended up having another guy, Jamie Nails, who played on the offensive line at Florida A&M and played for the Buffalo Bills and Miami Dolphins. Jamie and I grew up in the same church. Lewis Tyre, another guy from Baxley, played offensive tackle at Florida State. It was nice to see all those guys from a small town make it in college football and in the NFL.

That FSU summer camp was my first exposure to a college team. I told one of my high school coaches, Keith Johnson, who was my running backs coach and baseball coach and really was like a second father to me, that I wanted to go to a football camp. I knew he was going to come back with an application to go to camp at the University of Georgia, but he came back with only one application. It was Florida State, and I had never heard of Florida State. I filled it out and went to camp and that was it. I later asked him, "How did you come up with FSU?" He said he did his research, and, back then, Florida State was the only team that actually had their coaches teaching at the summer camps rather than having high school coaches doing all the instructing.

The closest thing to pulling me away from Florida State was pro baseball. I didn't get drafted to play baseball out of high school, but the Cincinnati Reds, San Diego Padres, and Pittsburgh Pirates each had scouts at my games during my senior season of high school. One of the scouts asked me if I had a problem starting in their minor league system, and I told him that I didn't have a problem with it. But then he asked me if I would still go to Florida State if I were drafted to play baseball, and I answered him the only way a naïve person would answer. I told him, "Oh, I'm going to Florida State." Kids are a little smarter now. I showed them my cards and the decision had been made.

I graduated from high school in the spring of 1986 and was enrolled at Florida State by the second session of summer school. I was already on campus getting acclimated to college. They thought it would benefit me to get adjusted academically and it was good to come into school early. When I got to FSU, there were three backs ahead of me: Sammie Smith, Victor Floyd, and Keith Ross. I ended up being one of only a few freshman who weren't redshirted that season. I was from Georgia, and call it being naïve, but I didn't know Sammie Smith was all-world. I didn't know who Keith Ross was. I just knew I was going to play as a freshman.

Back then, Coach Bowden used to give us index cards, and he'd have us write our goals on them. My goal was to start the first game of my freshman season. Coach Bowden laughs about it now, "Yeah, right, a freshman." Ironically, I ended up starting against Toledo in the 1986 opener because the other three running backs were hurt. I used to tell people that I hid out at the dorms and would hit the other backs with a billy club and eventually got all three of them. But I ended up starting that first game and playing as a true freshman.

Speed was always former Florida State star Dexter Carter's strength. He returned a kickoff 100 yards for a touchdown against Miami as a freshman in 1986, which still ranks as the longest in FSU history.

I had a 100-yard kickoff return for a touchdown against Miami during my freshman season, and I showed my shortstop skills on that play. Keith Ross made a lateral to me, and the ball bounced up. We'd practiced that play every day, but we never knew when we were going to run it. Coach Bowden told us on the sideline, "Run the lateral!" I remember catching the ball and all I saw was green grass in front of me. It was an opportunity for me to show off my speed. It was just a straight sprint. A lot of people talk about being in a zone where you don't hear anything, and that's how that play was for me. I just knew I was a little true freshman running down the field against Miami. It was tremendous.

During my sophomore season in 1987, Sammie and I were voted the best duo of running backs in the country. We ended up having 1,900 yards combined. I think I showed the work ethic, durability, and toughness that usually wasn't found in a small back. Sammie Smith was much bigger and ran a 4.4 [seconds in the 40-yard dash]. I was smaller and ran a 4.3. I ran between the tackles better than most people thought I would be able to do. I had played in a veer offense in high school, so I ran between the tackles all the time. Sammie could go into the game and pound between the tackles but also take it around the corner. I could pound it in there, too, but being a small back, they didn't want me running between the tackles all the time. The coaches did a great job of allowing each of us to take advantage of our skills.

253

We went 11–1 during the 1987 season, and that was the start of the FSU dynasty. I thought the 1987 team was the best team I played on. We were down one point to Miami and went for two points to win the game at the end. All the fans hated our going for the win, but we've always been 100 percent in support of the decision because we worked hard for a win, not a tie. We didn't make the two-point try and lost the game 26–25. What we didn't know at the time was if we had tied, we would have won the national championship at the end of the season. But we still didn't regret it. We never second-guessed Coach Bowden.

After losing to Miami, we won the rest of our games and finished 11–1. We beat Florida 28–14 in Gainesville later that season, and Sammie and I both had over 100 yards rushing. Miami won the national championship, and we finished No. 2.

During my junior season in 1988, Coach Bowden was starting Sammie Smith and Marion Butts, and he was really pounding them between the tackles to kind of wear the defense out a little bit. It wasn't like Sammie was playing the first half, then I would play the second half. But after those guys pounded them, he would bring me in to slash and run. We had a good season and finished 11–1 after losing to Miami 31–0 in the opener. We finished No. 3 in the country that season.

We lost our first two games during my senior season in 1989. We just didn't know anything about Brett Favre when we played Southern Miss in the opener [a 30–26 loss]. In the second game against Clemson, Terry Allen came to town and just out-manned us [in a 34–23 loss]. To take a team that was 0–2 and still have the schedule we faced, including games against Miami and Florida, to win them all was unbelievable. Arguably, that 1989 team could have been the best, even though we finished 10–2.

We beat Miami 24–10 in Tallahassee during the 1989 season. [Miami quarterback] Gino Torretta threw an interception on the first play of the game, and then I got a great block and took it about 40 yards [37] around the corner for a touchdown. Even though the stadium was about 20,000 seats smaller than what it is now, I still have people tell me that's the loudest they've ever heard Doak Campbell Stadium.

254

I had 142 rushing yards in the first three quarters against Miami, but then I had the memorable flag on the helmet. Peter Tom Willis threw an interception, and I was going to make the tackle when Bernard Clark clipped me from behind. I saw the flag on the ground, and Clark was standing over me talking trash. Trust me, I couldn't have planned that play in my wildest dreams. Looking back on it, it was perfect; then it was just stupid.

I set the flag on Bernard Clark's head, just to let him know the flag was on him, and it stuck perfectly. I've always been a smart player, so when I put the flag on his head, I walked away. But what people fail to realize is that wasn't the end of it. There were three 15-yard penalties on the play: the clip, my putting the flag on his head, and another one on me. Leon Searcy came up to me, talking trash, and I was already upset at what I had done, so I jabbed him in the chest. They threw another 15-yard penalty on me. When I got to the sideline, Coach Bowden looked at me and said, "Hey, buddy, what are you doing?" Coach Bowden benched me in the third quarter and I could have had 200 yards in that game.

Not being able to get past Miami those first three years was difficult. Having an in-state school stop you from reaching your goals was difficult. But the big thing was, we wanted to win Coach Bowden's first national championship. We were heartbroken. But being national runner-up in 1987 and

No. 3 in 1988 were both great accomplishments. It allowed Coach Bowden to keep building on the program he had worked so hard to build. I just wish we could have gotten by Miami. We got by Florida during those three years, but we couldn't get by Miami. Even when we did beat Miami in 1989, they still won the national championship.

When I got to the San Francisco 49ers after college, everything from practice to what the thought process was in the building was about excellence. If you lost a game, it really was heartbreaking. All we knew was we needed to get back on the field as soon as possible and win another game. That's the same thing I experienced at Florida State. We didn't realize at the time that we were doing something that would probably never be repeated, but we were prepared for every game, regardless if it was a small school or a big school.

I look back and I'm proud that we were able to set a standard and tradition. The younger guys who came after us knew they were being held to a standard. I think that's what we lost over the last couple of years. When I went to the 49ers, nobody had to sit you down and say, "This is how we do things." From a player's perspective, all you had to do was watch Joe Montana, Jerry Rice, and Roger Craig. All you had to do was watch their work ethic. We talked about finishing so much that it became a habit.

255

That's the kind of work ethic and standard we're trying to establish at Florida State now. When kids come into my office, they see all these plaques and awards on the walls. When they come into my office, I want them to know I played at the same school they're at, and I faced the same emotional, educational, and physical challenges they're facing. Then I want them to see the next step of what they can do. I came to Florida State at 150 pounds and played in the NFL at 175 pounds. I don't think I was the best athlete, but I believe I maximized my abilities, and that's what I'm trying to teach them.

But the biggest thing I want them to know is I have a bachelor's degree and a master's degree. I want them to know that everybody comes here with a dream to play in the NFL, but at some point it's going to end, whether it's going to be after college, after one season in the NFL, or after seven seasons in the league. As soon as my last year in the NFL ended, I came back the next available term and finished my bachelor's degree. I try to tell them not to make football their lives because at some point it will end.

Dexter Carter, a native of Baxley, Georgia, was a star running back and kick returner for Florida State from 1986 to 1989. Carter led the Seminoles in rushing as a senior in 1989 with 684 yards and eight touchdowns. When Carter left FSU in 1989, he was the school's eighth-leading rusher with 1,788 career yards on 327 carries. He still ranks 12th in career rushing yards, and his 17 career touchdowns rank eighth in FSU history. As a freshman in 1986, Carter returned a kickoff 100 yards for a touchdown against Miami, which still ranks as the longest in school history. Carter was drafted in the first round of the 1990 NFL draft by the San Francisco 49ers and played his first five seasons there. He played one season for the New York Jets in 1995, before finishing his pro career with the 49ers for two seasons. He won five NFC West titles and Super Bowl XXIX while playing in San Francisco. Prior to the 2007 season, Carter was named running backs coach at Florida State. He and his wife, Jennifer, have four children and live in Tallahassee.

# LAWRENCE DAWSEY

## WIDE RECEIVER

### 1986–1990

I ATTENDED NORTHVIEW HIGH SCHOOL IN DOTHAN, Alabama, and I was recruited by North Carolina State, Memphis, Southern Mississippi, and Florida State. Alabama and Auburn were recruiting me, but they pulled their scholarships during my senior season. I broke my arm as a senior and didn't play that much, and I was too slow for Alabama and Auburn.

But I wouldn't have gone to Alabama or Auburn, anyway, Auburn was still running the wishbone with Bo Jackson and Brent Fullwood. Alabama was running a pro-style offense with Ray Perkins, but they weren't throwing the ball as much as Florida State. I went to Florida State because they were throwing the ball and because of Coach Bowden. He was a Christian coach, and I was raised in a Christian home, so that was important to my mother.

Florida State was the closest school to Dothan, about an hour and a half away, so that was important, too. I have seven brothers and three sisters, and I wanted my family to be able to get to me easily. I couldn't have made a better decision. The best decision I ever made in my life was coming to Florida State.

I never came to Florida State for a camp or anything before I made my official visit. But I'd been watching them play on TV. Coach Mickey Andrews, who recruited me, was from Ozark, Alabama, and my high school coach played with Coach Andrews at the University of Alabama. They knew each other, so it was just a good fit.

Wide receiver Lawrence Dawsey was named a first team All-American after leading Florida State with 65 catches for 999 yards and seven touchdowns in 1990.

I came to Florida State in 1986 and was redshirted. I played with four different quarterbacks here. Each one of them was different, but I really didn't have to make an adjustment. We ran our routes so precisely and our timing was so much the same throughout the four seasons I played. Even with a different quarterback, we knew our steps and knew where we were supposed to be. We practiced so much with each of those quarterbacks during the spring and summer that it really wasn't that much of an adjustment.

Danny McManus was the quarterback during my redshirt freshman season. McManus was a great quarterback. I think he could have played in the NFL if he hadn't had all those concussions. He was the type of quarterback that when he got in the huddle, he had complete control. The guys believed in him all the way down to his last game in the Fiesta Bowl against Nebraska.

The 1987 team was probably the most complete team I played on as far as coming together. I think we came together that season and really started what was the dynasty. Everybody contributed, whether you were a freshman, sophomore, junior, or senior. We knew if we went out and competed, we could beat any team in the country.

In 1987 Herb Gainer was really the only upperclassman who started besides the guys who were the "Fab Four." Ronald Lewis was the fastest receiver we had. Terry Anthony had the best hands. I think I probably ran the best routes. Bruce LaSane was the other part of the "Fab Four," and he was another great receiver.

We finished the 1987 season with an 11–1 record. We lost to Miami and we were ahead 19–3 before they came back on us. We went for the two-point conversion instead of kicking the extra point for the tie. But we all wanted to go for the win. If we would have tied that game, I believe we would have won the national championship instead of Miami. On the two-point conversion, McManus kind of locked in on Pat Carter, the tight end, and Ronald Lewis was open in the back of the end zone. That play was a heartbreaker when they tipped and knocked the ball down. It shouldn't have come down to that play.

259

We opened the 1988 season against Miami, and they embarrassed us 31–0. We were preseason No. 1 and they made that Seminole rap video. But Jimmy Johnson had Miami motivated, and they were ready for us. They were like sharks going out for blood that first game, and we couldn't seem to do anything right. But after that game, we came back and regrouped. We had a lot of big-time athletes on that team with Deion Sanders and Sammie Smith, the kind of guys you can lean on to get the job done.

Chip Ferguson was our quarterback in 1988. He didn't have the strongest arm, so everything had to be timing with him. You had to run precise routes. He was a smart quarterback and put the ball in position where only the receivers could make the catch. He had confidence in his receivers that we weren't going to let the defense make a play on the ball. After losing to Miami in the 1988 opener, we won our last 11 games and finished 11–1. We beat Auburn 13–7 in the Sugar Bowl.

We had another great team in 1989. We opened the season against Southern Mississippi, and nobody knew their quarterback, a guy named Brett Favre. We made too many mistakes and they had a great game plan. We kept waiting on them to fold, and they never did. We'd beaten them so badly the year before [Florida State beat Southern Miss 49–13 in 1988] that they were just waiting for us. We ended up losing that game 30–26.

We played Clemson the following week, and we knew that was going to be a tough game. Terry Allen was their tailback, and they had some great athletes. We lost the game 34–23, and to go 0–2 was a complete shock. Even then, though, the guys who were sitting in that locker room said, "We're not going out like this. We've got to get it together."

We ended up winning our last 10 games that season and beat Miami 24–10. We beat Nebraska 41–17 in the Fiesta Bowl. The team rallied around Peter Tom Willis because he was a great quarterback. The defense started making plays, with LeRoy Butler stepping in and replacing Deion at cornerback. We had a great freshman come in on defense, Terrell Buckley, who was a great punt returner. Everything just started coming together. Even after we were 0–2, the coaches did a great job of keeping us motivated. We knew we had as much talent as everyone else.

During my senior season in 1990, Brad Johnson started the first five games of the season. Then Casey Weldon came in and started the rest of the season. We were a young team going into 1990 and didn't have that many seniors. But we had a lot of young talent. We played at Miami early in the season, and I don't think the young guys were prepared for that kind of atmosphere. I could look at the young guys' eyes and see it, and I kept telling them, "Hey, they're only going to be as good as you let them be."

The Miami game was one of those games where I was just in a zone [Dawsey caught 13 passes for 160 yards in the Seminoles' 31–22 victory in the Orange Bowl]. I didn't care who was covering me—if the ball was in the air, it was my ball. We went 1–3 against Miami during my career, and we should have at least gone 2–2 against them. They had great players like Michael Irvin, Brett Perriman, and Steve Walsh.

I had another big game against Florida, which was my last regular season game at Doak Campbell Stadium. It was a great way to go out. On the second play of the game, Casey and I hooked up on a 76-yarder down the right sideline. They had two All-Americans, Will White and Richard Fain, and both of them bit on Casey's pump fake. He just threw a great ball down the sideline and it seemed like it hung up there forever. I was just waiting for it to come down. It worked out and it was a great call. We knew how aggressive they were.

I'll never forget during my senior season, Coach Bowden came up to me on the sideline and said, "Dawsey, this is your drive." He probably called four or five straight passes to me, and I took the team right down the field. It gave me an opportunity to be an All-American that year. He just kept throwing me the ball.

To have an opportunity to come back to Florida State as a coach is a great opportunity. I see it as a blessing and a dream come true. I always wanted to come back to my alma mater and be a coach. I never thought it would happen. But when Coach Bowden called me and offered me the opportunity, it was something I couldn't turn down. I was fortunate to have played for a legend and now I'm coaching for a legend. It's truly an honor because, of all the people he could have considered for the position, he chose me. He told me I was the guy he wanted because he knew the type of guy I was and what I could do.

Coach Bowden is a great guy and he's well respected, but I know he doesn't like to lose and still has the fight to win. He's leaving it to us to get the program back to the top. With the coaching staff he's put together, I know we're going to get it back to where it belongs.

Lawrence Dawsey, a native of Dothan, Alabama, was a star wide receiver for the Seminoles from 1987 to 1990. As a senior in 1990, Dawsey was named first team All-American by the Associated Press after leading Florida State with 65 receptions for 999 yards and seven touchdowns. He also led FSU in receiving as a junior with 38 catches or 683 yards and four touchdowns. He finished his college career with 128 receptions for 2,129 yards, both of which currently rank eighth in school history. Dawsey was a third-round choice of the Tampa Bay Buccaneers in 1991 and was named *Sports Illustrated*'s NFL Rookie of the Year after leading the Bucs with 55 catches for 818 yards in his first pro season. He also led the Buccaneers in receptions in 1992 and 1994. Dawsey also played for the NFL's New York Giants, and New Orleans Saints before retiring after the 1999 season. Dawsey started his coaching career as a graduate assistant at LSU during the Tigers' 2003 national championship season, then worked three seasons as receivers coach at South Florida. He was named Florida State's receivers coach prior to the 2007 season. Dawsey and his wife, Chantel, have one son, Lawrence Jr., and they live in Tallahassee, Florida.

# The

# NINETIES

# CASEY WELDON

## QUARTERBACK
### 1987–1991

I GREW UP IN TALLAHASSEE and attended North Florida Christian School. The first college football games I went to had Jimmy Jordan and Wally Woodham playing quarterback for Florida State. Those guys were my heroes, with the way they were slinging it around. I'd go to the stadium and here "F-L-O-R-I-D-A-S-T-A-T-E!" echoing in the stands. I loved it.

We sold Cokes at the games as a fund-raiser for our football team. I remember when Pittsburgh and Dan Marino came into town and some of the other great games. Florida State was the team in town, and I didn't know any different. But growing up, I was actually a Georgia Bulldogs fan. I'm from Georgia and all my uncles and everybody were Bulldogs fans, and I grew up the biggest Herschel Walker fan. I had a chance to play with him with the Philadelphia Eagles later in life, and it was just a dream come true.

So when it came time to pick a college when I was being recruited, even though I loved the Bulldogs and Florida State was my second favorite team, it was a choice between Vince Dooley's offense and Coach Bowden's offense. It was a no-brainer, and Florida State was my number-one choice.

Brad Johnson and I got to Florida State in 1987. They told me Brad was probably just going to play basketball, and I'd probably have no competition from him. They told him I was just some little skinny kid from in town, who played at a local Christian school, and that I wasn't going to play much. When we got there, Danny McManus was coming off his injuries, Chip Ferguson had played as a freshman, and Peter Tom Willis was there.

Florida State went 11–1 in 1987 while we were being redshirted. Brad played basketball his first two years at Florida State, and we were scout team quarterbacks behind the older guys. In 1988 we got beat 31–0 by Miami in the opener. Coach Bowden didn't really have an audible system, and so [quarterbacks coach] Mark Richt said if we're not going to let Peter Tom use his brains and get out of bad plays, then we might as well have a better athlete back there.

I played a little bit against Southern Mississippi in the next game [a 49–13 victory], but I didn't play that well, and they put Peter Tom back ahead of me. Later that season, after Chip Ferguson got hurt, Peter Tom had a great game against South Carolina [a 59–0 win] and he was pretty well entrenched as the starter.

At Florida State back then, you just had to accept that the quarterbacks weren't going to play until their junior or senior seasons—at least I accepted it. We were all such good friends. Chip and Peter Tom used to play against Brad and I in tennis. We were all such competitors and good friends. It was tough. I remember after Peter Tom had a phenomenal game in the Fiesta Bowl [a 41–17 victory over Nebraska at the end of the 1989 season], I realized it was going to be Brad and me, going at it for the starting job the following season.

I went up to Brad on the bus and told him, "No matter what happens, I hope our friendship will never be affected by it." It was just accepted that you waited your turn. You always think you're going to be the guy, but with Brad and me, we weren't smart enough to think one guy was going to lose out. My daughter always asks me why I didn't let him play in college, so I could have played in the pros. It worked out pretty good for him, I think.

Brad started each of the first six games of the 1990 season. We lost to Miami [31–22] in the fifth game, and he started the next game against Auburn. Before that, I was going into the game and getting a series in the second quarter, whether it was three plays and out or a touchdown drive. I went into the game late against Miami and led us on a meaningless touchdown drive. But a lot of times coaches see what they want to see, so I guess it meant something.

Against Auburn, I think Brad threw an interception early in the game, and I think what got Brad in trouble after that was he was very conservative and

Casey Weldon grew up a University of Georgia football fan, but chose to play for Florida State after a stellar career at North Florida Christian High School in Tallahassee. After playing nine seasons in the NFL, he now coaches at North Florida Christian High School.

was dinking and dunking, which wasn't too much to Coach Bowden's delight. I was a guy who threw it down the field. I went into the Auburn game for my series at the end of the first quarter, and it was third down and eight on my first drive. Edgar Bennett made an unbelievable catch on the sideline for me on what was a pretty bad throw. It was just an unbelievable catch that kept the drive going, and we went down and scored. They left me in the game, and we went down and scored again. We lost the game 20–17, but I wound up having a pretty good game.

I started after that and won every game, until the first "Wide Right" against Miami the following year. My first start came against LSU the following week, and they turned the ball over twice on the kickoff. It was a great game in which to get your first start. Amp Lee was running the ball really well and scored early in the game, so we had a comfortable lead and won the game 42–3. We beat South Carolina 41–10 and beat Cincinnati 70–21. We played Memphis State in Orlando and won 35–3.

Three weeks later, we played Florida at home in Doak Campbell Stadium. We were going to throw a bomb on the first play of the game because Coach Bowden felt like their safety would bite on play-action. We missed on the first one, but I wasn't concerned about missing on two low-percentage passes. On second down, the bomb was there, and Lawrence Dawsey made a great catch for a 76-yard touchdown. It was a pretty fun game, and we won 45–30.

We finished the 1990 season by beating Penn State 24–17 in the Blockbuster Bowl. Penn State was probably the hardest-hitting team we played, and I had no idea Joe Paterno versus Bowden would be such a big deal. We had no idea what was coming with that matchup. It was the Blockbuster Bowl, and we weren't used to playing a bowl game that early, but it was a fun game.

In 1991 we opened the season playing against Brigham Young in the Pigskin Classic in Anaheim, California. Ty Detmer was their quarterback, and he'd won the Heisman Trophy the year before. I was excited about playing against him, and we were preseason No. 1. Having a team like we had, I was very excited about the season. There was a lot of motivation against BYU, and Detmer had dismantled Miami in what was a big upset the year before. We won the game 44–28, and it was good to get those guys.

We beat Tulane 38–11 and beat Western Michigan 58–0. Then we went to play at Michigan, and they had Desmond Howard, who was a receiver and kick returner. It was a huge game; we were No. 1 and they were No. 3. They said they were going to show us Big Ten football and they'd smash us. But we just had some great plays and the defense scored twice. Terrell Buckley intercepted a pass on the second play of the game and ran it back for a

267

touchdown, and Amp Lee just had a phenomenal game. Michigan was going to score before halftime, and Howard Dinkins intercepted a pass down near our goal line that really changed momentum. If Michigan had scored there, that game really could have been something. I got a shot of cortisone at half-time, after taking a shot to the ribs, but we came out and beat them pretty good in the second half.

We won the game 51–31, and it was a pretty quiet 100,000 people in Michigan Stadium. Years later, I saw a Michigan fan in the Bahamas wearing his Michigan T-shirt. I asked him what was the worst game he ever saw at Michigan, and he responded, "The Florida State game." I just kind of smiled and went on my way. It's still the most points ever scored by an opponent at Michigan Stadium, so I'm still pretty proud of that.

We went home and beat Syracuse 46–14 and beat Virginia Tech 33–20 in Orlando. We beat Middle Tennessee State 39–10, and were really rolling going into LSU. We went to LSU, and it was an absolute monsoon. It was the worst rain game I'd ever seen. It was unbelievable. I got hurt, Robbie Baker got hurt, Kevin Mancini got hurt, and a couple of other guys got hurt. We had five or six big injuries in the LSU game. We won the game 27–16, but I really feel like losing Mancini at our tackle position is what cost us in the Miami game.

We beat South Carolina 38–10 the following week, and everything was pointing toward that Miami game. We played them at home, and we were still ranked No. 1 and they were No. 2. Mancini tried to play but didn't last the whole game. We had the ball inside Miami's 10-yard line four times and scored 16 points. It was tough, and having a banged-up offensive line hurt us.

We got the ball back at the end of the Miami game and had plenty of time to go down and score. We just had to get into field-goal position. We had a third-down play, and Coach Richt called "68," which was a great call. We knew they were going to blitz us; we had a takeoff, and they jumped the hot route. If I could have back one throw in my career, it would probably be that one. I couldn't tell if the receiver was going inside or out, and I should have just thrown it to a spot and let him go get it. He wound up getting a pass interference penalty against Miami, but it should have been a touchdown pass, which would have ended the game right there.

We ended up having a chance at an easy field goal, and I thought it was good. That was the year they moved the goal posts in a foot and a-half on each side, and the kick just went right outside the right upright. It would have been good the year before. I thought the field goal at the end was good. I've had a pretty good life, but that's one of the worst things that has ever happened. It was tough.

We were done after that. We had nothing to play for after losing to Miami. We were an independent—we weren't in the ACC or the SEC—so there wasn't a conference championship to win. We had nothing to play for and had to play Florida in the last game of the season. During practice that week, I got hot with a couple of the receivers with the way they were practicing, but I knew we were done. Everything we were playing for was over, even though we were playing Florida.

I tell [former Gators defensive tackle] Brad Culpepper all the time that if I'd known the way they were going to celebrate like that after the game, we would have found a way to pull it out. We almost won the game. We had a fourth and nine at the end of the game and had a chance at a couple of throws in the end zone, but we lost the game 14–9. It was a hot day, and we were beat up and pretty much done.

We played Texas A&M in the Cotton Bowl after the 1991 season, and I think they had about eight or nine NFL first-rounders on that defense. Our defense just played unbelievably. I gave Texas A&M all their points when Quentin Coryatt tackled me in the end zone for a safety. We only scored 10 points, but our defense played unbelievably and won that game for us 10–2.

269

Desmond Howard won the Heisman Trophy in 1991, and I finished second. Going up to New York and being in the Downtown Athletic Club was a neat experience. I had friends who were doing "Casey for Heisman" kind of stuff, but we were just so focused on winning the national championship. I never even realized the importance of it until O.J. Simpson said, "Once you win the Heisman, you're like royalty. You're forever introduced as 'Heisman Trophy winner' then your name." It was cool to be there and just be a part of it. It was special.

Coach Bowden really had a knack for play-calling. It was neat to see how he attacked teams from a football standpoint. From a personal standpoint, he was just always an absolute gentleman. He loves what he does and loves being around his players. I hope he can stay healthy and keep going for another 10 years.

Casey Weldon, a homegrown product from Tallahassee, Florida, was Florida State's starting quarterback for much of 1990 and 1991. As a senior, Weldon completed 189 of 313 passes for 2,527 yards and 22 touchdowns. He led the Seminoles to an 11–2 record, beating Texas A&M 10–2 in the Cotton Bowl, and to a fourth-place finish in the Associated Press top 25 poll. Weldon finished second to Michigan receiver/kick returner Desmond Howard in voting for the 1991 Heisman Trophy and won the 1991 Johnny Unitas Golden Arm Award as the country's top quarterback. Weldon was named a second-team All-American by the Associated Press after his senior season and was a first-team selection by the Walter Camp Foundation and *Football News*. He was a fourth-round draft choice of the Philadelphia Eagles in the 1992 NFL draft and played nine seasons with the Eagles, Tampa Bay Buccaneers, San Diego Chargers, and Washington Redskins. He was inducted into the FSU Sports Hall of Fame in 1999. Weldon lives in Tallahassee, Florida, and is an assistant football coach at North Florida Christian School, his alma mater.

# BRAD JOHNSON

## QUARTERBACK

## 1988–1991

I WENT TO CHARLES OWEN HIGH SCHOOL in Black Mountain, North Carolina, and graduated in 1987. I was being recruited by Alabama, Florida State, North Carolina, and Georgia Tech to play football. Basketball was always my first love, but at that time, Georgia Tech had signed Dennis Scott on its basketball team. I was just bound and determined to play basketball. When they signed Dennis Scott, I knew I had to make a football decision. I thought I had more room to grow as a football player than a basketball player and had a better chance to reach the next level in football.

Florida State was kind of on the rise in football at the time. It was a top-10 program and was going to major bowl games every year. I thought the coaching staff was in a stable position, so I wouldn't have to go through firings and hirings and all that. I thought Tallahassee was a place I'd want to live after I graduated.

I got to Florida State in 1987 and sat behind Danny McManus, Peter Tom Willis, and Chip Ferguson. I was redshirted that season and didn't play much in 1988 or 1989, either. At that time, if you were playing quarterback at Florida State, you almost had to wait until your senior season to play. It was just kind of what was expected at that time. I ended up playing basketball my first two years at Florida State but was missing a little bit of spring football practice and a little bit of the beginning of basketball season. I knew I still had to make a major decision as to which sport I was going to play.

A ninth-round draft choice by the Minnesota Vikings in 1992, Brad Johnson has thrown for more than 28,000 yards with 164 touchdowns in 13 seasons with the Vikings, Washington Redskins, and Tampa Bay Buccaneers. He led Tampa Bay to a 48–21 victory over the Oakland Raiders in Super Bowl XXXVII.

Casey Weldon and I were juniors in 1990. I started the first couple of games in 1990, and then Casey came in and played the next year and a half. That was basically the end of my career at Florida State. There was so much competition at Florida State, and people don't understand how competitive it was. Danny McManus retired from the Canadian Football League in 2007. Peter Tom Willis played in the NFL for four years, and Casey played in the pros for nine years. Charlie Ward came in as a freshman when I was there, and Chris Weinke actually came in when we were juniors.

There was just so much competition between all of us. You didn't realize how good players really were until after they left Florida State. I feel like we all made each other better, but at the same time, we all kind of took playing time away from each other. Now you're seeing kids start as freshmen and sophomores, and they're getting to play for three or four years. At Florida State at that time, we were only getting to play one or two years.

Mark Richt was my quarterbacks coach. We had a great relationship and I really respected him from the first day. He was a graduate assistant when I got there, and then he became quarterbacks coach and was calling a lot of the plays in the passing game. Brad Scott was the offensive coordinator and was calling a lot of the running plays. I feel like they really just gave us a true understanding of football and helped us in every aspect.

I started the first five games of the 1990 season and got replaced by Casey in the sixth game, after we lost to Miami 31–22. I didn't think I deserved to be benched when you actually looked at the numbers and production we'd had. But it was a decision they made and it was one that worked out well for Florida State and Casey Weldon. He played great and was the Heisman Trophy runner-up the following season. He played tremendously, and you can't fault the decision they made. I didn't feel like I'd done anything wrong; it was just the decision they made.

After the 1990 season, I had a few decisions to make. I thought about transferring to a Division I-AA school so I could play right away and wouldn't lose any of my eligibility. I thought about declaring for the NFL draft or maybe going to the Canadian Football League. I thought about playing one more season of basketball and just quitting football altogether. But it came back to the same reason I chose Florida State and gave up basketball at Florida State, and I wanted to finish my football career and give myself a chance to play in the pros. I thought I might be a late-bloomer because of the time I spent playing basketball. I just said I was going to give myself one more season of playing football and maybe something good would happen.

I started only one game my senior year in 1991, after Casey got hurt. Casey and I, and Mark Brunell and Billy Joe Hobert [who were teammates at Washington] were the only quarterbacks to ever come out of the same school in the same year, get drafted, and make an NFL roster in the same year. It's a unique situation for both Casey and me to have made it and actually have careers.

Casey and I were best friends, and it was a hardship on our friendship, but we respected each other and rooted for each other. It was just tough. The way it went at Florida State, there was always a year where the quarterback was able to play his senior season. That was the first time in a long, long time that there were two senior quarterbacks in the same year, maybe since Jimmy Jordan and Wally Woodham in the 1970s. Basically, I felt like I took a half-year away from Casey being the starter, and he took a year and a half away from me. But we pushed each other in practice and were the best of friends.

Coach Bowden always preached that practices would be much harder than the games because of the competition level. It really was when you're out there facing Deion Sanders and Terrell Buckley and Marvin Jones. It was unbelievable. More than anything, Coach Bowden was up-front with you and gave you opportunities. I thought he had great vision of players in recruiting guys and where they could go. I thought he had a great vision with coaches in assembling his staff. We played for some great coaches at Florida State.

During my senior season in 1991, we were ranked the No. 1 team in the country the whole year. Then we lost at Miami 17–16 in the next-to-last game of the regular season. It was the first "Wide Right" [kicker Gerry Thomas missed a 34-yard field goal wide right at the end of the game]. It hurt because you just don't get many opportunities to win a national championship. We were a very good team, and, two weeks prior to that, we'd beaten LSU 27–16 in Baton Rouge. We had a bunch of injuries to a lot of starters on the team, so the LSU game really hurt us more than anything. We lost the Miami game, and it hurt because you don't get many chances to go undefeated. I think if we'd won that Miami game, Casey would have won the Heisman Trophy. [Michigan kick returner/receiver Desmond Howard won the Heisman Trophy in 1991.]

After leaving FSU, I was drafted in the ninth round of the 1992 NFL draft by the Minnesota Vikings. I actually thought the New York Giants were going to draft me. I thought New York would have been the best place for me. Phil Simms was getting older, and Jeff Hostetler was at the same age. The Giants had talked to me a bunch and worked me out, but they drafted [Ohio State quarterback] Kent Graham in the eighth round. Then they took [Duke quarterback] Dave Brown in the supplemental draft that summer and took four quarterbacks into training camp. So sometimes things are a blessing in disguise.

After the Giants didn't select me in the draft, I didn't think I'd get picked by any team. I thought the Giants were my best shot, and I could have been the third quarterback there and could kind of be groomed. I had a degree in education and thought I'd go back and be a school teacher. But the Vikings drafted me in the ninth round, and I ended up making the roster. I didn't play much at all during my first three seasons with the Vikings. Rich Gannon was the starter, and then Jim McMahon and Warren Moon came in. I was a late-bloomer and was just learning the game and becoming better as a pure passer. I was getting better and better and went to the World League and started 10 games. I actually played more over there than I did during my entire college career.

I always believed it was better to be prepared and not have an opportunity than to have an opportunity and not be prepared. During my fifth season with the Vikings, Warren Moon got hurt and I got an opportunity to play. I ran off with things and have been playing ever since. I won a Super Bowl title with the Tampa Bay Buccaneers in 2002. That was really a great experience. There have only been about 25 quarterbacks who have won a Super Bowl and to have your name among some of the all-time greats is special. That was definitely the highlight of my NFL career.

When I went to the NFL, I was just hoping to make a team and was almost ready to give up and go back to teaching. To be drafted and make a team and sustain that kind of career is just really incredible. I've been very fortunate. I never gave in to the circumstance, whether it was being a backup or being labeled a certain way. I've just never given in, and six of the seven coaches I've played for have had winning records. I just keep working at it, that's the bottom line.

I appreciate the hardships I've gone through. It made me tough in different ways, and I have a passion to play the game. Sometimes, things don't work out for different reasons. I just know that I was a worker, and things usually work out for people if you give yourself a chance.

Brad Johnson, a native of Black Mountain, North Carolina, started six games at quarterback during two seasons at Florida State, from 1990 to 1991. He played two seasons of basketball for the Seminoles, then spent much of the 1987, 1988, and 1989 seasons as a backup quarterback on the football team. Johnson started five games in 1990 and one game in 1991, when FSU finished 11–2 and beat Texas A&M 10–2 in the Cotton Bowl. He was drafted by the Minnesota Vikings in the ninth round of the 1992 NFL draft and has played the last 13 seasons with the Vikings, Washington Redskins, and Tampa Bay Buccaneers. Johnson signed a free agent contract with the Dallas Cowboys before the 2007 season. Johnson, a two-time Pro Bowl selection, threw for more than 28,000 yards with 164 touchdowns in his first 13 pro seasons. He led the Tampa Bay Buccaneers to a 48–21 victory over the Oakland Raiders in Super Bowl XXXVII. Johnson lives in Athens, Georgia, during the off-season.

# TERRELL BUCKLEY

## CORNERBACK

## 1989–1991

I WAS FROM PASCAGOULA HIGH SCHOOL in Mississippi. I was a *Parade* All-American and was getting recruiting letters from everybody. My final choices were Clemson, Auburn, LSU, and Florida State. The main reason I chose Florida State was because Mickey Andrews, the defensive coordinator and defensive backs coach, was recruiting me, and when I looked at their TV schedule, Florida State was on TV every week. Back then, if you were on TV five or six times a year, that was a lot.

I got to Florida State in 1989, and Deion Sanders had just left. Obviously, you saw what a guy like Deion was doing there, and it influenced you. You wondered if your game matched his game. I felt like my game was different, even though we played the same position. With the attention and what he brought to college football, I loved him. I actually got a chance to meet him before I went to Florida State. I'd driven over to the Senior Bowl in Mobile, Alabama, and was able to talk to him after the game.

The media in Mississippi had started calling me "Baby Deion." I played in the inaugural Mississippi–Alabama High School All-Star Game, and they did a big story on me going to Florida State, and the announcers were comparing me to the player they called "Prime Time." They hadn't started calling Florida State "Cornerback U" yet, but you knew the defensive backs were going to get a lot of attention there because of what Deion had been able to do.

I really liked Coach Bowden. He was already a legend by then. When you looked and listened to him, you couldn't help believe what he was saying because he was saying it with such conviction. It was almost like being in awe of the guy. It was like, *Wow! Is he actually talking to me and wanting me to come to Florida State?* It was kind of unbelievable. I've got to give a lot of credit to one of my high school coaches, the defensive coordinator, Jamie Kelly, who was a mentor of mine. He put the thing in motion when we went to Florida State's summer camp before my senior season of high school.

I was the MVP of the FSU summer camp, and I didn't know it at the time, but they felt like they had the best of the best talent at their camps. So if you could outperform the other guys at their camp, you were obviously going to be at the top of their recruiting list. I had a great opportunity to talk to Coach Bowden and really get to know him and Coach Andrews. After that camp, they were like, "We don't even need to see anymore. You're coming here." I was sold on FSU at that point, and I was going to Florida State no matter what. It was mind-boggling to me.

I went to Florida State before the 1989 season and was playing behind LeRoy Butler at cornerback. He was the guy who showed me around when I visited Florida State. He was my host during the recruiting visit. I played behind LeRoy that first season, but on third downs, I went into the game and played left cornerback. Errol McCorvey was the other cornerback, but as the season went on, I started playing a lot at boundary corner, which was the tough, run-stopping cornerback.

We opened the 1989 season against Southern Mississippi, and I still can't believe we lost that game 30–26. Brett Favre was their quarterback, and he made a lot of plays for his team and did a wonderful job. Being from Mississippi, I knew who he was. I was a fan of Brett Favre. At that time, nobody knew how good Brett Favre was going to be. I had a decent day returning punts, and a couple of our best players didn't play in the game because they didn't make weight. That was my first introduction to big-time college football, and I learned that there were consequences for your actions. No matter how good you were, even if you were an All-American coming back, if you didn't meet certain criteria, there were consequences to face. Not having those guys obviously hurt us in the game, and we ended up losing.

We played Clemson the following week and lost that game 34–23. I had another good day returning punts, but we were still reeling from the previous week. Coach Bowden gave us one of those great speeches after the game.

Cornerback Terrell Buckley is considered one of the greatest defensive backs in college football history with 21 career interceptions at Florida State. During his career, Buckley returned three punts for touchdowns and his 470 career punt return yards broke an NCAA record that had stood since 1974. His 501 yards in interception return yards also established an NCAA record.

It wasn't the kind of speech I was used to. There wasn't a lot of cursing and stomping and screaming. It was just a challenge to us, from a competitor to a competitor. With our backs against the wall, he wanted to know what kind of character we were going to show. It was a great speech and we went on a roll. We won at LSU 31–21 the following week, and it was huge.

It was rolling after that. We beat Tulane 59–9, Syracuse 41–10, and Virginia Tech 41–7. The Syracuse game kind of put me on the map as a player. I had a long punt return for a touchdown in that game. [Buckley caught a punt and stopped as if he had called for a fair catch, fooling the Orangemen's coverage team, then ran 69 yards for a touchdown.] Here it is, 17 years later, and people are still talking about the play I made in that game. Coach Bowden called me the "Foolah from Pascagoula" after the game.

It was a play that I had seen in high school. I think it was the third time Syracuse had punted, and I had never played on artificial turf. I didn't realize the speed of the game on turf, so guys were getting on top of me very, very quickly. I couldn't move to get behind the walls, and I knew if I could get to the outside wall I had a chance to make a big play. Before I went out on the field, I knew I had to slow those guys down to give myself an opportunity to get to the wall. We had a great blocking team on punt returns. I caught it and stood there, and the Syracuse guys slowed down. One guy even walked right beside me. I counted in my head, "One-thousand-one, one-thousand-two, one-thousand-three," and once I started running, Corian Freeman, another one of our cornerbacks, cleaned up the guy who wasn't hustling. Once he did that, it was just a foot race and clear sailing to the end zone.

We played Auburn at home, and both teams were ranked in the top 10. It was Auburn and it was a huge game. Even though it was one of the biggest games of the year, it wasn't quite as big as playing Miami or Florida for most of the guys. But along with playing LSU, it was one of the biggest games for me. They had Alexander Wright, who was a really good receiver, and Reggie Slack was their quarterback.

It was a really big challenge for us to continue our winning streak. That was one thing I really loved about Coach Bowden; he never shied away from top competition. He had this old saying, "We'll play them anywhere, any place, any time." It didn't matter to us. If you look at the schedule before Florida State went to the ACC, that was what we did. We had momentum before that Auburn game, but after we won 22–14, it was like we got a shot of adrenaline in the arm. We were just so confident after that game. It was a tough and physical football game.

We beat Miami 24–10 that season. Miami won the national championship later that year, and we felt like since we beat Miami, we should have been the national champs. We won our final 10 games that season and at least should have had an opportunity to play for it. That Miami game in 1989 was one of the greatest games I ever played in. I played in a lot of games where there was energy and electricity, but that particular game was unbelievable. There were probably 20 or 30 guys who were picked in the first couple of rounds in the

NFL draft who played in that game. I'll never forget that game. Miami's receivers were Wesley Carroll, Randal Hill, and Lamar Thomas; and Craig Erickson was the quarterback. They had a lot of speed, and I was covering Thomas and Carroll.

We beat Nebraska 41–17 in the Fiesta Bowl after the 1989 season, and it was a really exciting game. Nebraska jumped out on us and had a 7–0 lead in the first quarter. Coach Andrews made some great adjustments; he probably made the best adjustments of any coach I ever played for, even after playing in the NFL for 14 years. He made some adjustments to take advantage of our speed, and our offense started clicking. Lawrence Dawsey took over the game at wide receiver, and we just pounded them after that. We did a little bit of everything in that game. John Davis, one of my fellow freshmen, blocked a punt in that game. It was a big win, and it really started taking off for us after that.

The following season, we were still rolling and beat East Carolina 45–24, Georgia Southern 48–6, Tulane 31–13, and Virginia Tech 39–28 to start the season. We had a 4–0 record going into the Miami game. We were ranked No. 2 in the country, and they were No. 9. What I remember about that game is I had a high ankle sprain. When you're not healthy, you can deal with not performing. I had a good game tackling, but not being healthy really disappointed me because there were some opportunities for me to make plays that could have helped us. We lost the game 31–22.

We lost to Auburn the next week 20–17. It was another great game. In my three years at Florida State, all of our losses were close. There were two stadiums I played in that were just loud and pandemonium: Jordan-Hare Stadium at Auburn and Florida Field in Gainesville. We wore all white uniforms at Auburn that season. That was the last time we wore those uniforms, too.

We finished 10-2 in 1990 and played Penn State in the Blockbuster Bowl. It wasn't the biggest bowl game, but it was a great matchup of coaches. It was a great opportunity to play a great program like Penn State. How many guys got opportunities to play the teams we played? We won the game 24–17, and it was a great ending to what was a pretty good season.

During my junior season in 1991, we opened the season playing BYU in the Pigskin Classic in Anaheim, California. We won that game and beat Ty Detmer 44–28. We beat Tulane 38–11 and blew out Western Michigan 58–0. Everything was setting up for a game at Michigan, and we were 3–0. Michigan had Desmond Howard and Elvis Grbac, the quarterback. They were calling it "The Game of the Century." You could play 1,000 games in your career, and that's one of those games you'll never forget. Going up to Michigan, our goal was to have 100,000 people sitting on their hands. We were No. 1 and they were ranked No. 3. There was the Desmond Howard versus Terrell Buckley matchup. It was size versus speed. Michigan was big, and we were fast.

We went in, and it was kind of the same thing that happened against Nebraska. I picked off one of Elvis Grbac's passes on the second play of the game and ran it back for a touchdown. I leaped into the stands after scoring, kind of like the "Lambeau Leap." The game went back and forth for a while in the first half. Then Coach Andrews came into the locker room at halftime and told us he was throwing out the entire game plan. He said we were going to blitz them and blitz them. When they got tired of that, we were going to blitz them some more. It was great. [The Seminoles beat Michigan 51–31.] I already had the utmost respect for Coach Andrews and Coach Bowden, but I left that game with even more respect for them. It started at the top, and when the head coach has enough confidence in his players to make plays when everything is at stake, it was unbelievable. It was kind of like the way Coach Bowden scheduled games. A lot of coaches wouldn't schedule games against Nebraska, BYU, and Michigan. But Coach Bowden wasn't afraid to play those games.

We were 10–0 going into the Miami game and had been ranked No. 1 in the country the entire season. We drove up and down the field against Miami and controlled both sides of the ball. We did everything we were supposed to do against Miami—except win the ball game. It was the first "Wide Right," and it was the most disappointing loss of my career. It's a memory I want to let go, but I still can't forget it. I thought that was the best team I'd ever been a part of. I thought that 1991 team rivaled the New England Patriots team I was a part of that won the Super Bowl. We had as much talent, confidence, and depth as that New England Patriots team. I still can't believe we lost in 1991. We should have gone undefeated, and it shouldn't have even been close.

But we lost to Miami and had a hangover the following game against Florida. That's how bad that Miami loss hurt. You can have a hangover and really be hurting, but you've still got a job to do. You can hurt after the season. We didn't do our job against Florida and lost the game 14–9.

We came back and beat Texas A&M 10–2 in the Cotton Bowl. Texas A&M had the "Wrecking Crew" defense. We were playing in Texas and we

282

were at a luncheon, and all they were talking about was the Texas A&M defense. I think that helped us to get over the Miami and Florida losses. We left the luncheon thinking, *We know we've got a great defense.* We'd been one of the best teams in the country for a long, long time. We wanted to go out and end the season the right way. They had a safety, and that was the only points they scored. It was a classic defensive battle.

That 1991 team was special. We had so many talented players: Kirk Carruthers, Amp Lee, Edgar Bennett, Casey Weldon, Kez McCorvey, Lonnie Johnson, Marvin Jones, Derrick Brooks, and Clifton Abraham. We had so many talented guys out there.

Right after the Cotton Bowl, I declared myself eligible for the NFL draft. I was the fifth pick in the draft and was selected by the Green Bay Packers. I played 14 seasons in the NFL and won a Super Bowl with the New England Patriots. I played in a lot of big games and feel really blessed to have done what I've done. It started with the decision that Florida State made in giving me an opportunity to come play football there. People still remember all the things I did at Florida State, and I think it was just a great match with me. I've very honored and humbled to have played there.

Terrell Buckley, a native of Pascagoula, Mississippi, was a star cornerback and punt returner for the Seminoles from 1989 to 1991. He is considered one of the top playmakers in college football history, with an FSU record 21 interceptions during his career. Buckley was named a consensus All-American and won the Jim Thorpe Award as the country's top defensive back as a junior in 1991. He led the country with 12 interceptions in 1991 and intercepted a pass in eight of FSU's 12 games. In a 51–31 victory at Michigan, Buckley intercepted a pass on the first play from scrimmage and returned it 40 yards for a touchdown. During his career, Buckley also returned three punts for touchdowns and his 470 career punt return yards broke an NCAA record that had stood since 1974. His 501 yards in interception return yards also established an NCAA record. Buckley was inducted into the FSU Hall of Fame in 2003. He was the fifth selection in the 1992 NFL draft by the Green Bay Packers and played 14 seasons in the NFL with the Packers, Miami Dolphins, Denver Broncos, New England Patriots, and New York Jets. Buckley was part of the 2001 Patriots team that won Super Bowl XXXVI. He has returned to Florida State to finish his degree and lives in Tallahassee, Florida.

# KEZ McCORVEY
## WIDE RECEIVER
### 1991–1994

I FIRST STARTED PLAYING FOOTBALL IN EIGHTH GRADE, and when I got to high school in Pascagoula, Mississippi, we won the state championship. My football coach was Steve Mathews—he had a son named Shane Mathews, who quarterbacked at the University of Florida—and we went to football camp at Florida State every summer. That was the first football camp I had ever been to; the first time I had been to Tallahassee. I became a fan at that moment.

I wanted to be up on that top practice field with all the seniors. I was an upcoming junior and I wanted to be up there with those guys like [high school teammate] Terrell Buckley. The next year he signed with Florida State. I was excited about being with Florida State.

I remember Florida State being on TV at Clemson and Deion [Sanders] throwing his hands up in the air and taking the punt back for a touchdown. I was the biggest Seminole fan in the whole world. The next year I remember watching the guys play against Miami.

For me, Florida State was the only scholarship in the whole world, at least that's what it seemed like. I didn't get on the radar until I went to that football camp. Terrell was telling the coaches, "You've got a pretty good receiver over here." I was the 275th-ranked receiver in the whole state of Mississippi, it seemed like.

It was motivation. I went there to make the team; I needed to make the squad. I didn't go up there to learn anything or pick up any new moves. I went up there for the sole purpose of showing those coaches I could play. It was extra motivation for me because they had the number-one receiver in the nation, the number-three receiver, the number-one defensive back—all those people there at the same time.

I went there with a chip on my shoulder with a purpose to show these guys I could play football. I ran a 4.5 [seconds in the 40-yard dash] on the track, and I tore up every guy that was in front of me. After camp [wide receivers] coach John Eason came up to me and said, "Kez McCorvey, you've got a scholarship if you want it." It was like—job done. That's how the process went for me. I went to camp and tried out and showed them what I could do, that I could play at Florida State.

My first memory is playing BYU at the beginning of the 1991 season. I remember getting in the game and being so excited. Before the 1991 season started, I was the starter, but I got injured. I got a hip-pointer, and Coach Eason said, "Kez, you've never started here before and, if you were a veteran, I would just put you back in the starting spot." He put me down on the third team. What happened in the game, a couple of guys dropped balls. I think Matt Frier dropped a couple balls, and then Shannon Baker dropped a couple balls, and all of a sudden I'm starting again.

I caught two passes. I've always been a guy with a bunch of moves. When I caught one, instead of going up-field trying to make yards, I tried to cut back behind everybody and got tackled and lost about two yards. I remember going back to practice and having to run, like, 50 times, catching the ball and running up the field.

I have one of those crazy mentalities about football. I always look at the game and think I should have done something better. The best memory I have was my first touchdown catch in the 1992 opener. I actually had three in one game. We played Duke—everybody needs a Duke in their life—and the first time I touched the ball on a catch, it was about 25 yards. The next time I touched the ball it was a touchdown. And the next time I touched the ball it was a touchdown, and the same thing happened the time after that. For me, that was the most exciting.

The year before [in 1991] I caught 22 balls for 300-some yards but didn't get any touchdowns. I was close a couple of times, but it was like the end zone rejected me—"You can't come in." To catch three touchdowns in the first game of 1992 was like freedom to me. It took the monkey off my shoulders and just allowed me to go out and play football and not care about

285

Wide receiver Kez McCorvey was a key member of the 1993 FSU team that finished 12–1 and beat Nebraska 18–16 in the Orange Bowl to win the national championship. McCorvey's 74 catches in 1993 still rank as second-most in a single season by an FSU receiver and his 189 career receptions are third-most in school history.

how many catches I got or what people thought about me. [Quarterback] Casey [Weldon] didn't get me in the end zone in 1991. These were from Charlie Ward.

The whole thing about the 1993 season was really not about winning the national championship game, it was about the journey of getting there. That Notre Dame game, I know there was a whole bunch of hype, but we knew we could beat those guys. We knew we were quicker than those guys.

When we got to the game, we pulled up to the stadium and, as we walked onto the field, we noticed they had turned the sprinkler system on. I was thinking to myself, "Who would turn the sprinkler system on before a game?" Only at Notre Dame would they turn the sprinkler system on before the game.

When we came back outside for the game, everybody was hyped and ready to play the game. We scored on the first drive and really didn't notice it a lot. We felt we could run the ball. The wind was blowing pretty good, but as the game progressed, we kind of saw how that water advantage came into play. They were stronger up the middle, they were a bigger team; they weren't as fast but they were powerful up the middle. We were a quicker team, but we had bad footing the whole game.

They got ahead of us. We felt we could still beat them, but they were just stronger. They were going to keep the defense on the field because they were stronger up the middle. It put us in a bad situation.

At halftime we started to put our no-huddle offense in. Once we'd get our four-receiver personnel on the field, you were basically done as far as rushing the passer. My high school coach sent me some long spikes. I was the only one on our side of the field that had good footing. Everybody else was slipping and sliding and falling, but I had pretty decent footing. In the first half, I caught one pass for 14 yards. In the second half, I caught 10 passes for 124 yards. I told a couple of my friends from Notre Dame [about the advantage they had]—they watered that field so we couldn't run and use our quickness in the game. We lost the game 31–24 and thought we'd been knocked out of the national championship race.

287

But the following week, Notre Dame was upset by Boston College. It was a feeling of redemption. We felt we were good enough to win that game and be a part of the whole national championship process. We didn't know if we would get that opportunity, but it played out that way.

I was in the back of the bus sleeping and I saw Corey Sawyer running out like a crazy maniac, like he had lost his mind. I knew something good had happened, seeing Corey running around with his hands raised up. I was thinking to myself, *It must be good for us.* I was excited about the opportunity to play in the Orange Bowl, but I knew we had Florida after that [Notre Dame loss]. I was excited that Notre Dame lost, but I was still mad that we had lost to them.

We beat Florida 33–21 in the last regular season game, then we played Nebraska in the Orange Bowl. We were ranked No. 2 in the country and Nebraska was No. 1, so the game was for the national championship. We knew that they were tough and fast and the whole deal. I remember seeing Trev Alberts on film, and we knew it was going to be a tough game, but we felt like we could hold them off long enough to get the passing game going.

During the game we were getting open, we were just killing their defensive backs, but we just couldn't get the ball off. We just couldn't get their guys blocked.

They were just unblockable. And we were a little bit rusty, too, and didn't make the plays we needed to make. In the last part of the game, it was kind of like that Miami feeling, *They're not going to steal it from us, are they?* But it worked out our way and we won the game 18–16, when they missed a field goal at the end.

To look back on it now, Coach Bowden getting drowned [by the water cooler before officials put time back on the clock to allow Nebraska a winning field-goal attempt], was funny. You laugh at it. But at the time, it was not funny.

During my senior season in 1994, we played Maryland, and I separated my shoulder. I played the whole game with a separated shoulder, fought through adversity, and caught a touchdown pass. I was really proud of myself. I look back at myself as a tough receiver, and that's one game that marked me as being tough. It was 1994 when Danny [Kanell] was the starter. Danny got my shoulder separated throwing the ball so late. He got me smashed. I was fussing at Danny Kanell. I told him, "Hey, Danny, I'm your first and only read. If you see me, you throw me the ball." For me, it was a defining moment.

Coach Bowden took a chance on me and gave me a lot of opportunities to play football at Florida State. He also helped make me become the man I am today as far as holding me accountable. He was one of those people that no matter what you were doing, when you got in front of him you were going to straighten up. That was him for me.

He was kind of that father figure. You were careful about what you did in front of him. I really took what he said to heart and I never wanted to disrespect him or anything he felt was important. He was that to me—that father figure, or actually grandfather figure—when I was at Florida State.

I was kind of a lone guy. The first time having a deep conversation was before I got married. I got married when I was a junior in college. He asked me if I was ready. He said he wasn't going to let me move off campus unless I was ready. We got married, and my wife and I moved in together. That was the first conversation I had in his office.

This is the thing about Coach Bowden, the things you think he would speak about in private he would speak about in public. He would address the team and talk about issues on campus, girls and stuff like that. He would speak about that in public to the whole team. It wasn't a private issue.

He was really looking out for me. He wanted to make sure I did the right thing, too. We had gotten pregnant and were getting ready to have a baby, so he was making sure it wasn't just me moving out [of the dorms]. He really cared about my making the right decision. "Okay, Kez, are you getting married for the right reason? Is this the right decision for you?"

Kez McCorvey, a native of Gautier, Mississippi, was a three-year starting wide receiver at Florida State from 1991 to 1994. McCorvey led Florida State in receiving as a junior and senior, and finished his brilliant career with 189 receptions for 2,660 yards and 16 touchdowns. He was a key member of the 1993 FSU team that finished 12–1 and beat Nebraska 18–16 in the Orange Bowl to win the national championship. He was named a first-team All-American by United Press International in 1993, and his 74 receptions that season still ranks as second-most in a single season by an FSU receiver. McCorvey's 189 career receptions is third-most and 2,660 receiving yards is fourth-most in school history. He averaged 4.2 catches in 45 career games, the third-highest average in FSU history. McCorvey was a fifth-round draft choice by the Detroit Lions in the 1995 NFL draft and played three seasons for the Lions. He operated Titus Sports Academy and lives in St. Augustine, Florida.

# WARRICK DUNN

## TAILBACK

## 1993–1996

W E ALL GOT LETTERS IN HIGH SCHOOL, but I think Jimmy Heggins, the guy who recruited Louisiana for Florida State, was my first contact. I was an option quarterback in high school [at Catholic High in Baton Rouge, Louisiana), but I also took snaps at running back and cornerback. At first, I thought Florida State was recruiting my tailback, Kevin Franklin. He ended up going to LSU. The other schools showing a lot of interest in me were Tennessee, Texas, Alabama, Florida, Illinois, Miami, and Penn State. As far as Illinois and Penn State were concerned, those places were too cold. To schools like Florida, which wanted me to play defensive back, I said, "No, thank you."

At first, Florida State recruited me as an athlete. Then I talked to the defensive coordinator. He told me, "You could be the next Deion [Sanders] or Terrell Buckley. You've got great feet." I said, "Coach, I appreciate that, but I want to play offense." I talked to the offensive coaches, and I took a trip there after my mom had passed. [Dunn's mother, Betty Smothers, was a Baton Rouge police officer; she was working an off-duty job, escorting a convenience store manager to make a late-night deposit, when a gunman shot and killed her; Warrick soon accepted the role as legal guardian for his younger siblings.]

Considering the circumstances, it was pretty tough, but after I got back home from my visit, Coach Bowden came to my house, and I told him I wanted to play offense. They were still trying to push me to be a defensive back, but he listened to me and understood where I was coming from when I said I wanted to play running back. He told me I'd have an opportunity to do that.

My mom passed on January 7, 1993. When I lost my mom, I was supposed to visit Alabama that weekend, so I had to cancel that trip. I visited Florida State and Alabama, and I was supposed to go to Texas when Tennessee stopped recruiting me because they didn't think I wanted to go there anymore.

Florida State just felt right. Kez McCorvey was my host. He was a senior. If you know Kez, he's a fast-talker, and you can't understand him sometimes. He was from [Pascagoula], Mississippi, so that gave me a guy I could identify with, someone who wasn't from Florida. When he took me out and talked to me, he wasn't trying to pressure me to come to Florida State. He was just saying that you could do this, you could do that, but all that time for me was still just a blur.

That whole time, I was like, "Well, I don't even know where I'm at." Once you know Tallahassee, you realize it's not that big, and I think everything about the school and the town and the people just helped me feel at peace and gave me a sense that things were going to be all right.

Growing up in Baton Rouge, I didn't really follow Florida State. I mean I played the game of football, but when people would talk about a big game they were planning to watch, like Miami–Florida State, I would just chill. It wasn't like I had to be in front of the television. I watched LSU a lot and went to Southern University games, but that was fun because I knew a lot of those guys. They were people I could relate to.

I definitely remember watching Charlie [Ward] and the amazing comeback at Georgia Tech. I loved how they were opening up the spread offense, and it was exciting to watch what he was doing, but I don't think I really became a fan until I took my visit. That was when it hit me, that here was a place that felt like home, and I really needed that after losing my mom.

As far as what position I was going to play, the first week of camp was a whirlwind. I was, like, sixth on the depth chart, and on the first day, there was a guy [Sean Jackson] who blew out his knee. He was second-team. The first-teamer [Marquette Smith] had hurt his ankle. There was Tiger McMillon. Rock Preston was a tailback. We came in together as freshmen. Zack Crockett was a fullback. William Floyd was a fullback. Pooh Bear Williams was a fullback. There was another guy who was in [the coaches'] doghouse.

291

Warrick Dunn was a star tailback for the Seminoles for four seasons, from 1993 to 1996. He ran for at least 1,000 yards in each of his last three seasons at FSU, including a career-high 1,242 yards and 13 touchdowns as a junior.

292

So I was put with the first-team offense on the first day. You had all those big-time names, Derrick Alexander, Derrick Brooks, and others, and I busted a couple of long runs against our first-team defense. I was like, "I'm not going back [to another position]," and after that, they never approached me about making any kind of switch.

You couldn't compare it to what you experienced in high school. This was just so intense. Everybody was so competitive. There was no such thing as you play a game and take a couple of days to chill out. No, I had to prove myself every day. I was always competing. We practiced hard, and that was something I had to get used to really quickly.

I wasn't trying to get hit, and I wasn't trying to hit anybody [in various drills], but I was pretty frail coming out of high school, so I just tried to get in guys' ways. I was trying to show the fight that I had. If a big guy came at me [in pass protection], I would try to cut him.

When I was in high school, I would return punts or kickoffs and I could make a million people miss, but I was just out there being an athlete. I didn't really know what I was doing. I caught a few balls out of the backfield in high school, but it wasn't like I had good hands. I knew that was something that I would have to prove to the coaches, to Charlie and the other quarterbacks, that I could catch any ball they threw my way. In looking back now, it seems like it was just second nature. It just kind of came to me, but I still had to learn some things. I dropped some balls.

I'll never forget Charlie dropping back, and he's not even looking at you, and the next thing you know, he's throwing a wide route to you. I don't like being fooled, so I learned real fast to always be on guard. You never know. Always expect the unexpected. Once I dropped a ball from him in practice, he was like, "You can never let that happen again." It was what I needed to hear.

Leading the team with 10 touchdowns as a freshman wasn't something I set as a goal or anything like that, but we had a void to fill, and I wanted to prove to everyone I could get the job done. [The 79-yard touchdown catch-and-run that sealed the 33–21 win over Florida and set up the Orange Bowl game against Nebraska for the 1993 national title] was supposed to be a play-action, five-yard out, but after I did my thing there on a man route, if you watch it on film, you can see that I kind of drifted up-field. Charlie was moving to that side [left], so I just kept running to make sure I was open. He got me the ball, and I made it happen.

If you look back at my freshman year, I wasn't a starter, but I made plays when I had a chance to. Against Miami at Doak Campbell Stadium, I took a direct snap and ran for a first down. [The Seminoles were facing third-and-seven at their 42 when Dunn lined up next to Ward in the shotgun. Dunn ran for 27 yards, setting up Ward's two-yard touchdown run that gave Florida State a 21–7 halftime lead.]

In the second half [of a 51–0 win] against Georgia Tech, I had three touchdowns [one receiving]. At Notre Dame [a 31–24 FSU loss], Charlie hit me for a six-yard touchdown.

But if you think about it and look back at that part of my whole life, I was always going up against guys who were bigger, stronger, and more experienced. When I got to FSU, it was just more magnified.

With my situation, coming from Louisiana, I also had to overcome a perception that I might not be good enough because I didn't grow up in Florida. The players from Florida are arrogant. They think it's the best state and that they're the best players and that they go up against the best competition. I always had to prove myself, being from Louisiana, because I always felt that we had a lot of talented players in our state, too.

I think after two games of my rookie year, I earned their respect. But I will say that if you asked most Florida State people what they most remember me for, they would say that play against Florida. That's my play in Florida State history. I think that will always be my defining play.

Those few days after losing at Notre Dame [31–24 on November 13, 1993, a game that was called "The Game of the Century"] were kind of hard. We felt like we had practiced okay, but not great. Then we got up to South Bend, and everyone was slipping down on that field. We got in the locker room at half-time, and Coach Bowden called me out, telling me in front of everybody that it's time to step up and to realize I'm not a rookie anymore. I mean, everyone was falling down, and he was calling me out? So I just went back out there and caught the ball and scored a touchdown, but that was a tough loss.

That next week, when we saw that Notre Dame had lost to Boston College and we had a night game on national TV, I don't care who we would've played or if the game was up on the moon, that team was going to pay. [FSU beat North Carolina State 62–3.]

After we held off Florida down there [in Gainesville], it wasn't long before we began all the work for the Nebraska game [in the Orange Bowl]. It was a crazy week. My roommate, Charlie Ward, was the Heisman Trophy winner, but that helped me in lots of different ways.

I roomed with Charlie, even though he was a senior, my whole freshman year. It was a good situation for me because I needed that guidance. I remember talking to him on the telephone one time for, like, 30 or 40 minutes. I was still in high school, and it meant a lot that he really was interested in me and wanted to do what he could to take away some of the stress in preparing for my first year of college.

It was hard enough what I was going through and what my brothers and sisters were experiencing without their mother. Once the football season ended, I drove home every weekend to be with my family. During the season and looking back at my freshman year, I had some perks as Charlie's roommate. No hazing. No hassles. People left me alone, and since he was a Heisman candidate all year, he traveled a lot, making appearances. After football was over, he played basketball, and I ran track. So we didn't see each other all that much, but when we did, I had a chance to learn a lot from him.

That week leading up to the Orange Bowl was pretty crazy. It was my first time in Miami. There was all this media and all these fans and just people everywhere. I just tried to stay with some of my teammates who were from that area and learn a little about my surroundings. I didn't see much of Charlie because he was so busy.

It seemed like game day would never come. Finally, when we arrived at the stadium and got dressed, everybody was really quiet. It was really, really intense, but I felt better after I finally got in the game and got hit. That released a lot of stress, which was something I definitely needed. It was an eye-opening experience, that whole day and night, but once I got on the field, my nerves settled down. The game situation, and what Nebraska was trying to achieve on defense, didn't get me in for as many plays as I was accustomed to, but the bottom line is that we won the game, we won the national championship, and Florida State was the No. 1 team in the country when everything was said and done.

Going into my final game with Florida State, I had accomplished a lot of my goals. There were a lot of things I couldn't control, like beginning my senior year as a Heisman candidate or winning a big award like ACC Player of the Year, but I definitely wanted to go out with a 4–0 record in bowl games. We had already beaten Florida in Tallahassee a few weeks earlier, and everyone playing and coaching for Florida State saw no reason why we wouldn't do it again.

But in the week leading up to the game, the flu was going around, and a lot of guys were getting sick. Once the game started, I didn't feel anything unusual, but they thought I was looking fatigued at halftime. I started cramping up, so they gave me an IV. When I tried to jog back out on the field and get back in the game, I started cramping up again. They told me I had the stomach flu and that I couldn't keep playing. [When Dunn left the game, FSU trailed 24–20, but without him, the Gators scored 28 unanswered points to win the 1996 national title.]

My sophomore year against Florida wasn't the first time I played in the Superdome. We lost a state championship there in high school, but the atmosphere was nothing like what I experienced in my first Sugar Bowl. The game against Florida in Tallahassee had ended in a 31–31 tie after we were down 31–3 and came back.

Getting named MVP of the [1995] Sugar Bowl was a big surprise. [Dunn ran 14 times for 58 yards, caught nine passes for 51 and threw a 73-yard touchdown pass to 'OMar Ellison.] Even though it didn't happen chronologically, I can always look back at my college career and remember that 23–17 win over Florida to end my sophomore year.

I've been blessed to have a long and successful career in the NFL. When Tampa Bay drafted me in the first round in 1997, I believed it was a dream come true, but just like when I participated in my first practices in Tallahassee, I knew I had to compete like crazy. It was cool to have Derrick Brooks as my teammate with the Bucs. We were never close in college because he was the big man on campus, and I was always trying to take care of my family in Baton Rouge, do well in school, and still do everything necessary to produce on the football field.

I guess Derrick and I hit it off in the NFL because it was there that I realized that I had earned his respect. He told me that when the Bucs were looking at making their picks in 1997 that he wanted Coach [Tony] Dungy to know that I could do a lot of things to help us win games. Not just run the football but catch passes out of the backfield, pick up the blitz, protect the quarterback, even run-block.

He really embraced me when I needed him to. Like when I came down for my first minicamp, Derrick took me out to eat, and we really hit it off. We've been close ever since.

Obviously, I know my career in the NFL won't go on forever, but I want to keep playing as long as I'm productive and can help my team win. With the Falcons, we're hoping to turn things around after falling short and missing the playoffs the last two years. I will never accept losing, and we believe the pieces are in place for a great 2007 season.

My charity work, which is channeled through the Warrick Dunn Foundation, has become a major focus of my life. We work in Atlanta, Baton Rouge, Tampa Bay, and other parts of the country to help single mothers realize their dream of becoming first-time homeowners. We have a lot of great sponsors in retail, manufacturing, and real estate that help us give these women the head start they need to take their lives and the lives of their kids to a higher, better standard.

It's rewarding to have a chance to give something back. Playing at FSU and in the NFL has given me a life I never could've imagined as a kid growing up in Baton Rouge. But my family and I had lots of people step up and do what they could to reach out and give us a chance to stand on our feet. I'm grateful for the many opportunities I've had, and I hope I can keep giving back to others as well.

296

Warrick Dunn, a native of Baton Rouge, Louisiana, was a star tailback for the Seminoles for four seasons, from 1993 to 1996. As a freshman, he helped Florida State win the 1993 national championship. He scored a team-high 10 touchdowns, ran for 511 yards, and caught 25 passes for 357 yards as a freshman. He ran for at least 1,000 yards in each of his last three seasons at FSU, including a career-high 1,242 yards and 13 touchdowns as a junior. Dunn was named a first team All-American by the Football Writers Association as a senior in 1996 after running for 1,180 yards and 12 touchdowns. Dunn was a first-round draft choice by the Tampa Bay Buccaneers in the 1996 NFL draft and played five seasons there. He played the last six seasons with the Atlanta Falcons and has run for nearly 10,000 yards with nearly 4,000 receiving yards in his pro career. Dunn was named the Walter Payton NFL Man of the Year in 2005 for his charitable work.

# ANDRE WADSWORTH

## DEFENSIVE END

### 1993–1997

I WENT TO FLORIDA CHRISTIAN HIGH SCHOOL in Miami and my only scholarship offer was Stony Brook, a Division I-AA school in Long Island, New York. They recruited me because of my grades and test scores in high school. I was only about 211 pounds, and played tight end, middle linebacker, and kick returner in high school. It was a small school, and only one coach came to my high school—Chuck Amato of Florida State—and the only reason he came was because he said he went to every high school in his recruiting region.

My high school coach told Coach Amato that I was about the only player from my high school who could play as a walk-on at Florida State. Florida State sent me a questionnaire, and a lot of schools sent me questionnaires, but Stony Brook was the only school that offered me a scholarship. I wasn't sure what I was going to do.

During my senior year of high school, one of our assignments in English class was to write a five-page letter explaining what our goals were and where we thought we'd be in five years. We put it in an envelope and sealed it, and the teacher put it in a box and kept it in the box until he mailed it back to us five years later. I got the letter five years later at my mom's house, and I recognized the handwriting and realized what it was. It was pretty neat to remember what my goals and mindset were back then.

When I wrote the letter, it was right before homecoming weekend at my high school. I wrote that I thought it was going to be my last year of football and how much I enjoyed sports and playing basketball and football. Spiritu-ally, I wrote that I had a lot of things going on and wrote about how I wanted to grow as a person, both morally and ethically. I thought I was changing during that time, and I wrote about my relationship with my parents. I wrote that I wanted to graduate with a master's degree in business from Florida State. I had applied to FSU at the time, and thought I'd go there to concen-trate on academics and not play football. I never thought I'd play organized football in college because I knew I didn't want to go to Stony Brook.

I walked on the football team at Florida State in 1993, and my first prac-tice was pretty tough. They wouldn't allow me to attend two-a-days because I was a walk-on, so I joined the team once school started and after I had enrolled. That put me behind the eight ball against the other players who had already been there. When I got there, I went into the locker room, and they were fitting me for my pads and practice jerseys and everything. The head trainer, Jimmy Callaway, and his assistants were helping me get their stuff. It was raining that day, so they were giving us all sneakers to work out in the gym. When the equipment guys were helping me out, Callaway cussed them out and cussed me out and said, "You need to be helping players who are going to be playing around here!" That was my first experience in the FSU locker room: I got cursed out and kicked out.

299

Needless to say, I ended up getting the rest of my stuff that day. During practice, I almost got into a fight with Peter Boulware. I gave it all I had on my first day of practice on the scout team and we had conditioning afterward. There weren't too many scholarship guys who were friendly. Those guys had been together for three weeks already, and I was just trying to follow every-body. At the end of practice, we were doing conditioning drills.

I had been blowing myself out in practice, not knowing that we'd have more drills to do at the end. By the time we got to the last drill, I was suck-ing wind and about to fall over. Mickey Andrews, the defensive coordinator, was making me go back and do this drill over and over, and the other play-ers were getting punished for it. I told Coach Andrews he could run me after practice but he didn't need to be punishing the rest of the players because it was my first day. Peter Boulware got mad and came up to me and said a few words. We almost went to blows before a coach broke it up, and then they ran me after practice.

The next day was a new day. We had one-on-one drills with the offensive linemen. None of the scholarship guys wanted to go more than once, so the

Andre Wadsworth grew from a 211-pound walk-on to one of the most feared pass rushers in college football. He finished his Florida State career with 233 total tackles and 23 sacks, the fifth-highest total in school history.

scout team players were having to go every time. I knew I was going to play defensive end or linebacker. They had me going up against this guy named Marvin Ferrell, who was one of the starting offensive tackles on the 1993 national championship team. My first one-on-one drill against him, when all the coaches were looking, I knocked him back on the dummy. He probably weighed 315 pounds. Everybody was like, "Where did this guy come from?" Of course, they told me to go back up there and do it again because they thought I was just lucky. I did it again and did the same thing.

I redshirted during the 1993 national championship season, and they wouldn't allow me to travel to road games. I went home every week during the games, but I practiced very hard. Coach Brad Scott, who was the offensive line coach, probably saw me the most during that redshirt season because I was on the scout team and going up against the varsity offensive linemen. He was very nice to me and would go out of his way to encourage me. He told me he really thought I could earn a scholarship if I kept working hard, and at that time, not a lot of walk-ons were being awarded scholarships. It was a big hurdle at the time, but Coach Scott really made me feel like I was doing a good job out there.

They took me to the national championship game in Miami, where we played Nebraska in the Orange Bowl. After the game was over, Coach Scott announced he was leaving to become the head coach at South Carolina. I thought my chances of getting a scholarship were over because he was gone. Initially, I thought about asking him to help me transfer to South Carolina and I believe he would have allowed me to do that. But I had always grown up a Florida State fan, even growing up in Miami, so I decided to stick it out.

301

When I reported back to Tallahassee for training camp before the 1994 season, Coach Bowden and Coach Amato called me up to their offices. I had no idea what was going on, but they told me I was getting a scholarship. I was so excited that I called my mom right there. I remember that to eat at the training table in the cafeteria, you had to be a scholarship player. The director of the cafeteria was named Mrs. Betty. If you weren't on scholarship, you had to pay for your food and you weren't allowed in there unless there was someone collecting money. Right after I got a scholarship, I immediately went downstairs to eat. I told the people at the cash registers that I had just been given a scholarship, so they let me go ahead and eat. I was eating a turkey sandwich, and Mrs. Betty came right up to me, grabbed my sandwich, and threw it in the garbage can. She thought I'd lied to her workers about being on scholarship. I told her I was on scholarship, but she didn't believe me.

I started the 1994 season as a defensive end and outside linebacker in the 4–3 defense we were running. I was really low on the depth chart. I moved to defensive tackle and nose tackle because when I was on the scout team, you played every position they told you to play. I learned the whole defense the year before and felt comfortable playing anywhere even though I was small. I was backing up Peter Boulware, Reinard Wilson, Derrick Alexander, and Tyrant Marion at defensive end. I was maybe fourth- or fifth-string at defensive end, and fourth- or fifth-string at defensive tackle.

Our first game in the 1994 season was at home against Virginia, and we were beating them pretty good [FSU won the game 41–17]. Coach Amato let me go in the game and play nose guard. My first play, I blew by [fullback] Charles Way, sacked [quarterback] Symmion Willis, and caused a fumble. I shot the gap and ended up getting the sack, causing and recovering a fumble. I played about six or seven more plays that game. We played at Maryland [a 52–20 win] and at Wake Forest [a 56–14 victory], and I probably played about 20 to 25 plays combined in those games. I didn't play at all against North Carolina [a 31–18 win] in the fourth game. Enzo Armella, the starting nose guard, blew out his knee against North Carolina and had career-ending surgery.

The next game was at Miami, and I was only on the kickoff return team. I wasn't going to play on defense at all, even though we were short one defensive tackle. The guys in front of me kept jumping offside early in the game, and Connell Spain, one of the backups, had an ankle injury that was bothering him. After they jumped offside again, Coach Amato asked me, "Andre, do you know how to play nose tackle?" I think he just wanted to make a statement to the other guys in front of me because they weren't playing that well. I went into the game and had 10 tackles and a half-sack in that game. We ended up losing the game 34–20, which was our only loss that season.

We had a Sunday practice the following day, and we lined up for warm-ups by depth chart. The starters and captains were on the 50-yard line facing the team, and players were lined up every five yards behind them by where they were on the depth chart. I was all the way on the goal line. Coach Amato walked out onto the field and grabbed my face mask and pulled me all the way to the front of the line and moved everybody else back five yards. I was shocked because I was a walk-on who had just gotten a scholarship. I started the next game on the base defense and actually set an ACC record for interior linemen with 32 tackles in three games, against Miami, Clemson [a 17–0 win], and Duke [a 59–20 victory].

The game I remember the most was tying Florida 31–31 at the end of the 1994 season. We were down 31–3 going into the fourth quarter and scored four touchdowns to tie the game with less than two minutes left [the game is still affectionately known as the "Choke at the Doak"]. We could have gone for the win after Rock Preston scored the last touchdown, but we kicked the extra point and tied the game. It was an unbelievable comeback and an exciting game.

I ended up playing nose tackle in 1994, 1995, and 1996. I gained about 10 to 15 pounds in each of those seasons and was getting a little bigger. I almost left Florida State after my junior season because I was projected to go in the first round of the NFL draft. I thought the Chicago Bears were going to pick me with the eighth pick. But I decided to come back for my senior season in 1997 because I saw an opportunity to play defensive end, which is where I thought I would end up playing in the pros.

I ended up playing in three Sugar Bowl games and two Orange Bowl games during my career at Florida State. That's why you go to Florida State, to play in big bowl games like that. We played teams like Nebraska, Florida, Notre Dame, and Ohio State in bowl games. Those were all exciting games.

Coach Bowden was a father figure to all of us. The first day, he told us he didn't want us sleeping with women because he thought sex should be saved for marriage. He told us he didn't want us drinking, even after we turned 21. He told us he was going to treat all of us like his sons, and that's what he did. He cared about us—more than he cared about football.

I came out after the 1997 season and was the third choice in the 1998 NFL draft. I played three seasons in the NFL before I suffered a knee injury. There are no regrets because I couldn't have done anything to prevent it. I just feel blessed every day for the things that happened.

303

Andre Wadsworth, a native of Miami, Florida, is one of the most successful stories in college football history. An unrecruited player from tiny Florida Christian High School, Wadsworth went from a walk-on to a dominating defensive lineman in four seasons, from 1994 to 1997. During his senior season in 1997, he was named the ACC Defensive Player of the Year and was chosen as a consensus All-American after totaling 16 sacks. He finished his FSU career with 233 total tackles and 23 sacks, the fifth-highest sack total in school history. Wadsworth was the third choice in the 1998 NFL draft by the Arizona Cardinals—the highest a Seminole has ever been drafted—and played three seasons before suffering a career-ending knee injury. He lives in Scottsdale, Arizona.

# The
# NEW
# MILLENNIUM

# DAVID CASTILLO
## CENTER
### 2000–2005

M Y EARLIEST RECOLLECTION OF FLORIDA STATE was actually when I grew up in Miami. I grew up a Hurricanes fan and I remember all those tough battles that they had against FSU. The game was always marked on the calendar and everybody was excited. You'd go to school and see people from the neighborhood talking about it. You had your Miami fans, you had your Seminoles fans; everybody was always taking bets on the game and joking around about it—the heated rivalry that it was and how much respect there was between the two teams and the great traditions.

I don't really agree with the way that high school athletes are recruited a lot of times. A lot of these recruiting services, they put too much weight on how big a kid is size-wise; what team they play for. If you're on a really good football team and you're big, you are more likely to get a higher rating than a kid who might be as big but might not play at a good school.

That was kind of my thing. My first two years at Palm Beach Gardens High, we were terrible. A new head coach came and kind of moved it up a little bit my junior year, and my senior year we were pretty good. It was very hard for me at a school like Palm Beach Gardens—I was competing with offensive linemen from Tallahassee Lincoln that had the reputation for being a dominant offensive line, with all the kids going Division I. That was kind of tough. I did fly under the radar quite a bit. I had a lot of schools—Ivy

League schools after me, the military [academies]—but people were saying, "He's not big enough. He's not this thing, he's not that."

But Florida State stuck with me the whole time. They were the second letter I ever got. The first was Georgia Tech. I was up front and honest with all the recruiters who came in that Miami was my place to be; that's where I wanted to go. There was no doubt in my mind. It ended up not working out that way, and things happen for a reason. Even through all that—Coach [John] Lilly was the coach who had my area—he was on me from the beginning and let me know they were interested in me. He didn't waver at all, even knowing that if Miami had offered tomorrow, I was gone.

Now that it happened the way that it did and I ended up at Florida State; if I could go back and do it again, there was no way in the world that I would not have chosen Florida State. I am very fortunate and blessed for it to work out the way that it did, even though I didn't get the national championship that Miami got while I was playing. My career might not have turned out the way I necessarily dreamt of it once—with all the injuries and not getting to play in the National Football League—but I wouldn't change one thing about it.

I'll never forget how supportive everybody else was, our training staff with Randy Oravetz and Dave Walls, our team doctors—pretty much every one of our team doctors I kept in business, with as many surgeries as they had on me. They were always so supportive. They went above and beyond the call of duty to keep me on the field.

307

We have this family atmosphere here at Florida State. It's been that way since the day I got here, and it just gets stronger every year, it seems like. We had some rough times, a few tragedies when I was playing here, but it's so strong now. Especially my last season here; that kind of stuff just makes you appreciate things so much more. As a high school athlete, you end up going away to college, you leave your family, then you end up getting an even bigger family when you come to Florida State. It's definitely a great thing we had—we still have—here at Florida State.

It was tough. In high school I was never hurt, really. I might have had a couple of injuries, like a broken thumb. I never missed time. I got up here [to Tallahassee] and started hurting my hands, having hand surgeries left and right. This Monday [April 2, 2007] will be my sixth hand surgery. I've had two foot surgeries, a right knee surgery, torn a pec [pectoral muscle], pulled numerous hamstrings…had a couple concussions, bulged disks in my lower back. You name it, and I've probably had it.

I appreciate people always saying, "Oh, you're the toughest guy I've ever seen play." I still to this day have people tell me, "You're one of the guys with the biggest heart I've ever seen; you were a leader out there and people fueled off you." I appreciate hearing that, but that's not necessarily what I wanted. I would have traded all that for this team to be more successful or for other opportunities in football. I didn't want to be known as the guy who was injured all the time.

The 2003 Florida game, we went to Gainesville and we beat the University of Florida 38–34 on the Hail Mary from [quarterback Chris] Rix to P.K. Sam—it was a last-ditch effort and we ended up winning the game. The athletic training staff asked me to carry off the Gator head, which is a tradition when we beat Florida. They asked me to do that [because of] all the injuries I had played with that year. I was playing on a broken foot. I had to have a special cast made for my foot just to play; a metal shank put in my shoe.

308

Against N.C. State two weeks earlier, [wide receiver] Craphonso Thorpe went down, and, like, two plays later I tore my MCL [medial collateral knee ligament]. In the Florida game I was basically taped from toe to mid-thigh, all the way up. I could barely bend my leg. I had to block the biggest kid I had ever seen in my life. Mo Mitchell was his name. He was about 370. I had to push him around all game. To be able to win that game and just for them to have the respect to ask me to [carry the Gator head], when we had guys who had done that like Snoop Minnis and Chris Weinke; I'm nowhere near the caliber of player they were. For them to ask me to do that was quite an honor for me.

Another great memory was in 2005, beating Virginia Tech in the inaugural ACC championship game and getting to hoist the ACC championship trophy up on the stage, when no one in the world was really giving this team a chance to win that game after an up-and-down season. We lost three straight that year and kind of backed into it. Everybody was talking bad about Florida State. Virginia Tech was supposed to go out there and kill us, and we ended up pulling it off. That was very big for me.

Getting to be a part of Coach Bowden's 300th victory was quite a victory. Beating Miami my final year [10–7 in 2005]. I was 0-for-6 against Miami at the time; finally getting to beat my childhood team. Every year they had seemed to find a way to beat us with a missed field goal. Out of all those years there was one year that they legitimately just beat us. I think it was the

After playing parts of six seasons at Florida State, David Castillo earned an NCAA postgraduate scholarship and enrolled in medical school at FSU. He also worked for the Seminoles Booster Club.

2003 rain game we played against them. Every other game we played them, with one more bounce we would have easily won. It could have been turned so easily. To finally get that accomplished was really big because I think I was going to be the first player to ever lose to a team seven times.

I think I ended up 1–6 against them. That was big. My freshman year, the seniors at Miami hadn't beaten us in, like, six tries; Dan Morgan and those kinds of guys finally got it done against Florida State. I just remembered the elation that they had and all the emotion they had on the field when they finally beat Florida State with the last-minute drive they had and the screen pass that broke it. That was the year [2000] when we played for the national championship, and that was the only loss we had. It could have decimated our season. Beating Miami was really big because I always had those memories in my mind and what it would be like to finally beat Miami. It built up every year and got worse and worse.

I was in a medical [school] magnet in high school and actually one of my criteria was I wanted a school that had a medical program. That was one of the reasons I was so high on Miami. They were obviously very good in football with all the national championships and tradition they had, but they also had a very good medical school.

310

When I first got to Florida State, they had the PIMs program, where you could go to the University of Florida but there was a promise that they would have a medical school by the time I was done playing. So I kind of had to have a little trust in the university to say, "This isn't just a ploy to get me here. They really were going to have a medical school." Now it's a fantastic medical program and I can't wait to start it.

I think Florida State, oftentimes, gets the short end of the stick when people talk about academics. Florida State for a long time had the reputation of a party university and the academics weren't good. I don't think that's fair, especially in athletics. When you look at our graduation rates compared to other teams in the ACC, we're second only to Duke. Look at the amount of [NCAA] postgraduate scholarship winners, which I was a part of, and how many we've had. We've had more than any school in our conference.

When you look at that and our sports, the success we've had on the field and in the classroom, there are very few teams that can compete with us, and I don't think people realize that. Florida State athletics take the graduation rates and academics a lot more seriously than people want to give them credit for. Once you get a stigma about something, it's very hard to outgrow that.

I knew that they were known as the number-one party school in the nation and they had just won the national championship the year before I committed. They played for it in the Sugar Bowl against Virginia Tech, and I came on my visit January 15; they had played on January 4 and I committed on January 15. I knew they had all these stereotypes and reputations, but I knew they had a lot of good programs. I was promised by a lot of people that the medical school was in the works and, by the time I was done, it would be ready to go. They fulfilled that promise.

I definitely had faith in Coach Bowden and the kind of man he is. He definitely isn't going to lie to your face. I knew that right away. A lot of times you get tripped up in recruiting because coaches are going to tell you what you want to hear: "You're going to be starting next year. You're going to be doing this, that, and the other thing." That wasn't the case at Florida State. They were very open and honest with me from the get-go. They stuck with me.

I knew when I sat there with my parents in Coach Bowden's office and he offered me a scholarship and told me exactly what he expected from me, I knew it was the truth and he wasn't giving me any lines to get me here.

Coach Lilly was another. I had a very strong relationship with him during recruiting. He was a big reason I came here. Coach [Dave] Van Halanger, who is now at Georgia, was a big reason I came here. Clint Purvis, the team chaplain whom I'm still very good friends with, had a lot to do with my decision.

311

There's a certain level of trust you have to have with anything, especially when you're making a major decision, and I felt that at Florida State I had that trust. It was that family atmosphere that I was looking for, and I felt it was my best opportunity to succeed, not only athletically, but as a human being, academically, and everything else. It was the best thing for my future.

I've had a strong faith pretty much my whole life. Coming here, I was taking a big step leaving home, leaving my mom, leaving my brother. I was coming up here pretty much on my own. When Coach Bowden promises your parents he's going to take care of you, he's not going to force religion on you or do anything the player doesn't want to do, but he's going to make the opportunity available. He's going to try and lead the horse to water, so to speak, but he's not going to force it on you. I have such a high respect level for that and all the coaches.

It's very hard to put into words because Florida State means so much to me personally. Now that I get to sit back and reflect, think about my career and my experiences here, good and bad, you think you go to wear the same spear on your helmet and the garnet and gold as all the great players who came before and even those you played alongside. You get to play at Bobby Bowden Field at Doak Campbell Stadium. You get to represent the Seminole Tribe and those proud people and all they represent. You get such unlimited opportunity that so many people don't have. You'd do anything to be in the position we were in. I got to play for Bobby Bowden, the winningest coach of all-time in Division I and one of the greatest coaches of all-time—a legend. I got to be coached by him for six years and even today, anytime he sees me, he says, "Come in here. Talk to me. What's going on?" That stuff means more than anything. Even though I didn't make the NFL and my career didn't pan out necessarily the way I wanted it to, those are all things you sit back and reflect on, and it's just great. There is no better feeling in the world than running out of the tunnel before 84,000 people at that game—screaming fans, ripping that Seminole sign, running out between the cheerleaders and the band's going, taking the field and everyone's going crazy. The rush you get from that—if you're not ready to play when that happens, you shouldn't be wearing pads.

When Chief Osceola runs out on Renegade at the center of the field and throws the spear in the ground, that symbolizes everything Florida State is about. And also, the war chant. Even to this day, my mom has it on her Florida State computer screen-saver and when it comes on, it plays the war chant. When I hear that, chills run through my body, and I feel like I have to go strap my helmet on and get ready to go to battle.

That's what makes Florida State different; that kind of tradition—other teams might have more success than we have some seasons, but I don't think they have what we have, and I don't think we would trade what we have for that of another school.

David Castillo, a native of Miami, Florida, holds the distinction of being a part of the FSU football program for six seasons, twice enduring medical hardships over the course of a career which included three seasons as the starting center. A second-team All-ACC pick, he was a three-time ACC All-Academic selection, earned an NCAA postgraduate scholarship, and was a finalist for the Draddy Award, presented to the nation's top football scholar-athlete. Castillo was enrolled in FSU's medical school in June 2007 and also works in the Seminole Boosters office.

# BRYANT McFADDEN

## CORNERBACK

### 2001–2004

I GRADUATED FROM McARTHUR HIGH SCHOOL in Hollywood, Florida, and was pretty much being recruited by every Division I school in the country during my senior season. My final choices came down to Florida State, Miami, Georgia, Michigan, and Tennessee. I chose Florida State because it was close to home and they had a great tradition of cornerbacks, with guys like Deion Sanders, Samari Rolle, and Terrell Buckley having played there. FSU was coming off that national championship season in 1999, so I thought I could go there and have the chance to win another title.

I got to Florida State in the summer of 2000, and we had one of the best recruiting classes in the country. I came in with guys like Chris Rix, Greg Jones, Kendyll Pope, and Michael Boulware, so I felt like it was a class that could really keep Florida State's tradition going. I thought I was going to play as a freshman in 2000, but I ended up redshirting because I fractured a disc in my lower back. I didn't play the entire season. We ended up having an 11–2 record in 2000—we lost to Miami during the regular season and then to Oklahoma in the Orange Bowl. The Orange Bowl was the national championship game, but we just couldn't get anything going on offense.

In 2001 I played mostly on special teams and played some in the nickel and dime packages in the secondary. I thought I had a pretty good year after coming back from the back injury and had really started to work myself back into shape by the midseason. We lost at North Carolina 41–9 in the third game of the 2001 season, and that was really a big shock. Florida State had never been beaten in the ACC like that before. We lost to Miami 49–27, and they went on to win the national championship later that season. We won a couple of big games—against Virginia [43–7] and Maryland [52–31]—then we lost to North Carolina State, which had Philip Rivers at quarterback. They beat us 34–28. We lost to Florida 37–13 and beat Georgia Tech 28–17.

We ended up playing Virginia Tech in the Gator Bowl after the 2001 season, but I didn't play in the game because I broke a bone in my right foot during practices before the bowl game. It was another setback, but at least it happened at the end of the season and I had the spring and summer to recover. I was getting a little frustrated with the injuries, but I thought I'd played pretty well when I was healthy.

I came back for the start of the 2002 season and was still playing in the nickel package as a cornerback. We won our first four games in 2002, then lost some games we weren't used to losing. We lost to Louisville [26–20 in overtime], and it was just pouring down rain up there from a tropical storm. Then we lost to Miami 28–27 at the Orange Bowl after our kicker missed a field goal at the end of the game that would have won it. I think that one went wide left, after all the others had gone wide right against Miami. We lost to Notre Dame 34–24 the next week at home, but they actually had a pretty good team that season.

We came back and won our next three games—against Wake Forest [34–21], Georgia Tech [21–13], and North Carolina [40–14]—and thought we had the season turned around, although we were out of the national championship race. But then we lost to North Carolina State 17–7 up there, and Phillip Rivers beat us again. We came home and beat Florida 31–14 to end the regular season. We still won the ACC that season and played Georgia in the Sugar Bowl. We didn't have [quarterback] Chris Rix in that game and lost to Georgia 26–13. We finished 9–5 that season, which was a record that Florida State hadn't had in a long, long time. FSU wasn't used to losing five games in a season, and we really felt like we had to get it turned around.

I moved into the starting lineup at left cornerback at the beginning of the 2003 season. We felt like we had a good team coming back and we were pretty strong on defense. We won our first five games that season, beating North Carolina [37–0], Maryland [35–10], Georgia Tech [14–13], Colorado [47–7], and Duke [56–7]. With the way we beat Colorado, which still had a pretty good program, we really had our swagger and confidence back.

Bryant McFadden was a second-round choice by the Pittsburgh Steelers in the 2005 NFL draft and won a Super Bowl ring during his rookie season, following the Steelers' 21–10 victory over the Seattle Seahawks in Super Bowl XL.

We were ranked No. 5 in the country when we played Miami at Doak Campbell Stadium. They were ranked No. 2 in the country, but we were playing at home. We turned the ball over five times, and [safety Sean] Taylor had a big game for them. We lost the game 22–14, which was our first loss of the season. We just never had much luck against Miami while I was at FSU.

We came back and won our next three games, beating Virginia [19–14], Wake Forest [48–24], and then Notre Dame. We went up to Notre Dame and beat them 37–0, which was just an unbelievable experience. They'd beaten us the year before, so we were kind of looking for revenge. I don't think

Notre Dame had ever been beaten that badly at home. [Notre Dame's worst loss was a 40–0 pasting by Oklahoma on October 27, 1956.]

We were back in the national championship race after beating Notre Dame, but then we went to Clemson and lost 26–10. It was a loss that really hurt. We played North Carolina State at home the next week and won 50–44 in double overtime. That was just a wild game.

We beat Florida 38–34 in the last game, when Chris Rix threw a Hail Mary touchdown on one of the last plays of the game. I didn't play much in that game and didn't play much against Miami in the Orange Bowl because I'd strained my groin in the Clemson game. We lost to Miami 16–14 in the Orange Bowl, and it was really bad to lose to them twice in the same season. It really left a bad taste in our mouths.

I was playing pretty well during my senior season in 2004 and stayed healthy, which was a big deal before the NFL draft. There were some questions about my health and durability, but I played every game during my senior year. We lost to Miami 16–10 in the first game of the 2004 season in the Orange Bowl. The defense played really, really well, but it was a weird game all the way to the end. Then we got on a roll and won six games in a row until we lost to Maryland 20–17. We came back and beat Duke 29–7 and North Carolina State 17–10. We lost to Florida 20–13 at home in a game that we should have won. We played West Virginia in the Gator Bowl, the second time we played in that game during my career. We won the game 30–18.

After leaving Florida State, I was drafted by the Pittsburgh Steelers in the second round of the 2005 NFL draft. During my rookie season with the Steelers in 2006, we won the Super Bowl. I had an interception against the Indianapolis Colts in the playoffs, which really put me on the map with Steelers fans. It was a lot of fun, and I was very fortunate to win a Super Bowl in my rookie season because a lot of guys play long careers without ever getting the chance to win a Super Bowl.

Bryant McFadden, a native of Hollywood, Florida, was a two-year starting cornerback for the Seminoles in 2003 and 2004. Before signing with the Seminoles, he was one of the country's most heavily recruited high school football players, as he was named a *Parade* All-American and *USA Today* All-USA as a senior at McArthur High School. Plagued by injuries during his first three seasons at FSU, McFadden moved into the starting lineup at left cornerback in 2003. He finished his junior season with 28 tackles, three forced fumbles, and a team-high nine pass breakups. As a senior in 2004, McFadden had a career-high 36 tackles, one interception, and 11 pass breakups. McFadden prevented his assigned receiver from catching a pass in four games in 2005. He was a second-round draft choice of the Pittsburgh Steelers in the 2005 NFL draft. As a rookie with the Steelers, he helped lead the Steelers to a 21–10 victory over the Seattle Seahawks in Super Bowl XL.

# BUSTER DAVIS
## LINEBACKER
### 2002–2006

I GREW UP IN DAYTONA BEACH, FLORIDA, and attended Mainland High School there. I grew up a Florida State fan and always wanted to go to school there. During my senior season, I was being recruited by FSU, Ohio State, Syracuse, Tennessee, and Nebraska—or at least those were my final choices. I chose Florida State because it was close to home and I'd been a Seminoles fan my entire life.

I got to Florida State in 2002 and was redshirted. I really thought I'd have a chance to go in and play, but the coaches thought I needed another year to get bigger and stronger. Looking back at it now, it was probably the best decision for my long-term career. I got to sit on the sideline and watch some other great linebackers play during that season.

We had great coaches at Florida State. Coach Bowden was a man of his word. If he told you he was going to do something, he would do it. He really cared about his players, and it was about more than football for him. He was really a father figure for all of us. Kevin Steele was our linebackers coach my last couple of seasons there, and he really showed me how to play the game intelligently and how to use my mind on the field. Mickey Andrews was our defensive coordinator, and he was just a great coach and was really enthusiastic and intense. I'll never forget the coaches I had at Florida State.

During my redshirt freshman season in 2003, I was backing up Allen Augustin and Sam McGrew at middle linebacker, so I didn't play a lot on defense. I probably played in seven games late in the game and got a little bit of playing time on special teams. We went 10–3 in 2003 and won the ACC championship. But we lost to Miami twice that season [the Hurricanes defeated the Seminoles 22–14 during the regular season and also beat FSU 16–14 in the Orange Bowl], which is something I'll never forget. We should have beaten Miami both times that season.

I was still playing pretty much a backup role during my sophomore season in 2004, but I was playing more on defense. I remember I had 11 tackles against North Carolina [a 38–16 victory] and played really well against Miami [a 16–10 loss]. I was getting more comfortable in our defense and was starting to play more physically. We went 9–3 that season and lost to Miami, Maryland [20–17], and Florida [20–13]. I thought we should have won all those games, but we were just never consistent enough on offense.

If you look back at my four seasons at Florida State, I thought the inconsistency at quarterback is really what hurt us. We went from Adrian McPherson to Chris Rix to Fabian Walker to Wyatt Sexton to Drew Weatherford to Xavier Lee. There was just never any continuity on offense. We always played well enough on defense to win games, but we could never score enough points to win games. I thought the quarterback situation was always what really hurt us during each of those seasons.

I thought we had turned it around during my junior season in 2005. We won our first five games in 2005 and beat Miami 10–7 at Doak Campbell Stadium to start the season. I'll never forget how physical that game was played. It was Labor Day night on national television, and there were just big hits all over the field. It was one of those games that stayed with you for several days because you were so sore from the pounding you took in the game. It was nice to finally beat Miami after we'd lost to them four times in a row during my first three seasons at FSU. We were feeling pretty good about ourselves after beating Miami, even though the offense had struggled. It was just two great defenses playing that night.

We beat The Citadel 62–10 and Boston College 28–17. We played Boston College up there, and it was their first game in the ACC. It was a good win. We came home and beat Syracuse 38–14 and Wake Forest 41–24. So we were 5–0 when we went to play at Virginia. It was a night game, and we just never really got anything going during that game. They were fired up to play us because they had kind of struggled that season. They ended up beating us 26–21, and it was a loss that knocked us out of the national championship race.

319

Considered undersized by many college football recruiters because of his 5'9"
frame, Buster Davis became a star inside linebacker for Florida State. The Daytona
Beach, Florida native now plays for the NFL's Arizona Cardinals.

We had to bounce back pretty quickly to stay in the ACC race so we could
still get to one of the BCS bowl games. We beat Duke 55–24 and Maryland
35–27, so we were still pretty confident, even after losing to Virginia.
But then we started having more problems at quarterback, and the offense
wasn't playing very well. We finished the season with a three-game losing
streak, losing to North Carolina State 20–15 in the first game. Philip Rivers
was N.C. State's quarterback, and he was the most talented guy I ever faced

in college. He was just a guy who could really change a game, and he was always making unbelievable throws. He was just one of those guys who found a way to help his team win.

We lost to Clemson 35–14, and playing Clemson was always a big deal because Coach Bowden faced one of his sons [Clemson coach Tommy Bowden]. Those Bowden Bowls were always big games, and they got a lot of attention, but I don't think Coach Bowden enjoyed them too much. We finished the season losing to Florida 34–7, which was probably the worst loss I had while I was at Florida. It was their coach's [Ron Zook's] last game, and they were fired up for the game. We just didn't show up that day.

We had a 7–4 record, but we still won our division in the ACC and played Virginia Tech in the ACC championship game in Jacksonville. Virginia Tech was a big favorite in the game, and our backs were against the wall. I don't think they even thought we'd show up to play, but we won the game 27–22. Willie Reid had a big punt return for a touchdown early in the second half, which really gave us a spark. Our defense played great and really had their quarterback [Marcus Vick] on his heels.

Even though we finished the season with an 8–4 record and really didn't feel good about how the season went, we won the ACC and played Penn State in the Orange Bowl. It was a big game because Coach Bowden was going up against Joe Paterno, and they were the winningest coaches in college football. It was a great defensive game, and it took three overtimes to decide it. They kicked a field goal at the end to win it. It was really a tough loss because we had so many chances to win it. [FSU lost to Penn State 26–23.]

My senior season was difficult because I really felt like we'd made some changes to get it turned around. We finished with a 7–6 record, which is a record I never thought I'd see at Florida State. Hopefully, with some of the changes they've made on the coaching staff, they'll be able to get things turned around. I think the program might have needed some new blood, especially on offense.

Even though my four years there weren't as good as I'd hoped they be, it's an experience I'll never forget. I had four great years there and became a better player and person. I think the struggles we faced at Florida State will only make me a better player in the pros. It taught me that things don't always come easy, and you've got to work for everything you get. I'll always love Florida State.

Buster Davis, a native of Daytona Beach, Florida, was a three-year starting middle linebacker for the Seminoles from 2003 to 2006. As a senior in 2006, Davis led the Seminoles with 109 tackles and five sacks. He was named a first-team All-American by the American Football Coaches Association and second-team All-American by the Walter Camp Foundation and *The Sporting News*. Davis had 91 tackles and two sacks as a junior. He was selected in the third round of the 2007 NFL draft by the Arizona Cardinals.

ADAMS · BUDDY STRAUSS · LEE CORSO · BILL PROCTOR · RON S

KINDERMAN · WILLIAM "RED" DAWSON · DICK HERMANN · STI

SUMNER · RHETT DAWSON · BARRY SMITH · J.T. THOMAS · JOE C

· REGGIE HERRING · KEITH JONES · RICK STOCKSTILL · PHIL WIL

· DANNY MCMANUS · PETER TOM WILLIS · DEXTER CARTER · CAS

DUNN · ANDRE WADSWORTH · DAVID CASTILLO · BRYANT MCFAD

TOR · RON SCHOMBURGER · FRED PICKARD · BUD WHITEHEAD ·

ANN · STEVE TENSI · TOM WEST · JACK FENWICK · BILLY RHODE

AS · JOE CAMPS · WILLIE JONES · KURT UNGLAUB · JIMMY JORDA

PHIL WILLIAMS · ALPHONSO CARREKER · TOM MCCORMICK · G

ARTER · CASEY WELDON · BRAD JOHNSON · TERRELL BUCKLEY · KE

NT MCFADDEN · BUSTER DAVIS · HUGH ADAMS · BUDDY STRAU

WHITEHEAD · GENE MCDOWELL · KEITH KINDERMAN · WILLIAM

· BILLY RHODES · RON SELLERS · WALT SUMNER · RHETT DAWSON

Y JORDAN · MONK BONASORTE · REGGIE HERRING · KEITH JO

RMICK · GREG ALLEN · JAMIE DUKES · DANNY MCMANUS · PETER

UCKLEY · KEZ MCCORVEY · WARRICK DUNN · ANDRE WADSWORT

DY STRAUSS · LEE CORSO · BILL PROCTOR · RON SCHOMBURGER

WILLIAM "RED" DAWSON · DICK HERMANN · STEVE TENSI · TOM